I0763102

JAMIE WYETH UNSETTLED

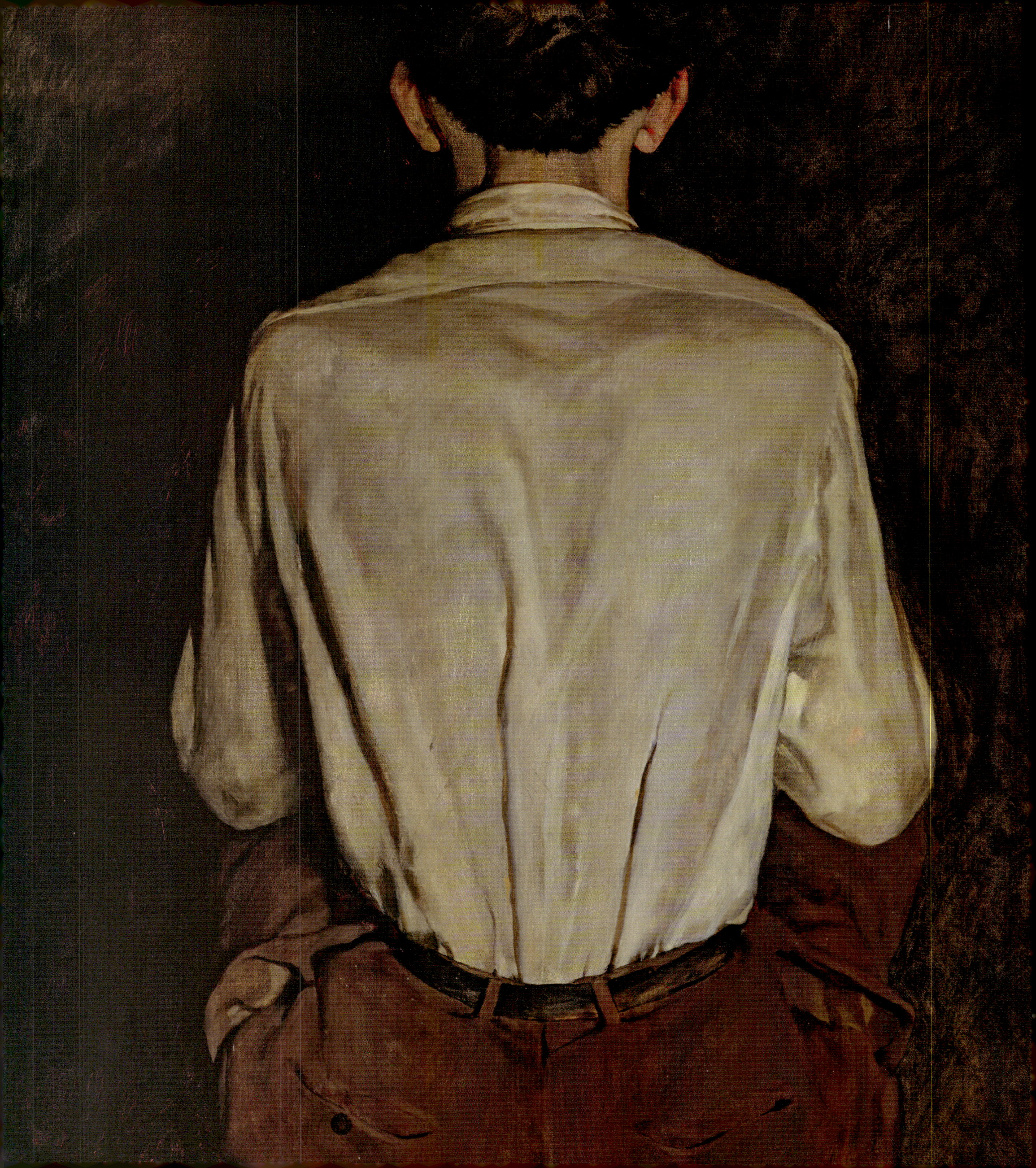

JAMIE WYETH

UNSETTLED

Edited by Amanda C. Burdan
With essays by
Jennifer Margaret Barker,
Amanda C. Burdan,
Rena Butler, Michael Kiley,
and John Rusk

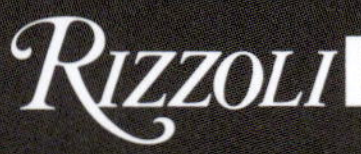

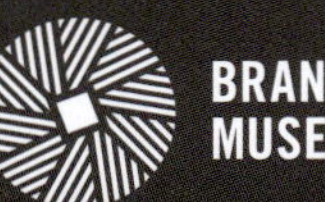

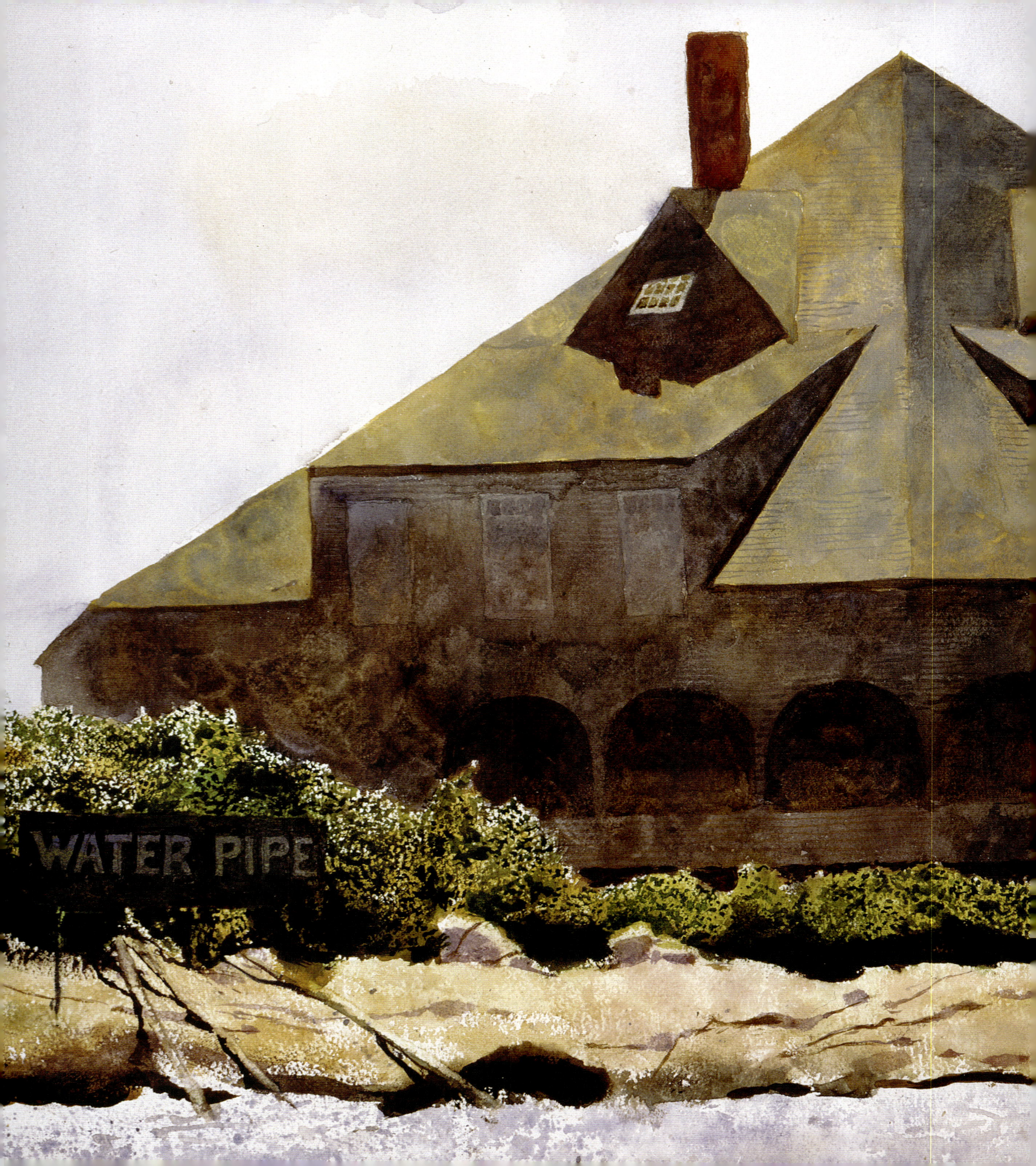
WATER PIPE

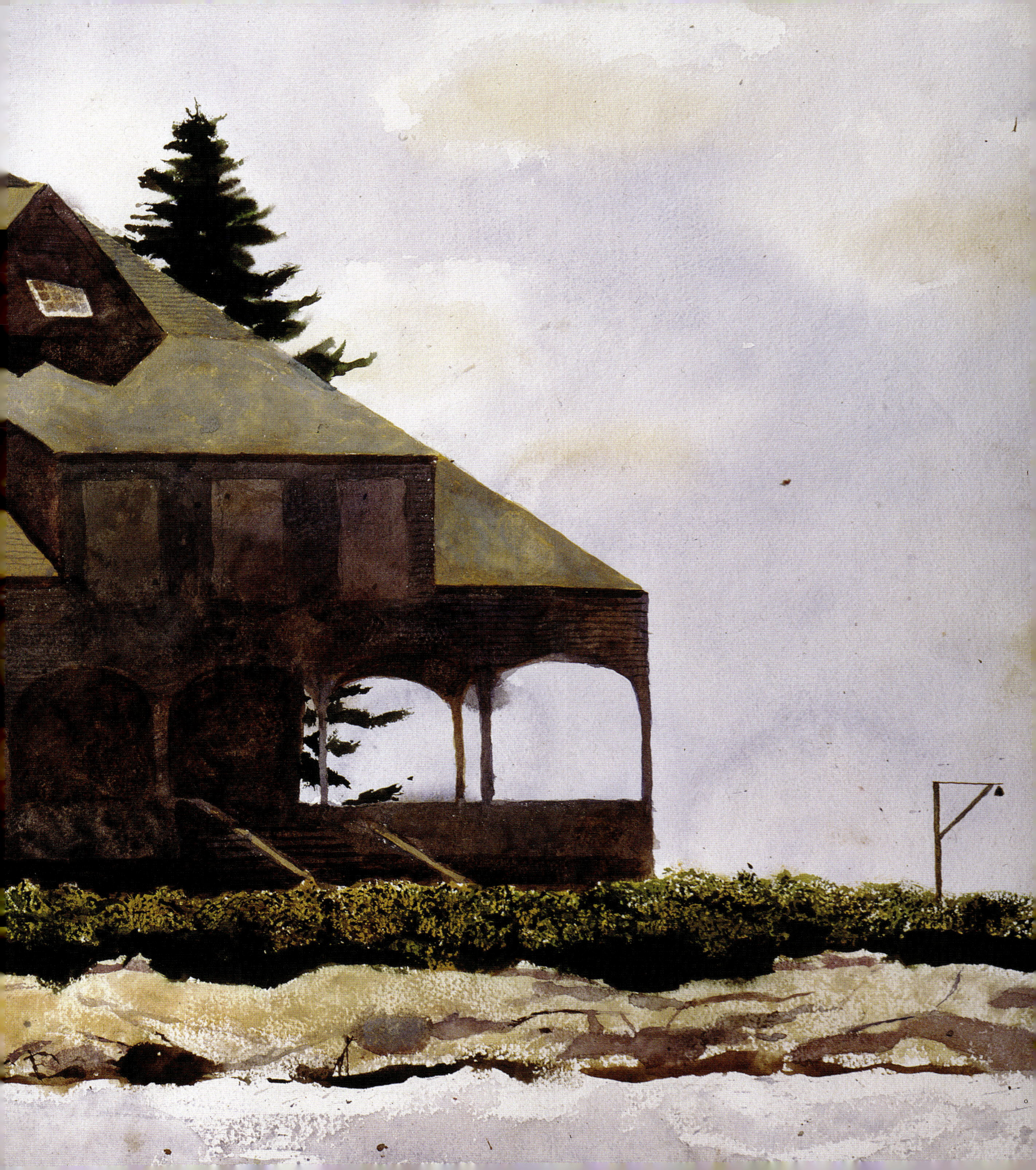

Published on the occasion of the exhibition
Jamie Wyeth: Unsettled, organized by the
Brandywine Museum of Art, Chadds Ford, PA.

Exhibition Itinerary

Brandywine Museum of Art, Chadds Ford, PA:
March 16–June 9, 2024
Farnsworth Art Museum, Rockland, ME:
July 4–September 29, 2024
Greenville County Museum of Art, Greenville, SC:
November 27, 2024–February 16, 2025
Dayton Art Institute, OH:
March 15–June 8, 2025
Frye Art Museum, Seattle:
July 12–October 5, 2025

First published in the United States of America
in 2024 by

Rizzoli Electa
A Division of Rizzoli International Publications, Inc.
300 Park Avenue South
New York, NY 10010
www.rizzoliusa.com

Brandywine Museum of Art
1 Hoffman's Mill Road
Chadds Ford, PA 19317
www.brandywine.org

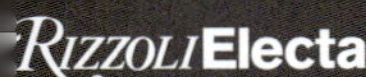

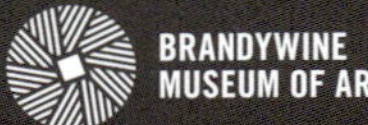

For Rizzoli Electa:
Publisher: Charles Miers
Associate Publisher: Margaret Rennolds Chace
Senior Editor: Ellen R. Cohen
Production Manager: Alyn Evans

Design: Barbara Glauber / Heavy Meta

2024 2025 2026 2027 2028 / 10 9 8 7 6 5 4 3 2 1

ISBN: 978-0-8478-9956-2
Library of Congress Control Number: 2023946961

Printed in Hong Kong

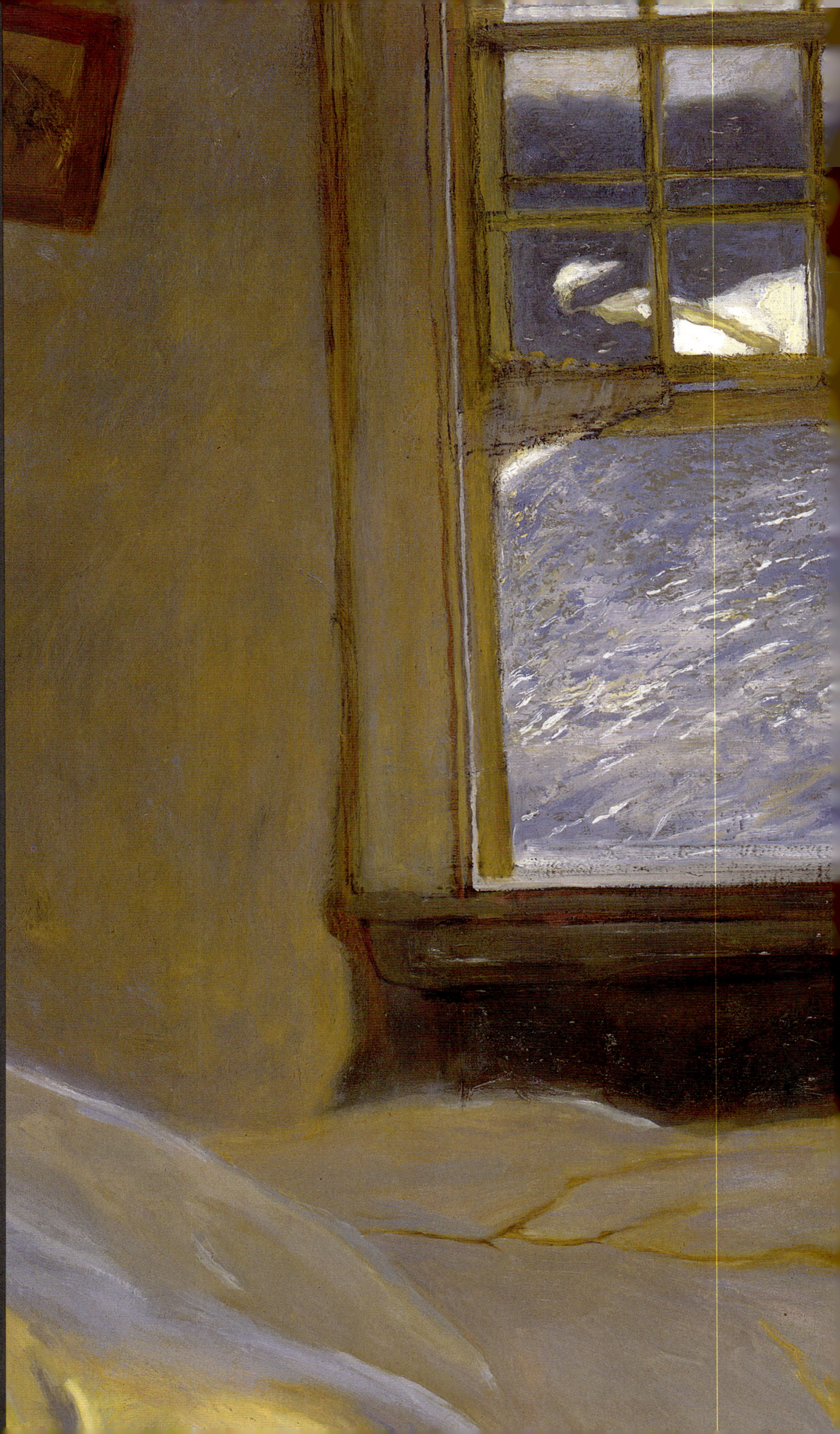

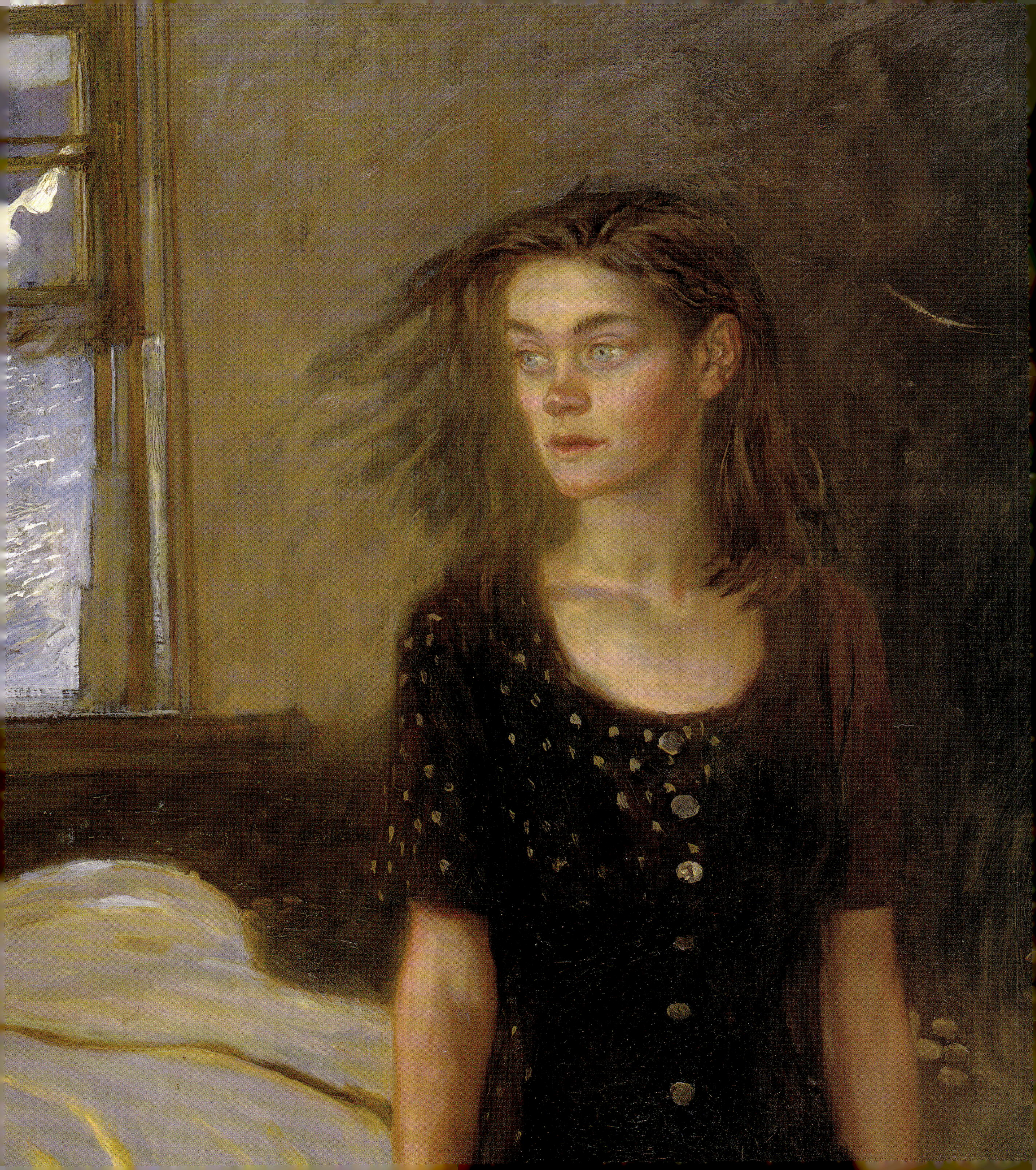

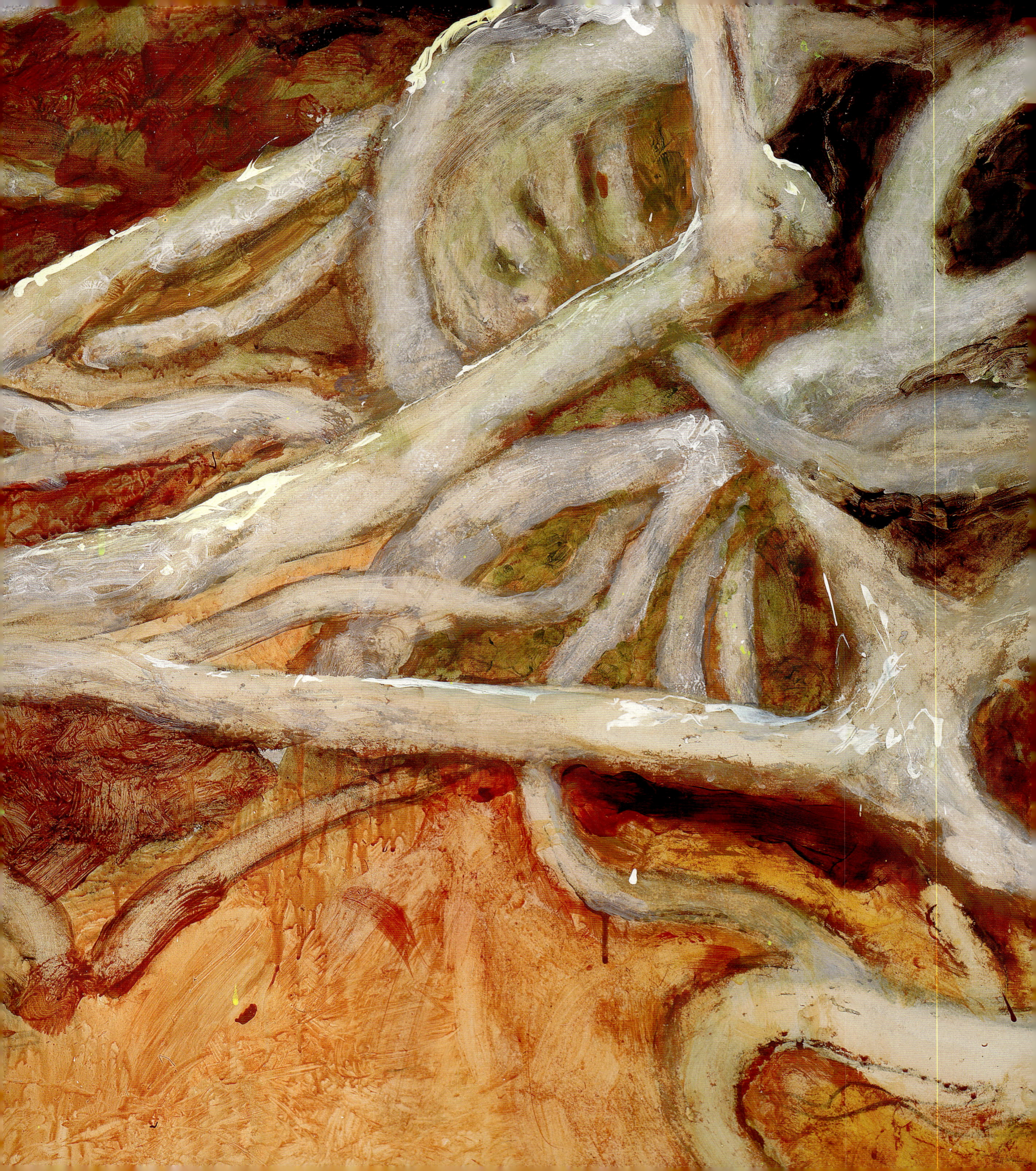

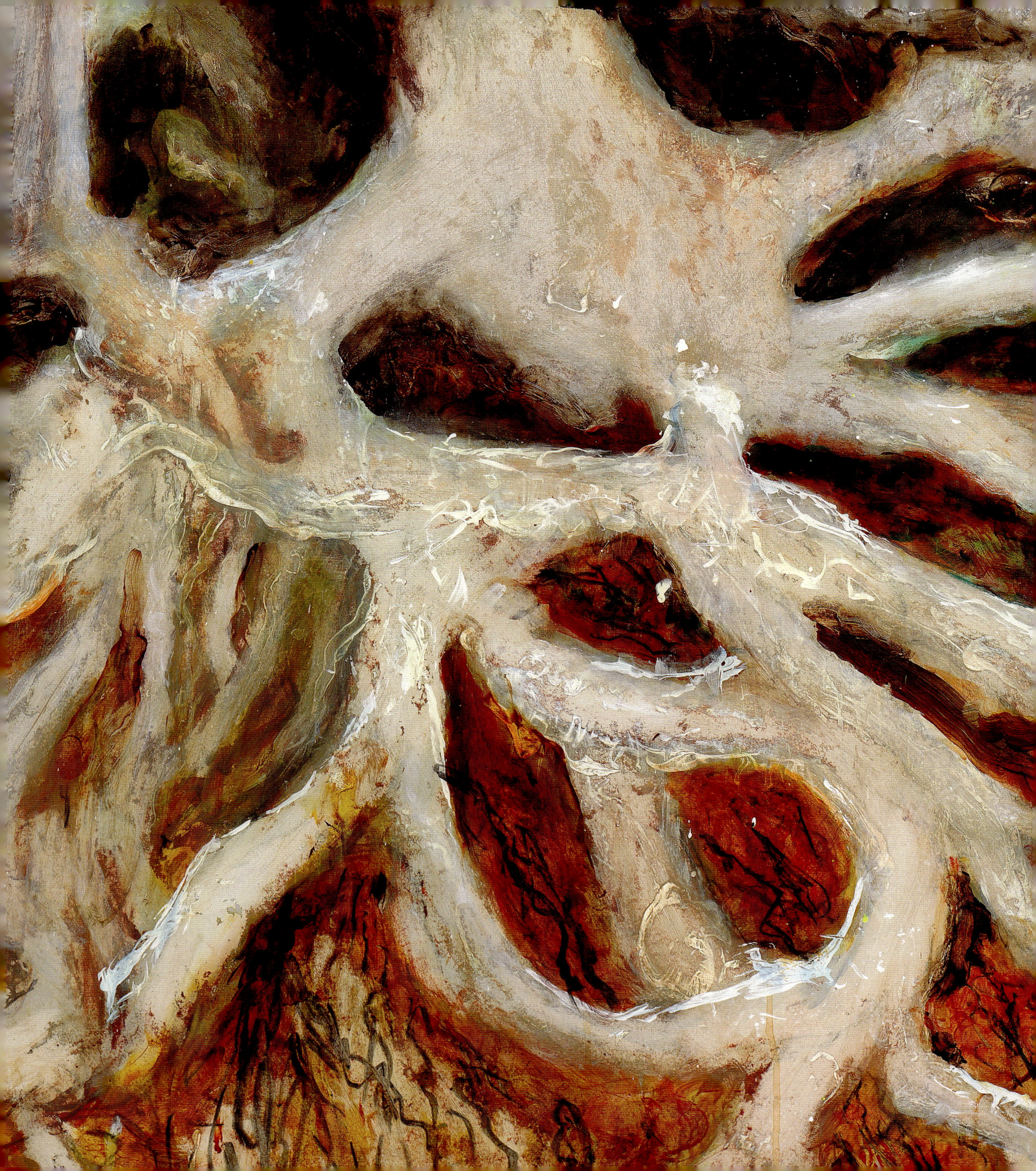

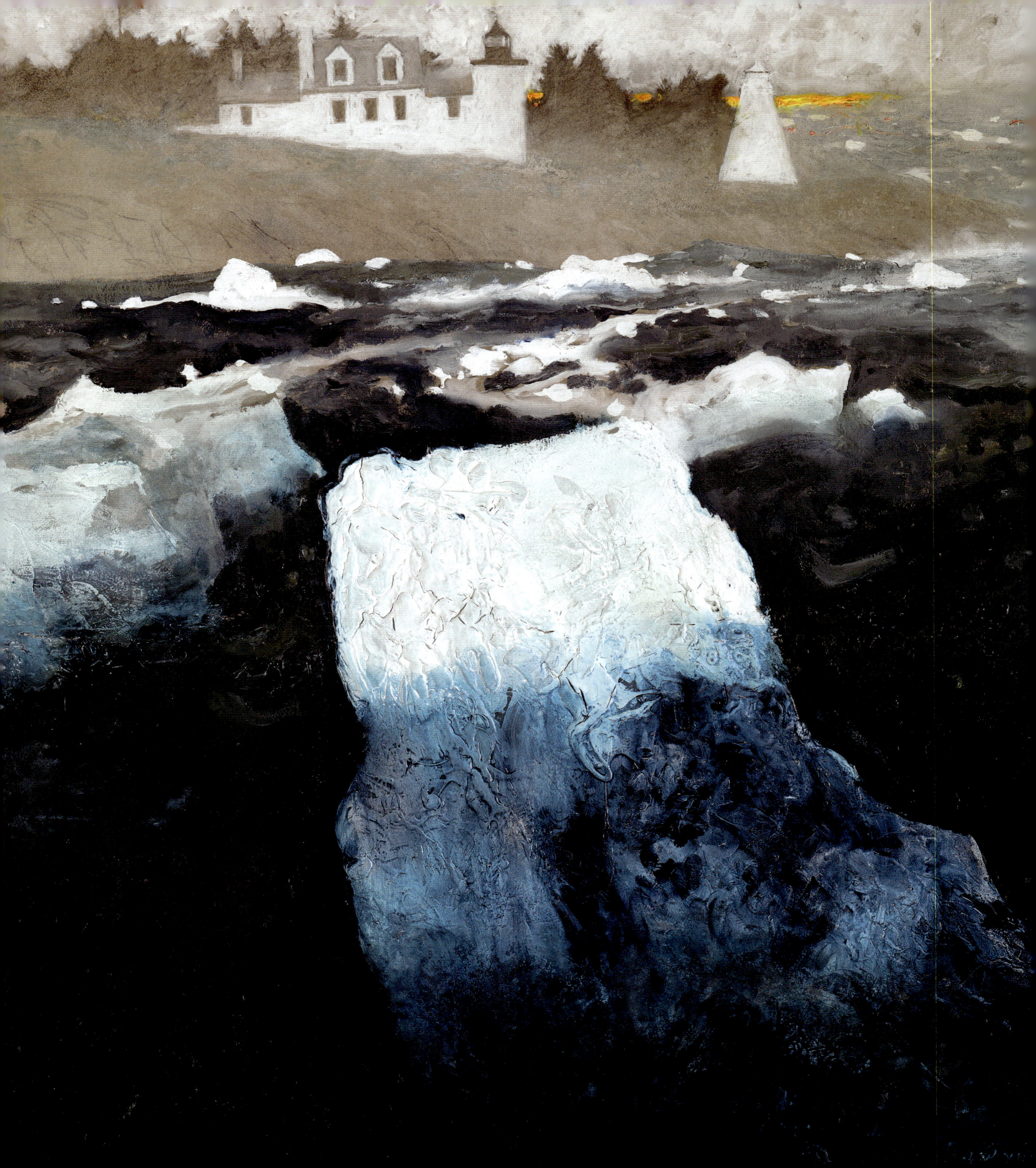

DIRECTOR'S FOREWORD

Jamie Wyeth is an American painter who defies the expectations of tradition and lineage. A familial apostate, he has distinguished himself from his renowned father and grandfather through development of a style decidedly darker, lusher, and more visceral and emotionally charged than those of his predecessors. Boundaries between the seen and unseen are blurred in the art of Jamie Wyeth. Through his startling compositions and a masterful use of media, color, and texture, the hyper-attuned Wyeth creates an immersive, synesthetic experience that both engages and upsets visual and emotional equilibrium. Everyday scenes become transcendental.

In this exhibition, Amanda Burdan, Brandywine's Senior Curator, brings fascinating new insight into the artist's oeuvre and with remarkable nuance plumbs a rich vein of the uncanny throughout his six-decade career. Not a retrospective (that was done brilliantly in 2014 by Elliot Bostwick Davis at the Museum of Fine Arts, Boston; Brandywine was one of four venues), the exhibition focuses on a single through line in his work, one in which ominous stillness, post-apocalyptic skies, frightening shifts in scale, and strange vantage points seem to highlight the vulnerability of the human condition. Through Wyeth's visual pyrotechnics, dreamscapes dissolve into nightmares.

Exhibitions such as this would not be possible without the generosity and cooperation of numerous individuals. First are the many museums and collectors who lent their works by Jamie Wyeth. To them goes our sincere gratitude. At Brandywine, I'd like to thank Virginia A. Logan, the Frolic Weymouth Executive Director and CEO of the Museum's parent organization, Brandywine Conservancy & Museum of Art, for her unflagging and enthusiastic support and for being a most excellent thinking partner on this project. Cuyler H. Walker, Chair of Brandywine's Board of Trustees, and D.D. Matz, Vice Chair, gave invaluable support to the exhibition in every sense of the term. Special recognition goes, of course, to Amanda Burdan. Her proposal for this exhibition six years ago was enthusiastically received, and her incisive inquiry ever since into the art of Jamie Wyeth provides a

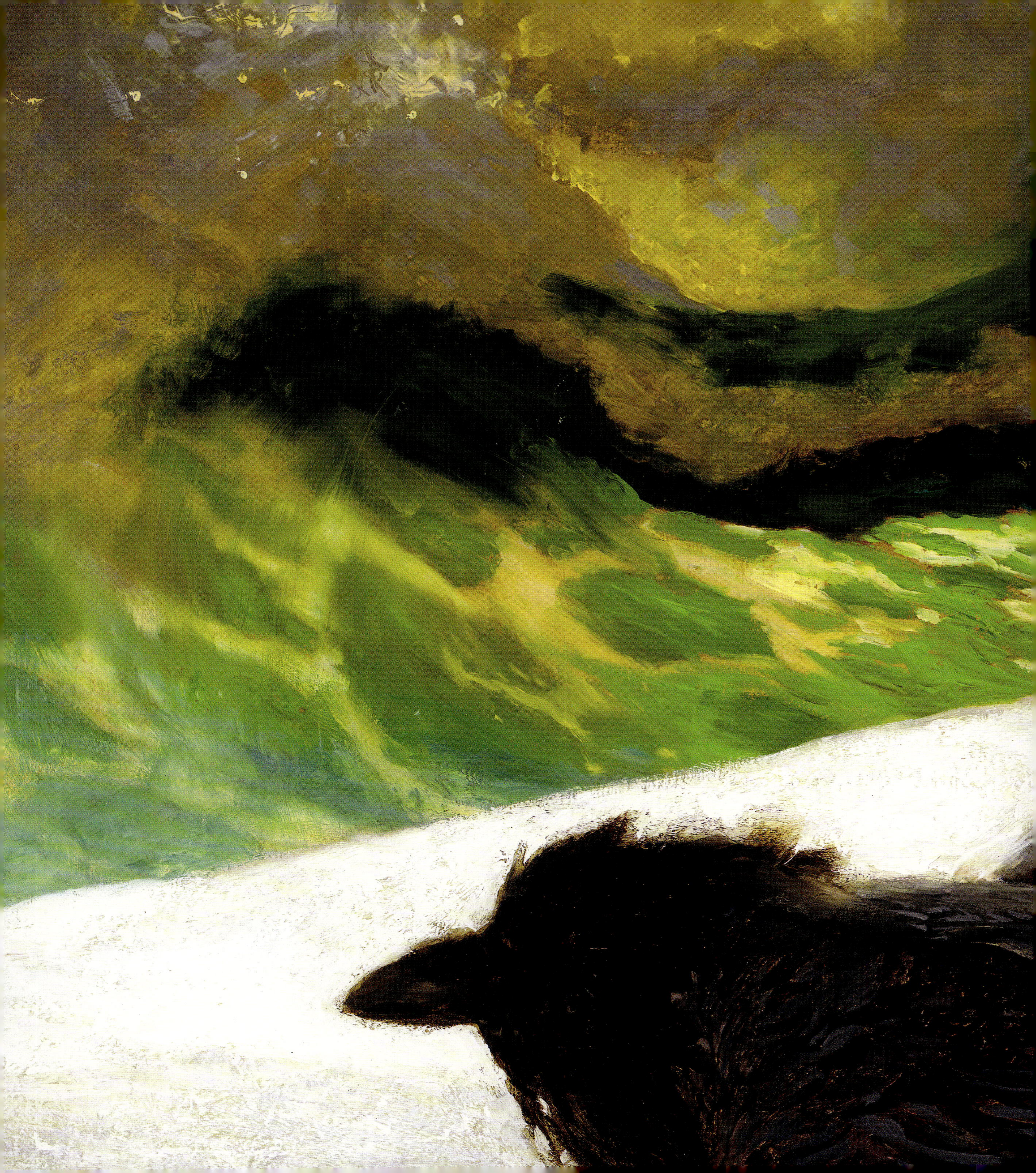

new lens through which to examine the artist's long career and put an aspect of his oeuvre into a wider context of visual culture.

To all the Brandywine staff that contributed to the project go my thanks, in particular Sara Buehler, Mary Cronin, Shawnna DeFilippo, Bethany Engel, Daniel Krull, and Michelle Moskal. I'd also like to acknowledge the four artists who have contributed essays to this publication and shared thoughts on creating the uncanny in their respective disciplines: Jennifer Margaret Barker, Rena Butler, Michael Kiley, and John Rusk. This publication represents another successful collaboration with Rizzoli/Electa, and I'd like to thank Margaret Chace, Associate Publisher, for her indispensable guidance and unerring commitment to excellence. We were also fortunate to have the wisdom and insight that Ellen Cohen, Senior Editor, brought to all the texts in these pages. In addition, sincere thanks go to Barbara Glauber at Heavy Meta studio for the striking design of this handsome volume that showcases the art of Jamie Wyeth so well. Finally, Mary Beth Dolan, Studio Manager to Jamie Wyeth, provided crucial and copious information incorporated in these pages, and we are grateful for her very warm spirit of cooperation.

We are delighted that *Jamie Wyeth: Unsettled* will have a wide reach as it travels across the United States after its presentation at Brandywine. I'd like to acknowledge and thank the directors and staffs at the Farnsworth Art Museum, Rockland, Maine; Greenville County Museum of Art, Greenville, South Carolina; Dayton Art Institute, Dayton, Ohio; and Frye Art Museum, Seattle. It has been a pleasure working with them all.

Major undertakings such as this exhibition and catalogue would not be possible without the support of our donors. We are indebted to our longtime partners at Chase for their sponsorship. My gratitude goes to Mac and Frances Weymouth for their lead gift and enthusiastic support. Deep appreciation is due to Linda L. Bean, Diana Bean, and an anonymous donor for their generosity, as well as Cina Alexander Forgason, Helen C. Alexander, D.D. Matz, and Morris and Boo Stroud. Most of all, I'd like to thank Jamie Wyeth for the goodwill, generosity, sensitivity, and humor he has shown during the years this exhibition has been in development. Though he abhors the spotlight, the sheen of his artistic brilliance is on display in this exhibition and publication. As they so clearly reveal, Jamie is a painter who has created his own legacy and redefined what it means to be a Wyeth.

Thomas Padon
The James H. Duff Director
Brandywine Museum of Art

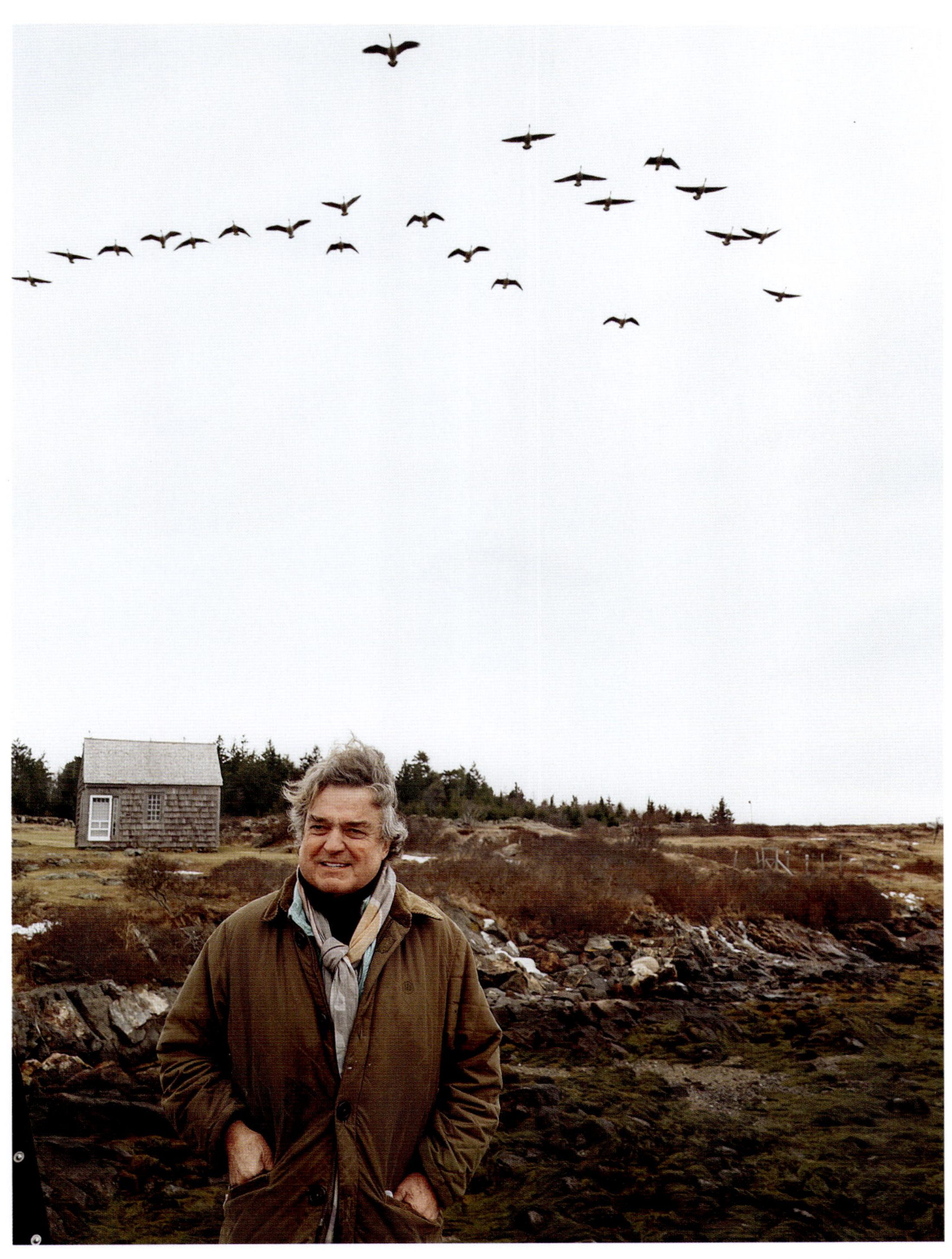

Jamie Wyeth on Benner Island, Maine, 2022

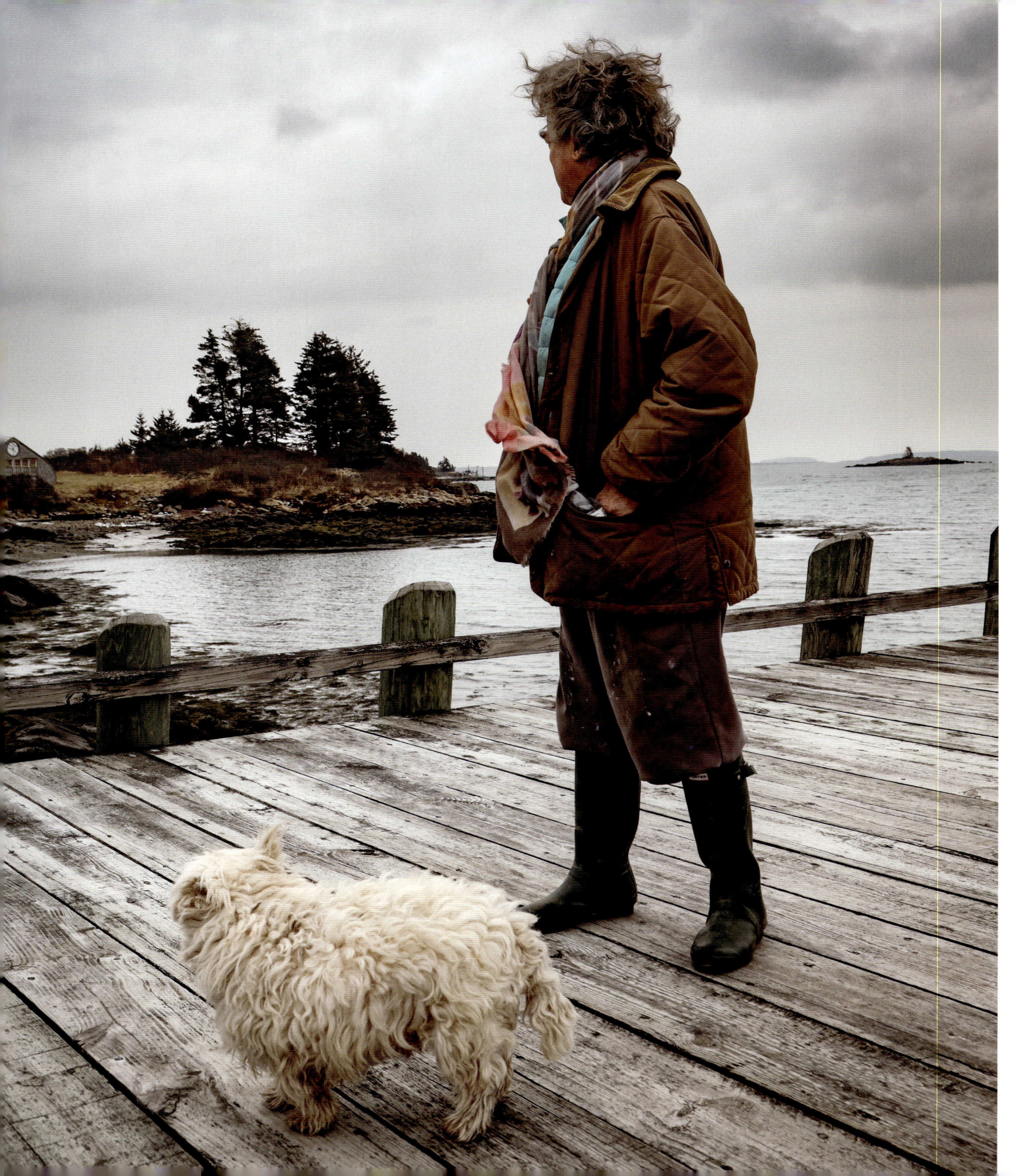

ACKNOWLEDGMENTS

My first encounter with Jamie Wyeth wasn't with his artwork, but with a short but provocative introduction he wrote for the exhibition catalogue *Call of the Coast: Art Colonies of New England* (2009). I was writing entries for several of the historical works of art in the exhibition—all the artists long dead and gone. His statement, as a living artist, explained the connection between himself and the ghost of Rockwell Kent, whose presence looms large on Monhegan Island in Maine, where Wyeth worked for many years. It was a peculiar point of view, but now one that I think is wholly fitting for Wyeth. He communes with a lot of ghosts in his work; the paintings are like seances summoning the spirits not always of people but of animals, places, and things. An art historian, such as myself, is not always the right person to write about and examine contemporary work by a living artist. After getting to know Jamie and his work over the last decade, I feel more conversant with his subjects, his stylistic shifts, and his compositional motifs. And it doesn't hurt that we're both highly conversant with the dead in our respective work.

My most sincere thanks go to Jamie Wyeth himself, for enabling this project to move forward. His open invitation into his personal archives, collection, and database of work was essential to finding my way through more than seven decades of his artistic output. His advice on works that might fit the exhibition's theme and flexibility in allowing me the leeway to explore the darker paths in his oeuvre is very much appreciated. In Tenants Harbor, Maine, Mary Beth Dolan was invaluable to my investigation and so very accommodating over the years of correspondence about this exhibition. Her personal knowledge of Wyeth's life and work helped to navigate the mysteries that were constantly presenting themselves. She arranged photography, sent dimensions in response to spur-of-the-moment shipping concerns, conveyed questions to Jamie when he was otherwise out of reach, and provided great hospitality and good company on my trips to Maine. Likewise, at Point Lookout Farm, Caroline O'Neil Ryan was so accommodating providing information and access to works in Pennsylvania.

Jamie Wyeth and his dog, Iggy, on the dock at Benner Island, Maine, 2022

I also want to thank our expert team of commentators for the exhibition catalogue. Each committed eagerly to this project, and their diverse perspectives on the arts makes the publication all the richer. Dr. Jennifer Margaret Barker, a Scottish American composer, is Professor of Composition/Theory at the University of Delaware. Her haunting and soul-stirring compositions have been performed around the world. In her commentary, she deftly walks us through the process of orchestrating an unsettling mood for her audiences with vivid details. Originally from Chicago, where she began her dance studies, Rena Butler has danced with and choreographed for prestigious companies worldwide, most recently the San Francisco Opera and the National Ballet of Canada. Her work with Philadelphia's BalletX, which she discusses in her essay, brilliantly engages with Black lived experience in an experimental film-based format. Michael Kiley, a sound designer, with whom Brandywine has previously worked, explores how sound can be anxiety-inducing in his commentary. His award-winning work in theater, as he explains, focuses on the "unseen" elements of a performance and is particularly enlightening in connection with the work of Jamie Wyeth and other visual artists. The examples of uncomfortable tension in narrative cinema recounted by filmmaker John Rusk have a striking affinity with Wyeth's compositional choices. Rusk's frequent work with M. Night Shyamalan—a master of the unsettling—and on the supernatural mystery *Stranger Things* attest to his facility in the discourse of the unnerving imagery.

At the Brandywine, our intrepid staff kept this project moving forward even in the face of major setbacks, including both COVID-19 and the devastating flooding brought by Hurricane Ida in 2021. Exhibition Manager Bethany Engel coordinated every detail of this ambitious project, setting and resetting exhibition schedules and coordinating many outside partners as planning evolved. Senior Registrar Sara Buehler and Associate Registrar Michelle Moskal likewise guided the ever-expanding checklist's loan agreements, shipping, and crating to five venues—Brandywine's most widely traveled exhibition—smoothly and professionally. The addition of Joshua Schnapf as Brandywine's new Head of Creative Services greatly advanced this project, both in terms of the catalogue and the visitor's gallery experience. Our photography coordinator, Todd Bradway, provided steady support, going with the flow of our changing checklists, new additions to essays, and last-minute brainstorms that kept the images in flux to the final deadline.

This striking catalogue is the product of many collaborations, and I am grateful that all our partners agreed to let this book be just a little bit weird. At Rizzoli Electa, Publisher Charles Miers and Associate Publisher Margaret Rennolds Chace championed this project early on and, with the help of Senior Editor Ellen R. Cohen, produced a handsome, if somewhat haunting, book. All the authors benefited from the guidance of Mary Ellen Wilson's copy-editing. Designer Barbara Glauber of Heavy Meta helped to define a style that echoed the catalogue's unsettling theme, gamely rising to the challenge of creating the book that makes the reader feel a little of the uneasiness of Wyeth's paintings.

I would also like to thank our collaborators at institutions across the country for helping this project to be a success. The Farnsworth Art Museum in Rockland, Maine, is a partner in many respects with our shared connections to the Wyeth family of artists. I am so pleased that they are both hosting the exhibition as well as lending a number of key works to the show. The Greenville County Museum of Art in Greenville, South Carolina, a deep repository of works by Wyeth, is the third venue for the exhibition and is lending a number of recent works to the tour. The Dayton Art Institute in Dayton, Ohio, and the Frye Art Museum in Seattle, each will host the exhibition in 2025, bringing Wyeth's work to new regions of the country. Their enthusiasm and support for the project have been most welcome.

This exhibition would not be possible without the generosity of institutions and individuals willing to share their works with audiences across the country. In addition to numerous loans from Jamie Wyeth's personal collection, other private individuals lending to the exhibition include Linda L. Bean, John Gardiner, Lindsay and Candice Hooper, Sherry Kerstetter, Frank McEntee, Lisa and David Spartin, Jim and Jocelyn Stewart, and several lenders who wish to remain anonymous. In addition to the Brandywine, Farnsworth, Greenville, and Frye, institutional loans have come from the Hunter Museum of American Art, the Kemper Museum of Contemporary Art, and the Saint Louis Art Museum.

Amanda C. Burdan
Senior Curator
Brandywine Museum of Art

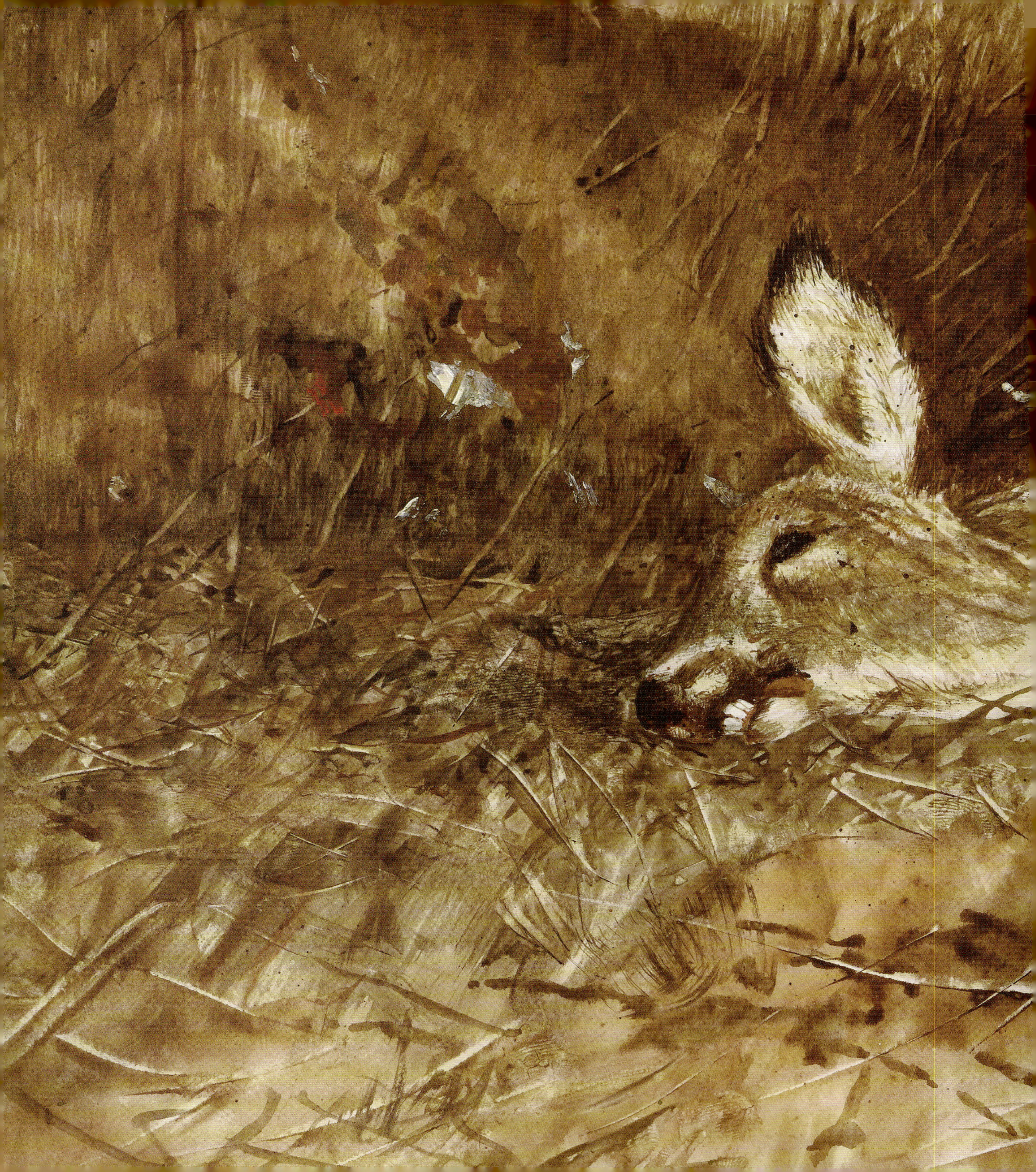

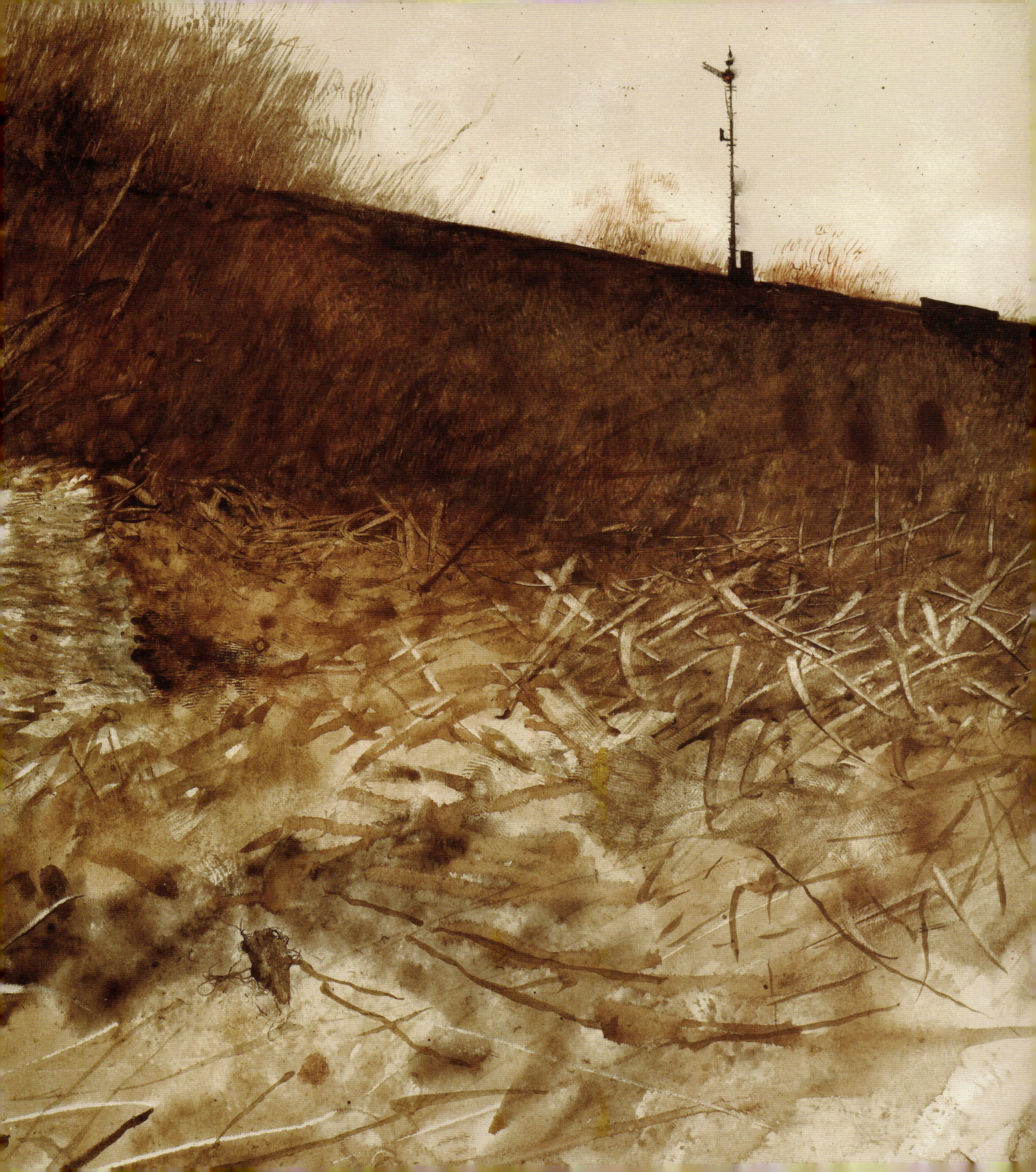

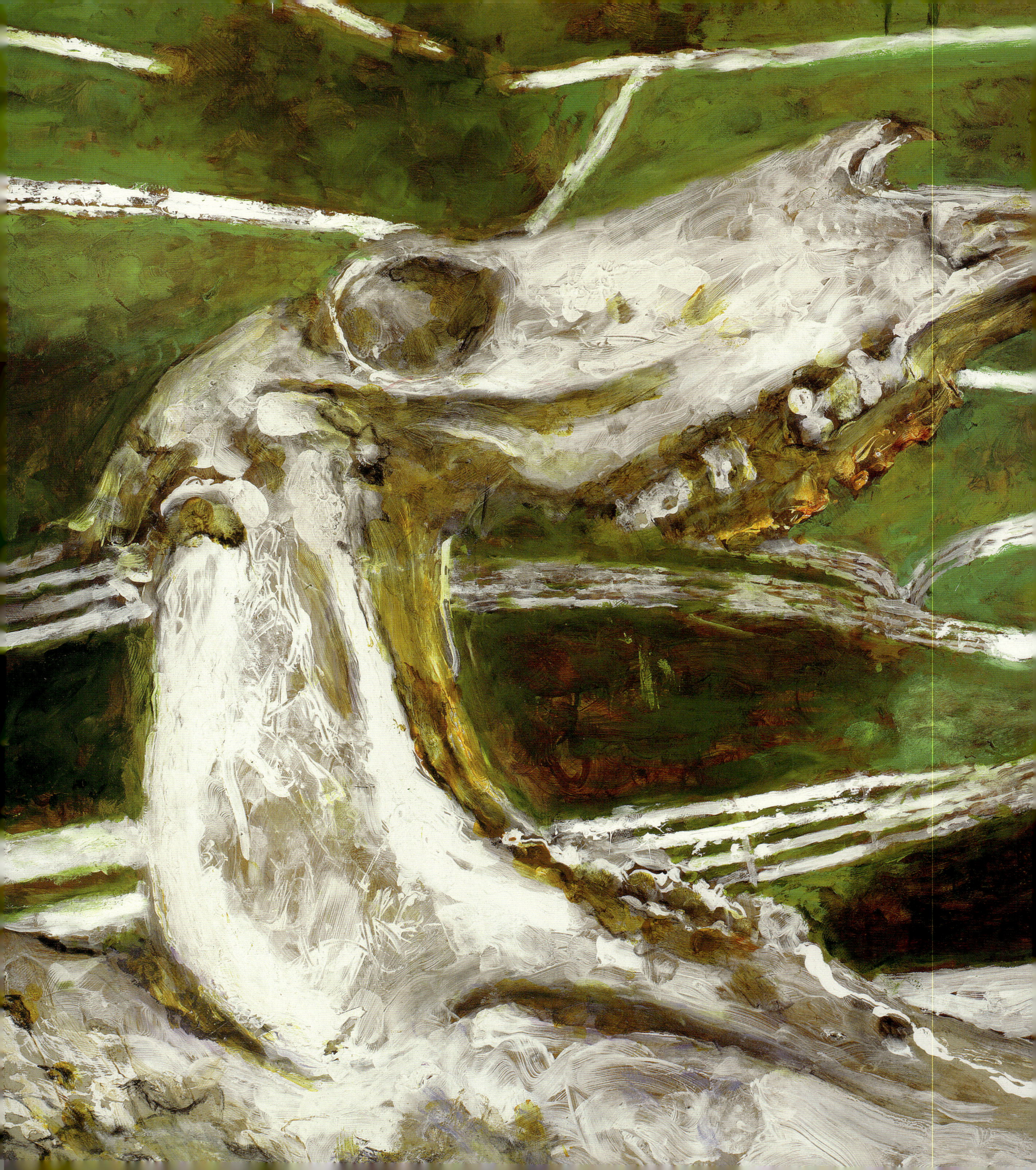

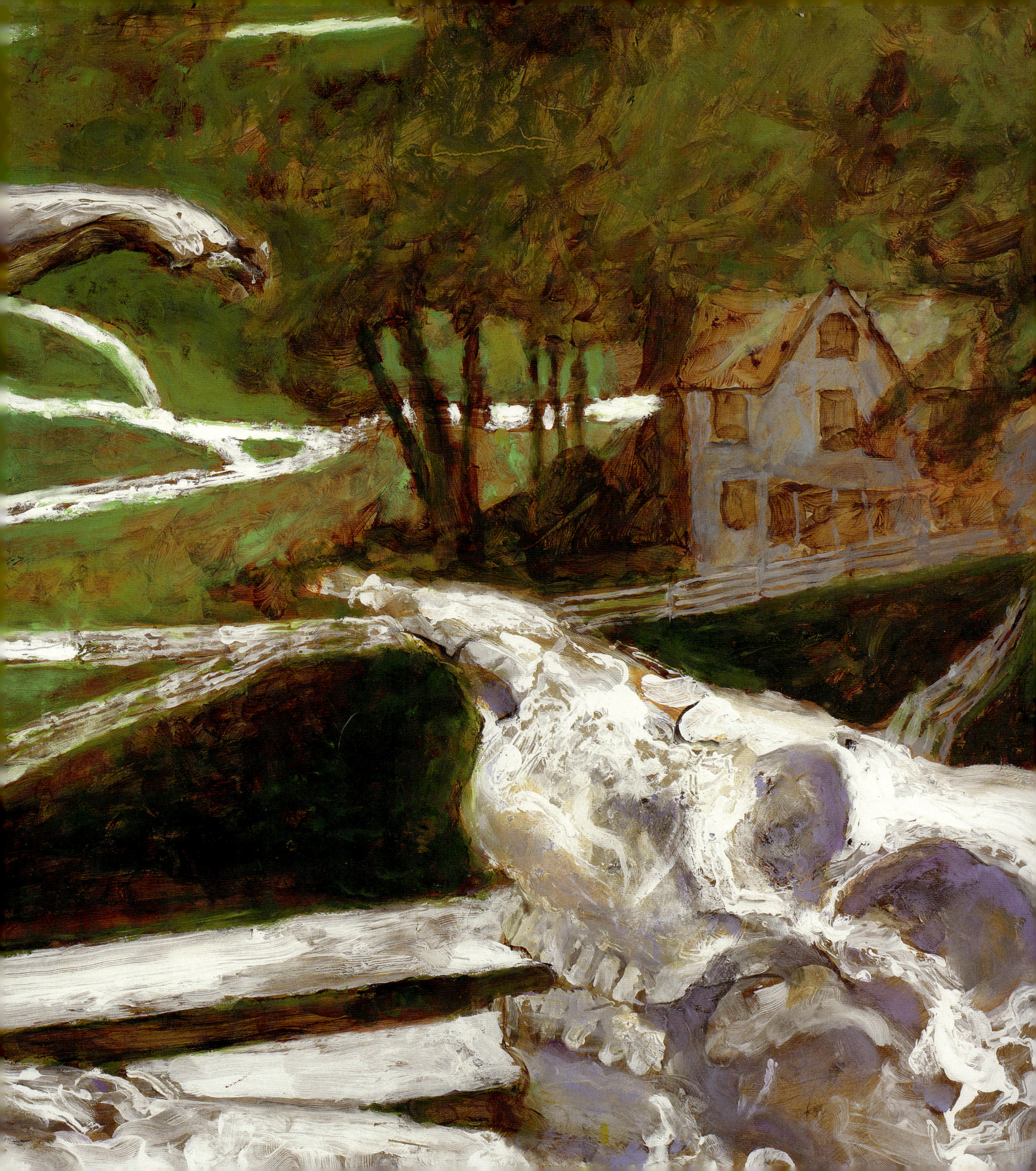

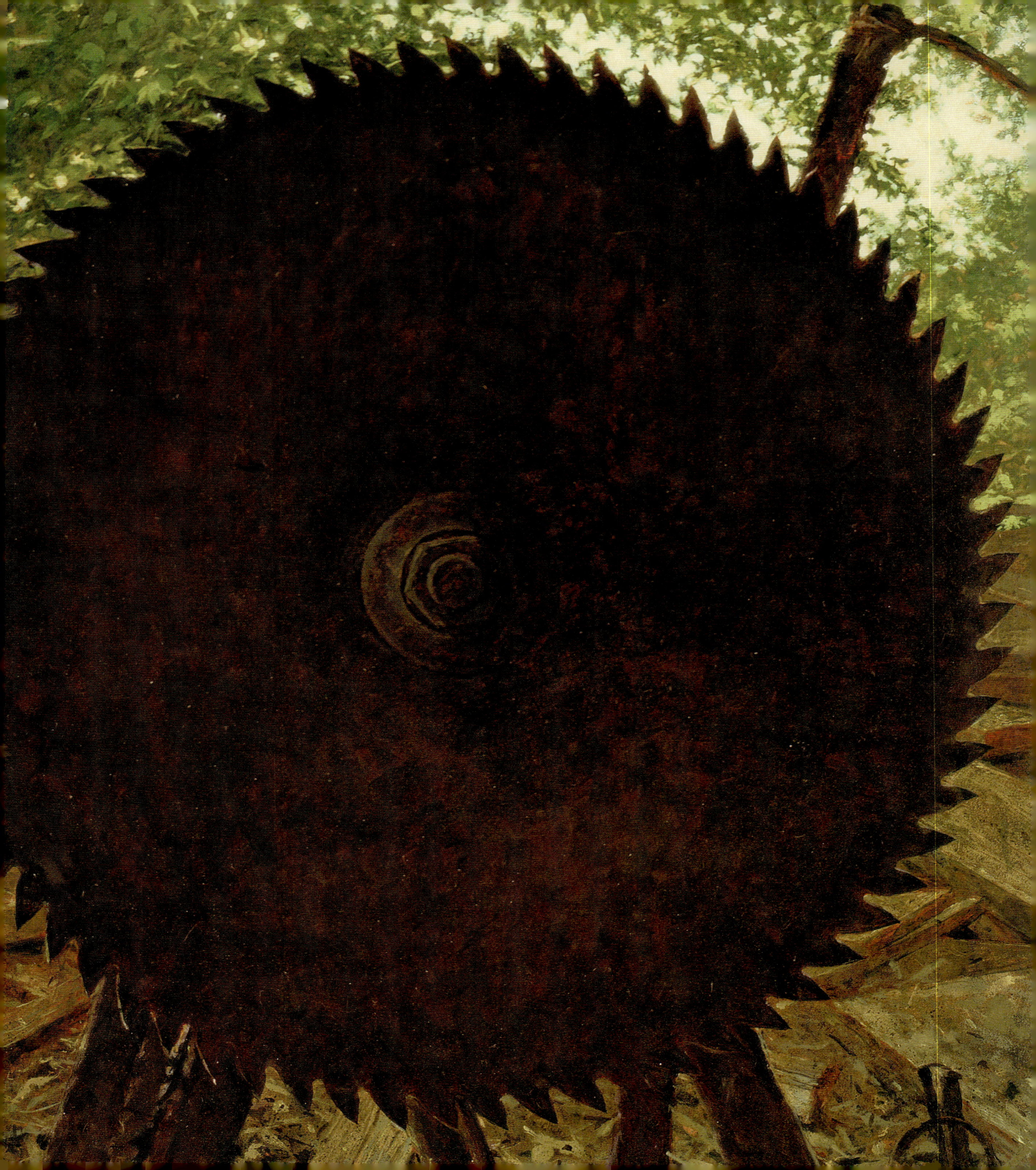

THE UNSETTLING, UNCANNY, UNNERVING WORLD OF JAMIE WYETH

AMANDA C. BURDAN

There are things in the world that are scary, even terrifying. Then there are things that are not quite frightening or upsetting—they are the prelude to fear, the unexplained feeling that something is not quite right. In the visual world, these are scenes that inspire dread, anxiety, or perhaps an uneasy calm. Sometimes we see something and, without conscious thought, get a certain chill we may not understand. An intuitive red flag is raised by our brains that warns us of impending danger. Across the decades of his career Jamie Wyeth has honed his attention onto these unnerving events, zeroed in on uncanny experiences, and become a master of the unsettled by marshaling a wide range of disconcerting elements—subjects, compositional approaches, and techniques—within his works. Developing a skillful, cinematic shorthand, Wyeth has the power to evoke anxiety in nearly every viewer. This focused look at his arresting, visceral imagery reveals fascinating insight into the artist and the art of visual storytelling.

Born into the third generation of one of America's most renowned artistic families, Jamie Wyeth grew up surrounded by creativity. He trained with his aunt Carolyn Wyeth in the studio of his grandfather, the illustrator N. C. Wyeth. Like his grandfather and his father, the realist painter Andrew Wyeth, before him, Jamie Wyeth splits his time between the Brandywine River valley of Pennsylvania and Delaware and MidCoast Maine. In these two locales he has passed through many "obsessions," as he calls his favored subjects. His style developed from the strict and meticulous realism of his teenage years to a more expressionistic variation characterized by Day-Glo colors, mixed-media techniques, and freer brushwork. Looking at Wyeth's oeuvre in isolation may still suggest affinities with the darker work by other generations of his family, such as the grim story evoked by N. C. Wyeth's *The Drowning* (1936; Brandywine Museum of Art) or the frozen corpse of Karl Kuerner in Andrew Wyeth's *Spring* (1978; Brandywine Museum of Art), but it does not form the starting point of this investigation.

This unsettling aspect has had moments of greater exposure over the decades. In his "Suite of Untoward Occurrences on Monhegan Island" (ca. 2012–present), each work rolls out a tantalizing but essentially weird partial narrative about the lore of this isolated island, leaving the viewer to imagine outcomes and meanings. His "Seven Deadly Sins" series (2007) and concurrent gull studies reveal the cruel and vicious nature of these birds, a subject that has preoccupied him for many years. Ravens and crows join the gulls in Wyeth's painted aviary as he explores a Hitchcockian fixation with our feathered friends. In the recent and ongoing "Screen Door Sequence," begun in 2015, he goes beyond the canvas to create haunting three-dimensional works that incorporate found objects and blur the line between painting and sculpture, the real and the imagined, this world and the next.

The persistent vein of intriguing, often ominous imagery in many of Wyeth's paintings is frequently countered and even hidden by his fuller body of work—particularly his immensely popular coastal views, farmscapes, and portraiture—but the darker and more troubling imagery is constant. A chilling thread runs through his work from the past sixty years, present but not overwhelming and ever evolving with his style and subjects. Whether introducing curious characters, exploring otherworldly places, or surveying peculiar landscapes, he is very much at home with uneasy subjects, standing apart in a shadowy and strange world of his own creation.

← *Buzz Saw*, 1969 (pl. 71). Detail

STRANGERS AND SPECTERS

As we enter Wyeth's unsettling world, we find his strongest means of evoking disquieting moods is perhaps via the straightforward presentation of eccentric portraits. The subjects in *Bean Boots* (1985), *Light Station* (1992), and *The Bones of a Whale* (2006) all conjure, with the artist's keen eye for outward signs of inner peculiarities, strikingly strong, if unnerving, character studies. Even more disturbing than some of the people we meet in full in Wyeth's paintings are the figures left partially hidden, which lend such works as *Record Player* (1964), *Channel 12* (1992), and *Other Voices, Study #1* (1995) an added air of mystery and perhaps peril.

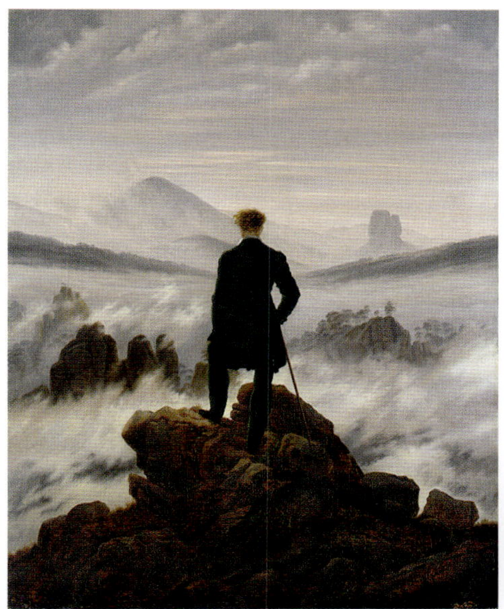

1

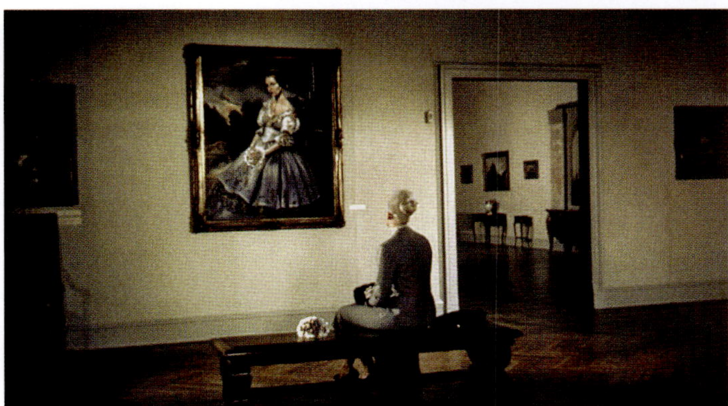

3

To accomplish this effect, Wyeth effectively deploys the compositional device of the *Rückenfigur*, a backward-

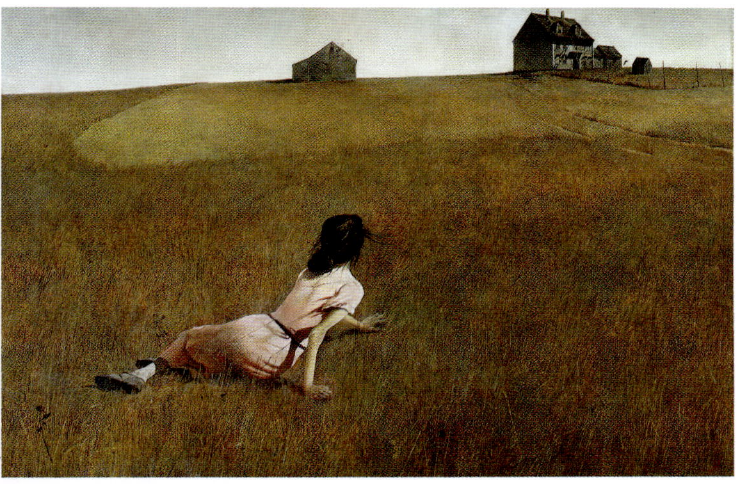

2

turned figure. As with his German Romantic predecessors who embraced the use of this trope, he engages it as a means of inviting a viewer into the world of his painting. With Wyeth, however, the invitation often seems more of a provocation to come closer if you dare. When Caspar David Friedrich painted his *Rückenfiguren* in the nineteenth century, the subject was frequently placed as an intermediary between the audience and a tempting view in the background, as in *Woman at a Window* of 1822 (Alte Nationalgalerie, Staatliche Museen zu Berlin) or *Wanderer above a Sea of Fog* from around 1817 (fig. 1). Perhaps the best-known American example lives very close to home. In Andrew Wyeth's 1948 tempera painting *Christina's World* (fig. 2), the physical and emotional yearning of the subject, Christina Olson, for her home perched high above on

1 Caspar David Friedrich, *Wanderer above the Sea of Fog*, ca. 1817. Oil on canvas, 37⅜ × 29½ in. Hamburger Kunsthalle, Hamburg, Germany. On permanent loan from the Foundation for the Promotion of the Hamburg Art Collections

2 Andrew Wyeth, *Christina's World*, 1948. Tempera on panel, 32¼ × 47¾ in. Museum of Modern Art, New York

3 Film still from *Vertigo* (1958), directed by Alfred Hitchcock

the horizon is palpable. Yet in none of these examples is an element of fear or dread intimated.

Wyeth's use of the *Rückenfigur* is more akin to the suspense-inducing practice of filmmakers. When Alfred Hitchcock revealed the clues of Madeleine Elster's unusual behavior in the psychological thriller *Vertigo* (1958), he directed the camera to view her character (played by Kim Novak) from the back, adding to the tension. As Scottie Ferguson (James Stewart) follows Madeleine, he lurks behind her, putting together elements of the puzzle (fig. 3). Like Hitchcock, Wyeth engages with voyeurism in *Record Player* (pl. 1), in which the crouched figure of Lester Stanley fills nearly the entire picture plane. Stanley, a local man who occasionally modeled for Wyeth in the early 1960s (fig. 4), is shown transfixed by an unseen record player in Wyeth's studio. The viewer is placed close to the subject, even more so than in many of the shots in *Vertigo*, which magnifies the sense of the danger of being discovered by the person being observed. The *Rückenfigur* is used to great effect in many thrillers and horror movies, paying off in shock when the figure turns to face the camera. The anxiety is frustratingly heightened by a painted *Rückenfigur* as the viewer awaits a reveal that never comes.

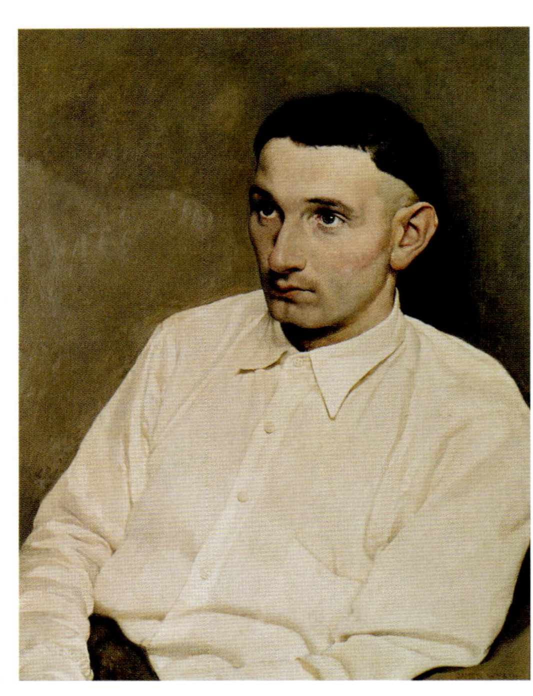

4

A similar composition is used in *Channel 12* (pl. 3), in which two small girls are viewed from the back while seated in child-size antique chairs. They appear to be twins, based on their matching size and outfits, though without seeing their faces the viewer is left unsure. Unlike in Friedrich's works, there is no view in the background to occupy the girls' or the viewer's attention. We are left to contemplate the similarities and differences (the chairs, the hairstyles, the shoe colors) between the two figures. As the desire to see their faces increases, so too does the concern about why we are not shown them in the first place. Our suspicions about the scene rise as well. Looking long enough, we question our first impressions. Is the child on the left real or a doll sitting with a human companion? The painting evades categorical understanding and ultimately confounds the viewer.

Perhaps just as unsettling as the unknown or unknowable *Rückenfigur* is its polar opposite: the confrontational figure viewed head-on. In life, the experience of catching a glimpse of a figure as presented in *Bean Boots* or *Light Station*, one whose posture challenges your perception and who meets your gaze so directly, can range from surprising to heart-stopping. The backward-turned figures grant visual power to the viewer, who seemingly controls the interaction.

4 Jamie Wyeth, *Lester*, 1963. Oil on canvas, 26 × 20 in. Private collection

Here the scopic power dynamic shifts in favor of the frontal figures, whom we might think of as "watchers" in Wyeth's work. They surveil, guard, startle, and generally unnerve the viewer with their intense stares and foreboding postures.

Wyeth composed *Bean Boots* (pl. 7) in a manner that places the viewer amid a disconcerting scene. The footwear from which the painting draws its title is the most innocuous aspect of an otherwise ominous narrative suggested by the elements of the composition. The oilskin-clad figure's piercing stare is muted by the brim of his cap, but the gauntlet on his hand connects him to the caged raptor at the left, which is partially hidden by the same shadow that falls across the figure's face. The bird's eye is prominent and acts as a surrogate for the gaze of the falconer. Above hang the trophies of this seemingly skilled hunter. Rather than just a display of the antlers of his prey, entire skulls with gaping eye sockets and snarling grins add menace to the scene. We appear to approach this sinister hunter not at his front door but from an interior space, turning us into a trespasser in a dangerous situation. To the right, two long guns hang on the wall, and now the hunter has us in his sights. The question remaining is, who will reach the weapons first?

Like his other works of island children, including *Dead Cat Museum* (1999) and *Cat Bates of Monhegan* (1995; pl. 8), the portrait titled *Light Station* (pl. 6) dwells on the sometimes-strange quirks of local life. Here, Orca Bates is seen posed in the role of lighthouse keeper, though the Tenants Harbor Lighthouse on which he perches was decommissioned in 1936. This character created by Wyeth is eerily motionless, and though he might survey the vast surroundings of the harbor or turn to look out to sea, his eye is instead fixed upon the viewers. In an uncomfortable exchange, the viewers become interlopers who discovers themselves under surveillance by this guardian of the light. The painting captures well the eerie sensation of being watched. The suspicion proves true—you are being watched—but that realization is immediately followed by disbelief. Who guards a decommissioned light? Perhaps someone out of touch with reality and living in a fantasy state, a nefarious figure guarding something kept within the lighthouse, or, more supernaturally, the spirit of a lighthouse keeper now gone. None of the potential answers are particularly reassuring.

There is no shortage of haunted and haunting beings in Wyeth's figurative work, including portraits of friends and relatives who have passed on as well as more anonymous figures who appear to be enchanted in some way. The otherworldly nature of these individuals is indicated in various manners. Perhaps the most straightforward among them is the physical transformation of Rudolf Nureyev into an animal in *The Faune* (2002; pl. 9). Rather than appearing to wear a costume, as he does in many other portraits by Wyeth, here the ballet dancer becomes a satyr-like mythological creature, complete with horns and furry hindquarters. In other works, figures appear to be mesmerized by some ancient spell or curse. The figure of young Kyle Murdock in *Dead Cat Museum* (pl. 5) stares as if in a trance, directly at the viewer, while pointing ominously at the placard inviting you to enjoy his offerings—both morbid and mundane. Behind him, a window presents a distorted reflection obscuring the view into the house/museum, adding further mystery to the otherworldly experience waiting beyond the door. The young woman with the piercing gaze in *If Once You Slept on an Island* (1996; pl. 17) illustrates the theme of the poem from which the painting's title is drawn; it describes an uncanny and vaguely magical change that comes over a person after sleeping on an island. The figure here awakens, newly enchanted, seeing the world with different eyes. It is not unusual for Wyeth to paint what appear to be half-dreaming, half-waking scenes.

From these eerie but otherwise fully comprehensible images we move to figures that are more difficult to reconcile with logical explanations. Rendering paranormal presences is a challenge for a painter who might struggle to convincingly depict the distinction between the visual and the spirit worlds. Take, for example, Morris Kantor's *Haunted House* (1930; fig. 5), which depicts an antique New England sitting room harboring a human-shaped shadow. Within the silhouette a dim nighttime scene emerges, showing tightly tucked-together houses with many windows glowing from within. The surreal phantom, however, calls the entire scene into question, leaving us to wonder which parts are "real" and which are meant to be ghostly illusion. As soon as we question our own perceptions, we enter into the uncanny valley that heightens suspicions to the edge of paranoia. Contemporary horror and suspense films are particularly adept at leading audiences down this path because filmmakers, like painters, traffic in visual imagery. One need only think of the masterful scene from Stanley Kubrick's 1980 film *The Shining*, based on a novel by Stephen King, one of the most unsettling American authors, in which the psychically inclined child Danny Torrance rounds the corner in a hotel to see twin girls at the end of the hall (fig. 6). Are they real or his psychic vision? Much of the larger plot of the film revolves around telling the "real" world from the spirit world, which gradually merge as the narrative unfolds.

Wyeth's ghostly figures are identified in a variety of paintings through the different techniques used to set the supernatural world apart from reality. In *The Steeple Salesman* (2012; pl. 18), the central figure is depicted *en grisaille* while the remainder of the scene is in full color. The effect of the monochromatic rendering is that of an old photograph, a visual cue easily connected conceptually with the past or with memories. The distinction between the earthly and unearthly realms is also technically distinct in *Spring, the Hanging of the Tree Rocks* (2017; pl. 16). The foreground figure of Wyeth's wife, Phyllis

5 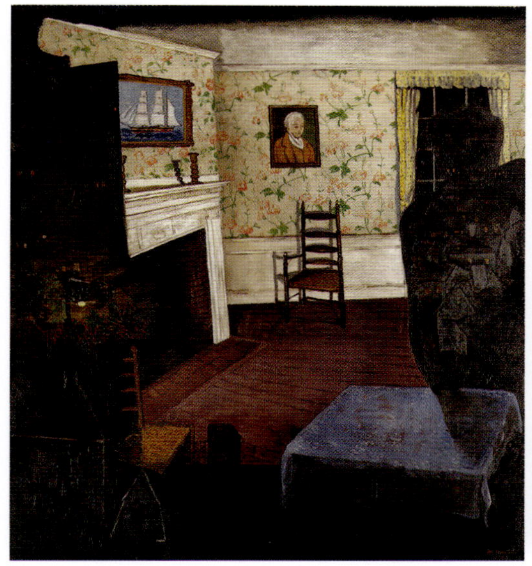

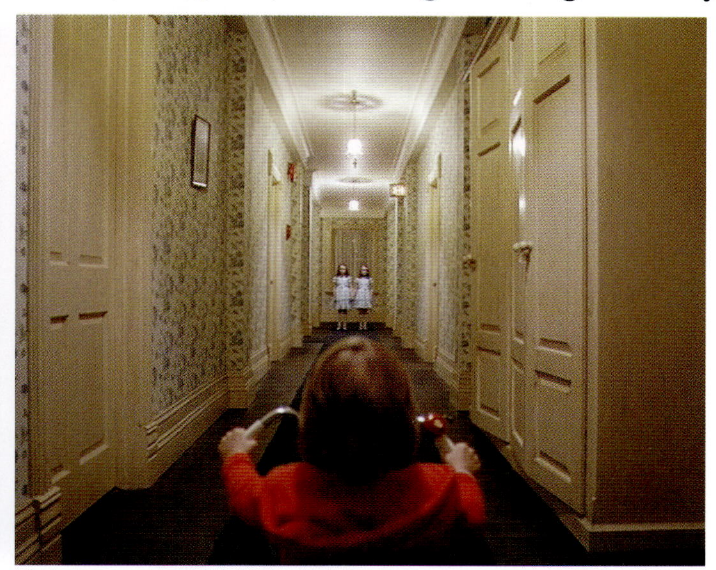 6

Mills Wyeth, and the trees represent an actual scene that captures her annual attempt to tame branches of blossoming trees by weighing them down with rocks. The other figures intertwine with the branches, half emerging from the blossoms but lacking full bodily articulation. In Wyeth's imaginative world, the simplest interpretation of these apparitions is as tree nymphs or other spirits embodying nature or spring.

In *Consommé* (2013; pl. 11), Wyeth relies on more traditional practices to render ghostly forms. The hazy, glowing figure of Andy Warhol perches awkwardly on a chair as he sips from a bowl. This is no vengeful specter or restless spirit seeking closure here on earth. Such a relatively mundane action may well represent Wyeth's memory of Warhol, who was a friend until his death in 1987. The very ordinariness of the image, which is much how Warhol might have acted in life, points out the fact that this is not Warhol. It is his double,

5 Morris Kantor, *Haunted House*, 1930. Oil on canvas, 37⅛ × 33¼ in. The Art Institute of Chicago, IL. Mr. and Mrs. Frank G. Logan Purchase Prize Fund, 1931.707

6 Film still from *The Shining* (1980), directed by Stanley Kubrick

his ghostly twin, an image that makes us blink twice to reconfirm our vision. Like Nureyev, who died in 1993, Warhol makes frequent posthumous appearances in Wyeth's paintings. The continued practice of making portraits of these two people suggests that their memories may be intellectually haunting the artist and that this repeated imagery represents their persistent invisible presence in his life.

Wyeth also conjures the spirits of the departed as part of his series "Screen Door Sequence." In these works, life-size figures are painted as part of an assemblage that includes a found door or window. The constructions utilize internal lighting that illuminates a figure who stands just beyond the threshold. Although the subjects include figures from the entertainment world, the most powerful of these works depicts Wyeth's father, grandfather, and friend Warhol. In the earliest, simply titled *First in the Screen Door Sequence* (2015; pl. 13), Warhol and his dog Archie are tucked inside an antique wooden screen door embellished with stars and stripes. The glare of the overhead lighting accentuates the stark white of Warhol's wig and ghostly pallor. As in *Consommé*, the screen door draws upon the memory of an ordinary action, but its appearance emphasizes the fleeting nature of just such an encounter. As in real life, a figure momentarily appears in a doorway; he passes through and is gone.

Two other highly significant figures in Wyeth's life also received the screen door treatment: his father and his paternal grandfather. In *Dormer: Third in the Screen Door Sequence* (2017; pl. 14), Andrew Wyeth reaches out through a broken pane within a shuttered window frame. The addition of a painted cast-bronze hand breaks the illusory effect of the picture plane: the work enters into the third dimension, crossing over into the viewer's realm. The window frame is Gothic in style, made up of a pointed arch and tracery segmenting the glass. Its design is identical to, though not quite as elongated as, the window in Grant Wood's *American Gothic* of 1930 (Art Institute of Chicago). The elder Wyeth is glimpsed as if transitory, about to disappear again into the world behind the window. In *Apples: Fifth in the Screen Door Sequence* (2021; pl. 15), Wyeth evokes his grandfather N. C. Unlike the other two constructions, in which the figures appear to be inside an imagined building with relatively little to indicate the interior atmosphere, this portrait of the eminent illustrator seems to capture him outdoors, collecting apples from an orchard. However, given the ethereal appearance of the landscape, in which a brilliant green haze encompasses the trees and the apples seem to fall weightlessly to the ground, one may also read the scene as a hallucination or illusion taking place within a house. The door then becomes a passageway not to the indoors or outdoors but to another world in which N. C. Wyeth goes about the task of gathering fruits in an eternal autumn.

HAUNTED PLACES AND DISTURBING SPACES

The framework of the screen door series, which suggests Wyeth's paintings are part of a larger, unseen or presumed architectural structure, introduces a classic subject used by purveyors of the uncanny: the haunted house. In a string of what might be called house portraits, Wyeth excels at presenting buildings in an unsettling light. He carefully chooses the lighting, perspective, architectural style, and other aspects of his subjects to create extremely unwelcoming spaces. The roots of the very concept of the "uncanny" lie in the German word *unheimlich*, which literally translates as "unhomelike." The comforting, familiar feeling of being at home is thus reversed to make one feel uncomfortable, ill at ease, suspicious, and ultimately fearful. An image of a house that raises the hairs on the back of one's neck is the ultimate in unsettling experiences. Wyeth is by no means the first artist to seize upon the house portrait's potential for eerie effect. Film has entire genres devoted to horror and suspense that rely on setting tense scenes via establishing shots of creepy houses. In the realm of American painting, two artists were especially adept at creating images of brooding architecture: Charles Burchfield (1893–1967) and Edward Hopper (1882–1967).

7

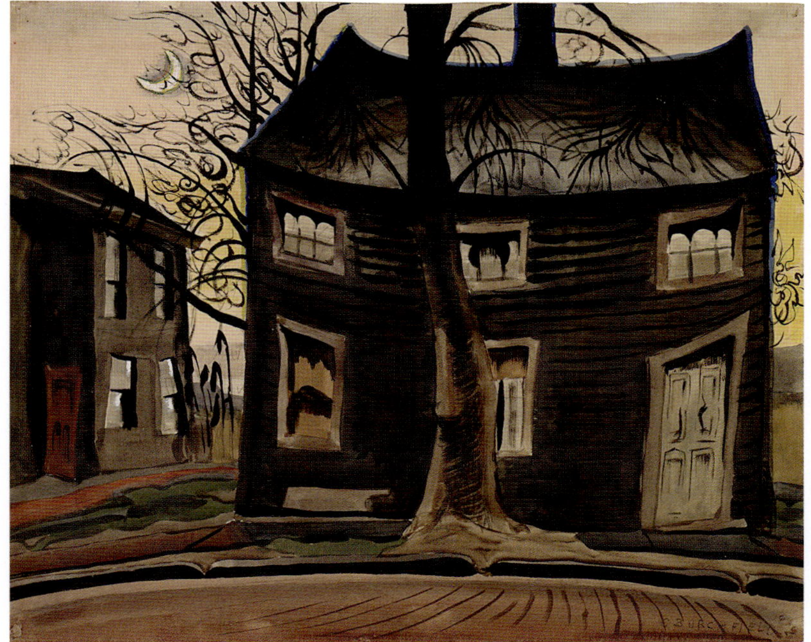

Burchfield is a master at depicting buildings in a way that brings them to life. Their facades are true faces, with window eyes and porch mouths. They stretch and yawn and moan, rarely appearing bright and cheerful. *New Moon* (1917; fig. 7) is one of many examples of houses Burchfield painted that appear less as if they are inhabited by ghosts than as if the house itself were a living, enchanted being. Here, the roofline curves into two hornlike peaks; that same invisible force stretches the windows and door into a taut grin. The warped architecture extends to the street, which is bowed toward the facade, caught in the house's thrall. The bare tree in front rustles its expressively sinuous

7 Charles Burchfield, *New Moon*, November 1917. Watercolor and opaque watercolor with graphite on wove paper, 18⅛ × 21⅝ in. The Cleveland Museum of Art, Anonymous gift in Memory of Henry G. Keller, 1954.569

branches, seeming to ensnare the crescent moon above. Even the neighboring house is impacted by the shadowy force, as seen in its distorted first-floor windows. Burchfield infuses the house with a menacing power that warns viewers and visitors to keep their distance.

Wyeth captures the same haunted house spirit, notably in *Squirrel Island* (1986; pl. 63), which may be the most direct example of a home that appears alive in his oeuvre. Unlike Burchfield, Wyeth does not obviously distort the subject to turn it into something fearful. His approach is to make the spirit of the structure emerge through realistic rendering. He relies on what is known as pareidolia, the human tendency (or desire, even) to see faces in everyday items. In making sense of the visual world, some people are apt to try to

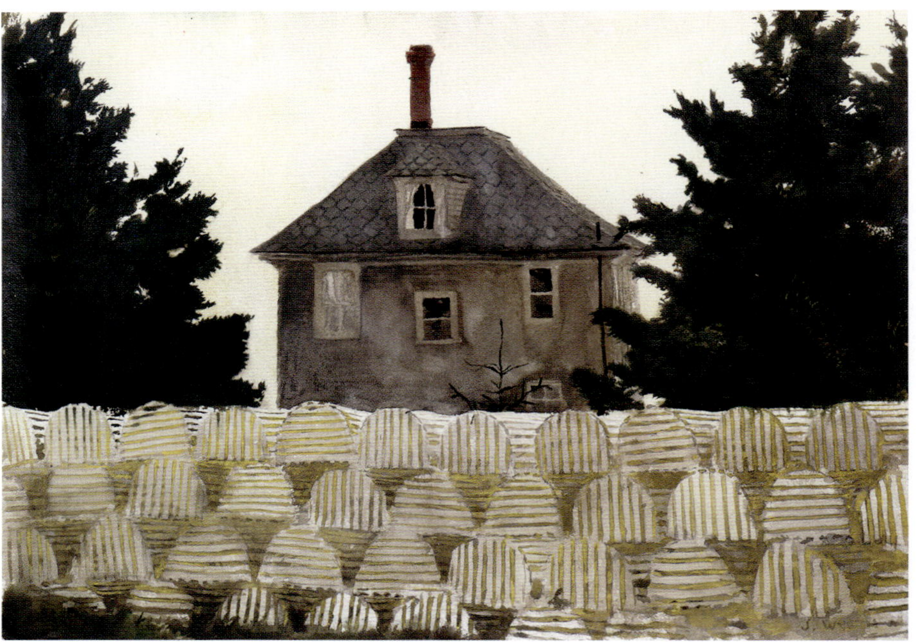

8

see familiar patterns (a human face, for example) as a way to impose order and assign meaning. In Wyeth's world, the faces that are revealed veer toward the disturbing. The house on Squirrel Island is fashioned like a sharp-edged jack-o'-lantern, with the dormered windows turning into two triangular eyes above a broad triangular nose. The posts and arches of the expansive wraparound porch form a gaping smirk. Looking further we see the chimney at the left is matched by a tall pine tree rising behind the house on the right. Together they create uneven horns, drawing the visage toward that of the devil. The house is its own warning to passersby: turn back.

A slightly more erratic character is perceived in *Hudson House* (1978; fig. 8). The house at the center of the composition, with its asymmetrical fenestration and off-center chimney, contributes to the structure's disorderly appearance, despite the crisp geometric outline. If the facade here forms a face in the mind of the viewer, it is a disoriented one, with one eye obscured by a white haze (the shaded window) and blank stare. The resulting face gives the impression of being disturbed, broken, and misfit. The house is barricaded by an expanse of lobster traps (a technical device that will be discussed later) and appears guarded by two flanking evergreen trees. The isolated quality of this peculiar structure raises the question: are these protective measures meant to keep intruders out or to keep something even more dangerous in?

The artist Edward Hopper is often recognized for his special talent of depicting lonely people, but he also excels at imbuing his architectural subjects with a spirit of anxiety and mystery. The quintessential Hopper house portrait is *House by the Railroad* (1925; fig. 9), which coincidentally hung alongside *Christina's World* for many years at the Museum of Modern Art in New York, forming a disquieting vignette near the escalators. Set against a stark sky, the Victorian-style home stands isolated from other buildings, nature, and people. The point of view Hopper selected, with the ground hidden by the rise of the railroad bed, elides any indication of human presence—there are no potted plants, no bicycle on the lawn, no wash hanging out to dry. A narrative of neglect is formed in which the grand house was abandoned when the railroad cut so close to it. Moreover, for those who recognize this structure as a model for the Bates house in Alfred Hitchcock's 1960 film *Psycho* (fig. 10), the imagined narrative could also be far more disturbing.

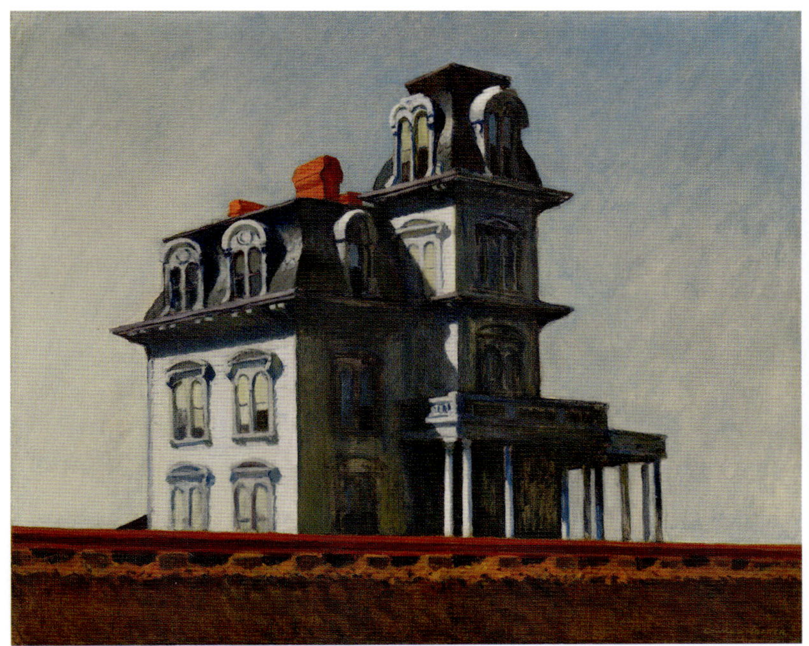

9

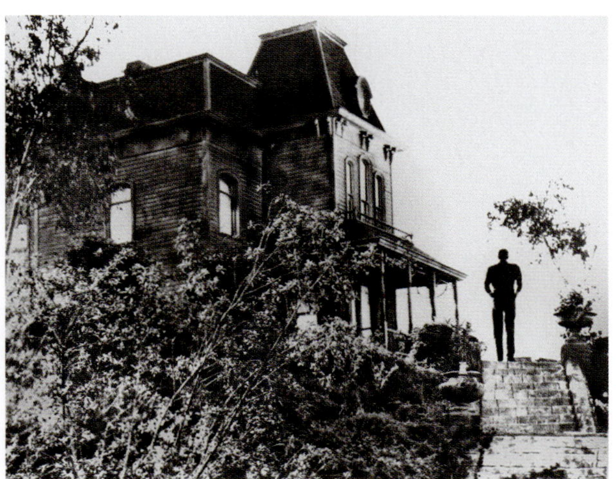

10

8 Jamie Wyeth, *Hudson House*, 1978. Watercolor on paper, 21½ × 30 in. Private collection

9 Edward Hopper, *House by the Railroad*, 1925. Oil on canvas, 24 × 29 in. The Museum of Modern Art, New York

10 Film still from *Psycho* (1960), directed by Alfred Hitchcock

The visual framing device of cutting off access to a structure is one that Wyeth uses to great effect. In *Island Church* (1968; pl. 65), the obstruction is not a railroad track but the aforementioned battery of lobster traps. With their shapes echoed in the arched bell tower above, the traps bar our physical and visual entry into the scene. We approach not as worshippers to the front door but as interlopers in the landscape. By using this perspective, with only the roofline visible, Wyeth ensures that the structure is still identifiable as a church but is cut off from its function of welcoming the faithful. Like Hopper's Victorian, the lack of a human presence casts this religious house of worship into dysfunction. A similar but even more extreme example of this compositional device is found in *Hekking House* (1968; pl. 64). The structure, which stands on Monhegan Island, is viewed from a vantage point that makes it appear to have sunk into the sands below. While the island is filled with visitors in the summer season, here we are shown what seems to be an off-season moment. The house sits empty, resting on the ground, silhouetted against the sea, waiting for its inhabitants to return. The imagination is eager to fill it with ominous occurrences, and the house, it appears, is ready to accept them.

Wyeth does not lead the viewer to haunted houses only to leave them on the doorstep. In fact, the screen door sequence may be his own explicit way of inviting the viewer inside. From early in his career, he has been breaching the thresholds of ominous spaces to explore uncertain interiors and the visions they may bring. Two mid-1960s paintings, *Barn Door, Broad Cove Farmhay* (pl. 61) and *Traps* (pl. 68), position the viewer inside a questionable space, looking toward a door or, more fittingly, toward a potential escape route. Wyeth offers us clues to our unlucky fate in the sparse elements of each composition. The grids of the barn door windows suggest the bars of a jail cell, while literal cages stand forebodingly at the egress in *Traps*. Given the tenor of so many other works by Wyeth, it seems safe to presume that we are meant to feel shut in, as if the doors are closing on us and we are being given a final glimpse of the outside world.

The concept of imprisonment also arises in a later work, *Gull and Windsor* (1993; pl. 4). A view inside Wyeth's lighthouse on Southern Island, the painting shows a tightly cropped scene consisting of the back of a Windsor chair and a window. The empty chair echoes the body that once sat there (and possibly will again). Gone is the inhabitant, who drew the chair up to the window to keep watch (indeed, that room in the lighthouse is called the watch room). The identity and whereabouts of the person remain a mystery while the gull on the windowsill replaces the human element. Why and how is this bird inside? Is it injured and under someone's care? Is the house abandoned and now reclaimed by nature? As with the girls in *Channel 12*, we question whether this is even a real bird or a decoy or work of taxidermy. Wyeth confirms that it was in fact the pet of his longtime model Orca Bates. Trapped inside by a thin pane of glass, the gull peers out the window. His confinement is further emphasized by the many spindles of the chair, functionally meant to wrap around a human form but which now compose a partial cage for this forlorn creature.

In *Traps* and *Barn Door, Broad Cove Farmhay*, the viewer stands in a work space curiously absent of workers. Always one to explore dark corners, Wyeth also turns his attention to what some brave soul might encounter farther inside these structures. What he finds and chooses to share is a series of portraits of tools, the sorts that are naturally found around the farms he explored as a young man. While many artists have found beauty in everyday objects, Wyeth is adept at drawing out the anxiety inherent in them by suggesting a backstory. The subjects in *The Axe* (1964; pl. 70) and *The Scythe* (1966; pl. 69) are placed within expected work spaces, as if momentarily put to rest at the end of a day's work. *Buzz Saw* (1969; pl. 71), by contrast, is a focused study of the blade itself, whose minimal surroundings are represented only by a flurry of yellow and green brushwork. Significantly, Wyeth depicts each tool in a state of disuse, enticing the viewer to picture their individual functions. In that act of envisioning the uses of these objects, however, thoughts drift from the legitimate to the nefarious.

11

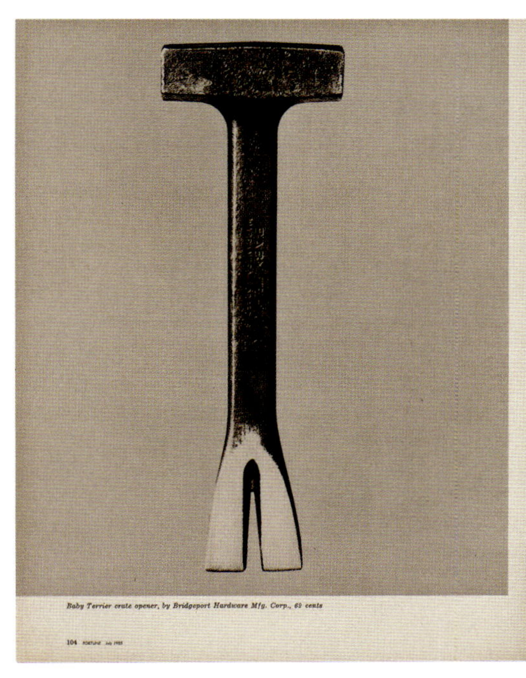

Baby Terrier crate opener, by Bridgeport Hardware Mfg. Corp., 69 cents

104 FORTUNE July 1955

The American photographer Walker Evans (1903–1975) similarly examined the material culture of work in a portfolio he created for *Fortune* magazine in 1955. In "The Beauties of the Common Tool," he elegantly showcased a chain-nose pliers, an open-end crescent wrench, and a Baby Terrier crate opener (fig. 11), among other hand tools. In his accompanying commentary, Evans extolled the classic lines, the "tough simplicity," and the aesthetic purity of each, comparing a hardware store to a museum for these "undesigned" forms.[1] All of these tools were positioned and photographed against a seamless backdrop, making them appear to float in space. The even, frontal lighting emphasized their symmetry, casting no shadows. The tools were oriented strictly, vertically or horizontally, using no illusionistic angles. A generous amount of empty space surrounds each one, and

11 Walker Evans, "Baby Terrier crate opener, by Bridgeport Hardware, Mfg. Corp., 69 cents," from "The Beauties of the Common Tool," *Fortune*, July 1955, 104

below the images, simple captions denote the name of the tool, the name of the manufacturer, and the price. The result of this direct objectivity is that each tool is elevated, taken out of the world of work and thrust into the realm of art.

Wyeth's meditations on tools are far less objective, and although he also elevates them out of the world of work, their destination is more akin to a crime scene. These objects are common enough for a farm environment, but they are also implements of great violence. In one respect, his paintings create in the viewer an instant vision—an imagined portrait—of the laborious lives of the people who used them. Nothing about that interpretation, however, explains the unsettling experience of viewing these works. Perhaps it is the current popular fixation with true crime, forensics, and the psychology of murder that adds to the disturbing perception of the dangerous potential such objects possess. Seen as weapons, the subjects of these paintings are accomplices to crimes. They are the pieces of evidence that may link an assailant to an attack. They are agents of mayhem that have been deployed in countless horror films to bloody effect. In this interpretation, when we imagine the tools as portraits of the people who have used them, we no longer see toiling farmhands. Instead, we see executioners, torturers, and psychopathic killers.

THE NATURAL AND SUPERNATURAL WORLDS

The use of the *Rückenfigur* is not the only comparison to be made between Wyeth's paintings and those of the German Romantics. The reaction among the Romantics to the industrialized Enlightenment venture reinvigorated attention toward nature and landscape, and other subjects that may transcend the limitations of human understanding surfaced in the work of many artists. To take another example from Caspar David Friedrich, *Abbey in an Oak Forest* (1809–10; fig. 12) directly compares the Age of Reason with other temporal frameworks. The small figures of the monks, moving in a procession through the ruined abbey graveyard and entrance, represent the passage of humanity's dependence on the explanation of phenomena based in Christian ideology. The age of Christianity is brief compared to the timescale of nature, as represented by the gnarled oak trees, and even the cosmic timescale referred to by the crescent moon. The wonder of the natural world stands in magical opposition to the rationality of Enlightenment thought. The Romantics, Wyeth among them in some ways, pay tribute to the vast, mysterious, sublime natural world.

Wyeth's work in Maine frequently acknowledges the power of the sea and its fearsome ability to challenge and overcome the accomplishments of humanity. In *Portrait of a Moon Curser, Fifteenth in a Suite of Untoward Occurrences on Monhegan Island* (2020; pl. 38) and *My Mother and the Squall* (2016; pl. 41), the sea churns and threatens human figures. In *Berg* (2011; pl. 39) and *Spindrift* (2010; pl. 40), Wyeth's small island and its lighthouse are engulfed from all angles in

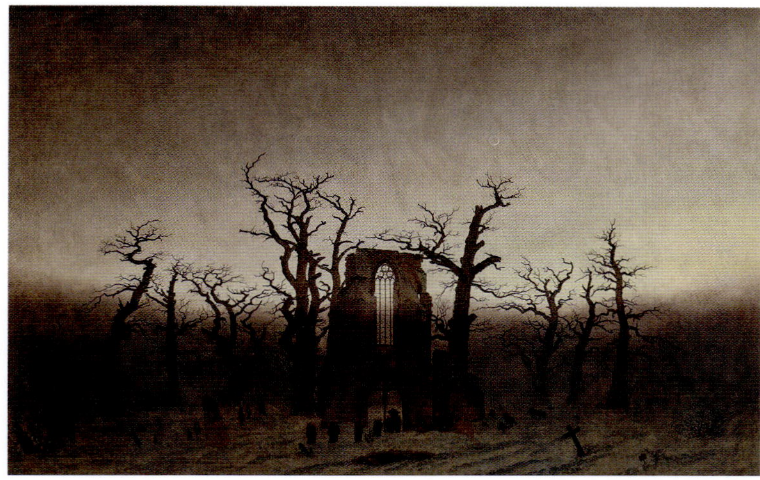

12

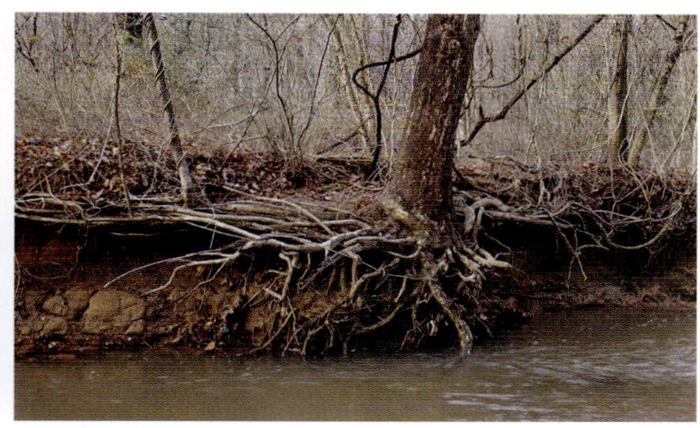

13

the onslaught of coastal storms. However, it is the earlier forest-based works from Pennsylvania that represent a more supernatural side of his landscape paintings. In these, the imagination is unleashed on a walk through the woods or along the banks of the Brandywine Creek into a mystical world inhabited by enchanted sycamores.

The often exposed and elaborate structure of a sycamore's writhing and serpentine root system suggests a chaotic tangle of activity (fig. 13). The massive trees support themselves by spreading their roots out, not down, allowing observers to see what, for most other trees, is hidden well below the surface. Not surprisingly, Wyeth's compositional perspective often casts attention downward to the roots, rather than up at the canopy in a more traditional point of view. *Roots* (1971; pl. 31) and *Roots, Revisited* (2019; pl. 32) provide excellent examples of the artist's stylistic change over time while remaining focused on the bases of the persistently captivating sycamore. The twisted tangle becomes a springboard for Wyeth, as in *Where W. Rat Lives* (1978; pl. 33), to use the reflective river surface to mirror the

12 Caspar David Friedrich, *Abbey in an Oak Forest*, 1809–10. Oil on canvas, 43⅜ × 67⅜ in. Nationalgalerie, Staatliche Museen, Berlin

13 Roots of a sycamore tree (*Platanus occidentalis*) exposed by floodwaters

exposed roots, indicating an enchanted world underneath the forest floor. Not surprisingly, the shallow root system of such a massive tree often fails to provide adequate ballast in a flooded area, but the uprooted specimen provides even further opportunities to explore the underworld, as seen in *Fallen* (1975; pl. 34).

More than the simple observation of a natural phenomenon, Wyeth's tree paintings lean toward the paranormal, their curious organic forms endowed with an animating spirit. Like the trees in Friedrich's painting of an oak forest, Wyeth's trees become ancient creatures with a life force of their own. In the popular imagination, trees have often been granted the ability to come to life—frequently in unsettling ways. From the feisty talking apple trees in *The*

14 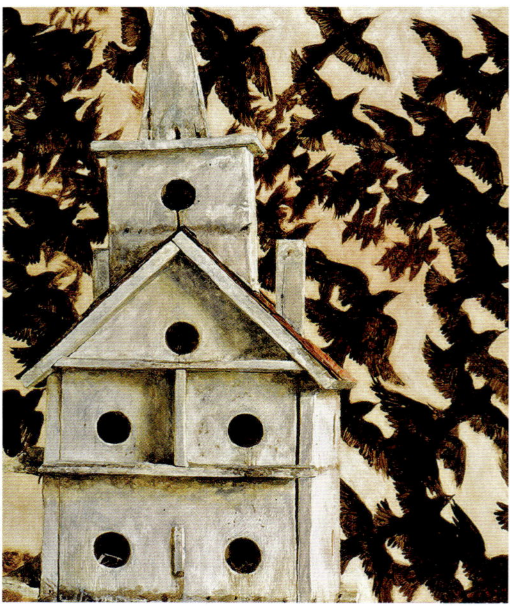

Wizard of Oz to the Whomping Willows of the Harry Potter universe, magical trees exist in many supernatural worlds. Wyeth's versions make up a rather sinister woodland world. For example, the original title for *Fallen* was *Torso*, compelling the viewer to see an anthropomorphized form—a body, undoubtedly dead and possibly dismembered—lying on the ground. Wyeth's arboreal creatures are more akin to the nightmare tree in the 1982 film *Poltergeist*. Before it develops overactive prehensile branches and attempts to devour a boy named Robbie, the child sees it as a threat, saying to his father: "I don't like the tree, Dad." His father reassures him, "That's an old tree. It's been around here a long time." To which Robbie persists: "I don't like its arms. It knows I live here, doesn't it?" The father's attempt to comfort his son prefigures the terror to come when he ominously states: "It knows everything about us, Rob." After becoming possessed by spirits, the suspicious tree proves Robbie's apprehensions were preternaturally accurate.

Within the broader natural world, the animal kingdom looms large in Wyeth's unsettling works. Acknowledging his self-proclaimed obsession with birds, he made them the subject of many works over several decades, including a meditation on the seven deadly sins, as embodied by seagulls who enact the baser natures of humanity. His gruesome work to reintroduce ravens to Southern Island in Maine involved transporting a cow carcass to attract the birds to a new habitat there. Popular culture readily lends an unsettling interpretation to his images of birds, just as Hitchcock's terrifying 1963 film *The Birds* served to raise suspicions about

15

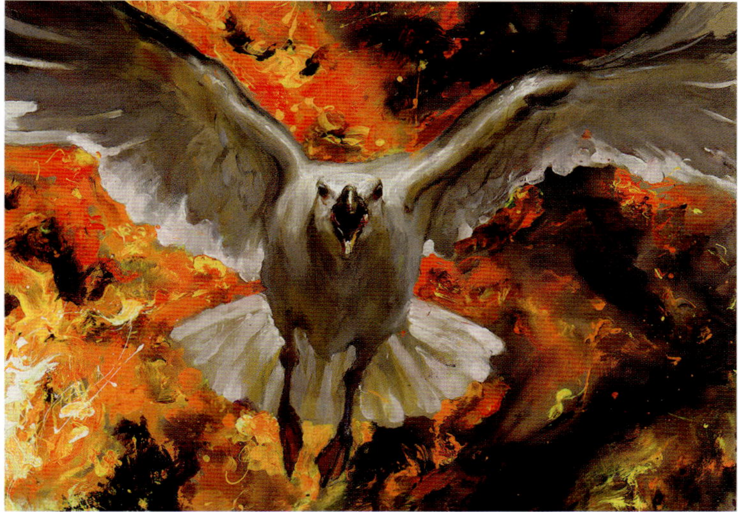

avian behavior, which was calculating, vicious, and ultimately left unexplained. In Wyeth's paintings, a variety of unnerving activities are observed in our feathered friends. Hitchcock's gathering of birds begins rather innocently, but their aggressive behavior rapidly renders groups of birds—murders of crows or unkindnesses of ravens, as they are fittingly termed—suspect. In *Birds' House* (1989; pl. 47) and *Bird Church* (1989; fig. 14), their sheer number instantly recalls scenes of the swarming creatures in the film. Though the elegant, solitary, and still predator in the foreground commands attention in *Snow Owl, Fourteenth in a Suite of Untoward Occurrences on Monhegan Island* (2020; pl. 46), the dizzying swirl of birds above provides a foil. Their behavior appears frenzied, causing the viewer to consider what disturbance may be just out of view.

The gulls in *Wake* (2008; pl. 50) and *Carney Gull #3* (2009; fig. 15) are related to a broader study of both the playful and fearful nature of these common birds. This pair of harrowing images of

14 Jamie Wyeth, *Bird Church*, 1989. Multimedia on paper, 35½ × 29½ in. Private collection

15 Jamie Wyeth, *Carney Gull #3*, 2009. Combined mediums on paper, 34½ × 48 in. Crystal Bridges Museum of American Art, Bentonville, Arkansas, 2009.12

seagulls, set alternately against foggy and fiery backdrops, portrays the ferocity of animals in their uncontrollable natural state. The two gulls, wings outstretched, bear down on the viewer so close that the tips of their wings are just out of view. The hooked beaks are poised to make imminent contact, and one can imagine their screeches rising over the roar of the ocean or the flames in the background. This provoked state is most like the horrifying telephone-booth attack sequence in *The Birds*. While Tippi Hedren's character Melanie Daniels is feebly protected by the shattering glass, Wyeth's gulls descend upon the defenseless viewer.

Perhaps none of Wyeth's birds are as sinister as his ravens—a bird with a reputation that predates Hitchcock's classic. Instead, this creature calls to mind the timeless poem by the American Gothic master Edgar Allan Poe. In *Saltwater Ice* (1997; pl. 48), the pair of ravens pose, ever watchful, against a backdrop of snow and a bilious green sea that appears otherworldly. These glossy black, blue, and iridescent guardians are rendered with frightful intelligence, suggesting that though they may be small, they will defend their territory against all predators, including us. The intriguing *Rudolf Hess and the Raven* (1997; pl. 49) creates an unsettling effect with its extreme conflict of scale. The stark silhouette in flight against a Technicolor sky appears to be a monstrous creature when we notice that it carries a human body in its claws. Upon closer observation, it becomes clear that the body is a military figurine, not a human being. As soon as this visual conundrum is sorted out, the bird shrinks in our apprehension to a normal size. Causing perspective to shift in such a way is a sophisticated move, forcing us to question our own perceptions, a very discomforting experience.

Winged creatures are not the only animals prowling Wyeth's canvases. The bodies, blood, and bones of sheep, cows, whales, sharks, and deer make up some of the most disturbing imagery. Beginning as early as 1968 in a group of studies related to *Portrait of Lady* (private collection), Wyeth's interest in the sinister side of the animal world begins to emerge. In *Sheep Drawing with Letter* (1968; pl. 42), he gives evidence of how even a purportedly gentle creature might evince menace. Below a black ink and wash rendering of a sheep's head, he wrote, "His face is the blackest of blacks and his eyes an unearthly pale—he terrifies me." Those terrifying features form the basis of *Sheep Eyes* (1968; pl. 44), which layers and repeats the central motif of the animals' black masks and glowing eyes bisected by horizontal slits. Though unusually shaped, the pupils are nonetheless accurate and directly tied to the sheep's survival: grazing animals require a broad scope of vision to guard against ambush. In *Portrait of Lady, Study #1* (1968; pl. 43), the eyes remain a focus, but the full upright body of the animal (now given a name) alludes to the importance of vigilance with its alert posture. Even in the relatively safe confines of a farm, Lady is fully prepared against attack.

Wyeth grew up immersed in life on a farm—although his parents did not have their own, he frequently visited and worked at the farm of Mattie Ball in Chadds Ford, Pennsylvania. Many of his teenage works revolve around this site. In a 2011 interview, he remarked: "Through this whole farm obsession of mine, I sort of viewed myself as a latter-day Dorothy, my life filled with real and imagined creatures."[2] Wyeth compared his experience to Dorothy's realization that she's "not in Kansas anymore," and it is important to recall that Oz was a frightening dreamscape, with its flying monkeys, melting witches, and dismembered scarecrows. Among the potentially traumatizing events Wyeth witnessed on the Ball farm was the burning of a cow carcass. The cow, which had died in the night, was dragged into a field and set on fire; the smoke billowing across the landscape drew young Wyeth from his home. In *Below the Barn* (1965; pl. 55), the artist framed a composition that not only highlighted the grisly remains, charred and still smoldering, but also included live cows in the background. These can be interpreted in a variety of ways. They are, perhaps, nonchalant witnesses to the immolation of a fellow creature, a somewhat disturbing behavior. Or, given a more anthropomorphic reading, they might be seen as mourners at the funeral or guardians of the corpse.

The death of a cow on a farm may be a natural occurrence, but the intentional slaughter of an animal provides an opportunity for Wyeth to create some of his darkest works to date. Anyone living or driving through rural areas is apt to be familiar with the sight of roadkill. However, the animal that Wyeth captures in *Deer Head I* (ca. 1965; pl. 57) and *Deer Head II* (ca. 1965; pl. 56) is not a typical victim of a roadside collision. The deer in these two studies has been decapitated, making this scene either the site of a particularly violent accident or the evidence left by a hunter, perhaps even a poacher, after an intentional kill. In either scenario, Wyeth would have been working among the blood and viscera that was left behind.

Sketching from real bodies—both human and animal—is relatively common in traditional art training, although it usually takes place in a controlled clinical or classroom environment.

Naturalists of the nineteenth century, most notably John James Audubon, studied their subjects by first killing and then mounting them. Among his many unusual collections, Wyeth owns several taxidermied animals. The practice of mounting a dead animal in the guise of a living one creates a commonly agreed-upon uncanny experience. The resulting specimen—if done well—can look convincingly real but often fails to capture the spark of life that is now gone from the animal. The study of human anatomy is also standard art-training practice, and though Wyeth did not attend art school, he found a way to examine corpses by working in a morgue alongside a doctor. Several sketchbooks of his morgue studies (pls. 58 and 59) bear witness to the depth of his knowledge of the human form with flesh and tissue removed.

Skeletal remains of animals—another of the artist's creepy collections—also appear frequently in Wyeth's paintings, although after viewing his more visceral works, they might seem somewhat tame. In *Great White Shark* (2011; pl. 54), for example, a small dog bravely lifts his chin under the grisly shadow of the enormous mammal's gaping jaw. Wyeth makes the shadows more ominous with intense raking light, and the settee veritably quivers with energy, threatening to transform into a living beast. Rather than simply posing with the monstrous jawbone, the dog asserts a kinship with this distant evolutionary cousin of the ocean. In *The Bones of a Whale* (2006; pl. 53), pieces of the oversize skeleton contribute to the bizarre scene unfolding on the canvas. A young woman dressed in red stands like a pagan priestess surrounded by an array of bones yet evinces no fear of her surroundings. In *Farm Talk* (2016; pl. 52), the grinning skulls in the foreground appear reanimated in a macabre conversation. The use of bones as common props in Wyeth's world, where death and decay have become ordinary and unremarkable, is in itself unsettling.

The culmination of Wyeth's blood and bone works is, quite fittingly, the site where animal innards are part and parcel of a grisly but routine commercial enterprise. His spectacular tableau *Butcher Shop* (2015; pl. 60) features all the elements one would expect to find in such a gory interior—not just slabs of bloody meat, a decapitated head, and headless bodies but also a cleaver, an axe, meat hooks, and bone saws. The overall effect is more reminiscent of a horror-movie torture chamber than a grocery-store meat department. The butcher is a hulking man whose gray-tinged skin accented with pink tones indicates his exertion over the brutal task at hand. He grimaces, baring decaying teeth, as he brings down a meat cleaver while dipping his other hand into a bucket of blood. As in the screen door series, Wyeth's tableaux bring a three-dimensional realism to his visions, entering the viewer's physical world in the way a two-dimensional painting or drawing does not. *Butcher Shop* stands out as the terrifying pinnacle of the artist's unsettling interior world.

INTO WYETH'S WORLD

Perhaps not surprisingly, Wyeth's eerie imagined creations are countered in the real world with the oddities in his everyday life. He surrounds himself with unusual collections, many of which consist of precisely the types of objects that the average person might generally find strange. However, several of his most striking collections are textbook illustrations of the psychological concept of the uncanny as popularized by Sigmund Freud in a 1919 essay.[3] Automatons, robots, puppets, dolls, taxidermy, prosthetics—anything oddly real or in imitation of life has remarkably uncanny potential. Those familiar with the Wyeth family know that a particular passion for dolls and toy figures is seemingly part of their genetics. Ann Wyeth McCoy, Jamie Wyeth's aunt, collected dolls of children and had a nine-foot-tall dollhouse, which is still frequently displayed at the Brandywine Museum of Art. Beginning in his childhood, Andrew Wyeth collected military miniatures, thousands of which are still on display in the Andrew Wyeth Studio. Jamie Wyeth continues this tradition with a large collection of one-sixth-scale figures and their highly detailed dioramas, many of which are devoted to World War II–era vignettes. As miniature versions of human figures, these dolls usually rank fairly low on an interpretive scale of uncanniness. When such figures grow larger, approaching life-size, or move on their own, their strangeness increases exponentially.

Wyeth's collections reach another level of disquiet in a wide array of taxidermy, featuring birds and dogs, a bear, a fox, and more. In addition to the lifelike appearance of well-done taxidermy, the unnatural stillness of the animal compounds the unsettling effect. The viewer must reconcile that the object is both real (flesh, fur, and bone) and unreal (dead, frozen in place). A typical reaction is to check, in an apprehensive moment, to see if the animal is breathing. When a questionable object also has the ability to move, as with a robot

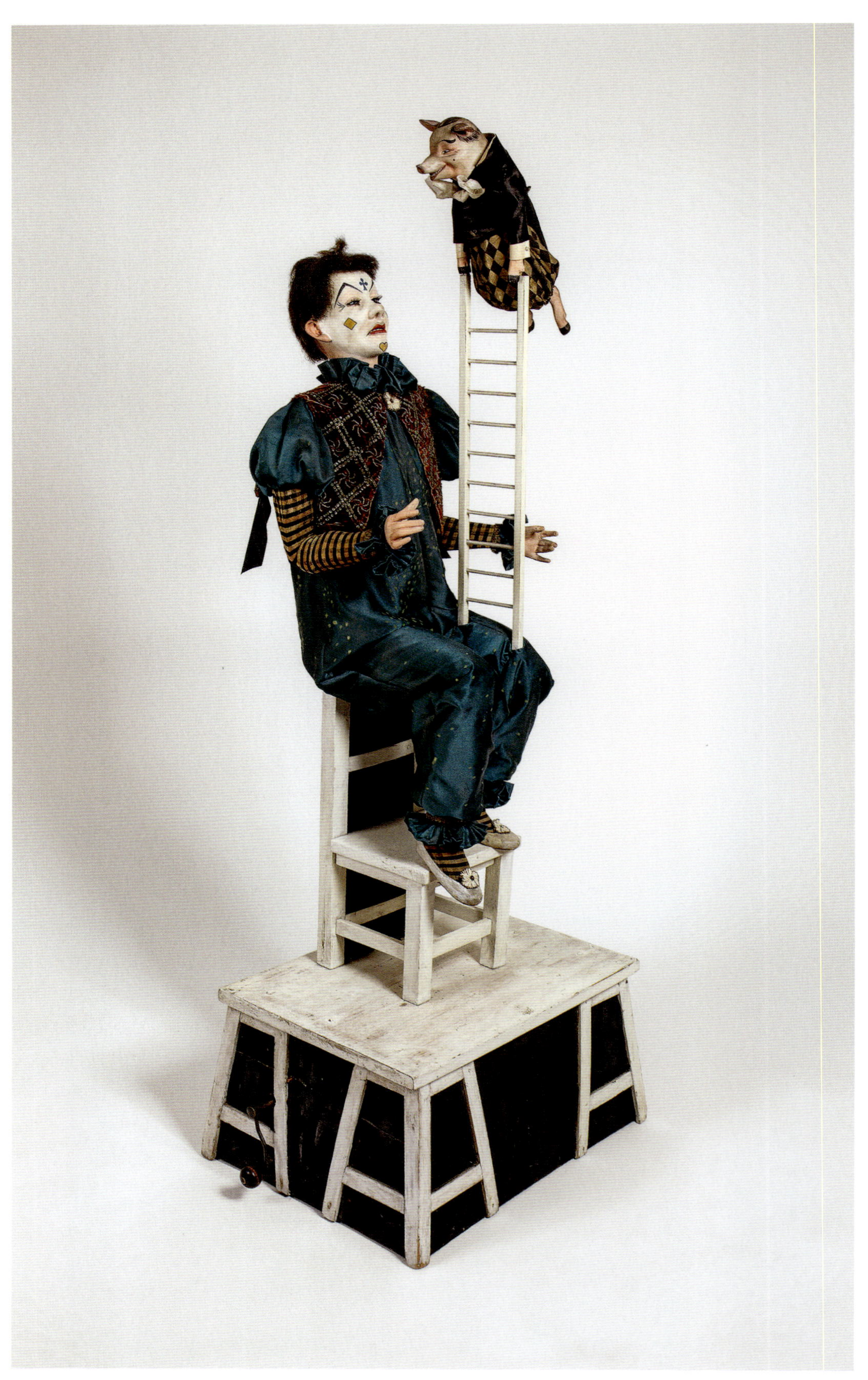

16 Gustave Vichy and Maria Teresa Burger, *Bob et son Cochon Savant*, ca. 1880. Papier-mâché and mixed-media musical automaton, 55½ × 22¼ × 15¾ in. The Phyllis and Jamie Wyeth Collection **16**

or automaton, the unnerving qualities reach their highest limit. In Wyeth's most unsettling collection—a small group of automatons—one particular piece rises to the peak of the Freudian uncanny.

Bob et son Cochon Savant (fig. 16) is a masterpiece of late nineteenth-century automatons. The largest and most complex automaton produced by Gustave Vichy and his wife, Maria Teresa Burger, in France around 1880, this fantastic fifty-five-inch tall, musical clockwork clown and his porcine friend perform over twenty nuanced movements to the accompaniment of four songs. One of only four known to exist, Wyeth's version still executes its acrobatic routine: the pig balances on a ladder, twisting and twirling, while Bob taps along, ready to catch the little gymnast should he lose his balance. The mechanism that drives the work is sophisticated enough to produce relatively smooth movements during its unexpectedly complex operation.

In his essay, automatons are specifically cited by Freud for their uncanny qualities. To explain the phenomenon, he uses as his primary example E. T. A. Hoffmann's 1816 tale *The Sandman*, which in its original form is much more elaborate than the shorthand version we know today. In both renditions, the Sandman visits children who should be sleeping. Rather than helping them along the road to the Land of Nod, as he does in twentieth-century retellings, the nineteenth-century Sandman plucks out the eyes of wakeful children. In the original story, a boy named Nathaniel has an encounter with the Sandman that later colors his perceptions of the world. As a grown, somewhat disturbed man, Nathaniel falls in love with an automaton named Olympia, whom he believes to be a real woman. The inability to tell the difference between the real and the replicant has a maddening effect on Nathaniel. Among the key themes shared by the Hoffmann tale and the Freud essay is the fear of being unable to trust one's own eyes and, as the ultimate consequence, one's own interpretation of the world. As a visual artist, Wyeth thrives on the suspension of disbelief that draws viewers into his carefully crafted pictorial illusion in all of its weird, haunting, unsettling glory.

Notes

1 Walker Evans, "The Beauties of the Common Tool," *Fortune*, July 1955, 103.

2 Quoted in *Farm Work* (Chadds Ford, PA: Brandywine River Museum, 2011), 49.

3 Freud's essay has been published many times over. For a standard English translation, see Sigmund Freud, "The Uncanny," trans. David McLintock and with an introduction by Hugh Haughton (London: Penguin Classics, 2003).

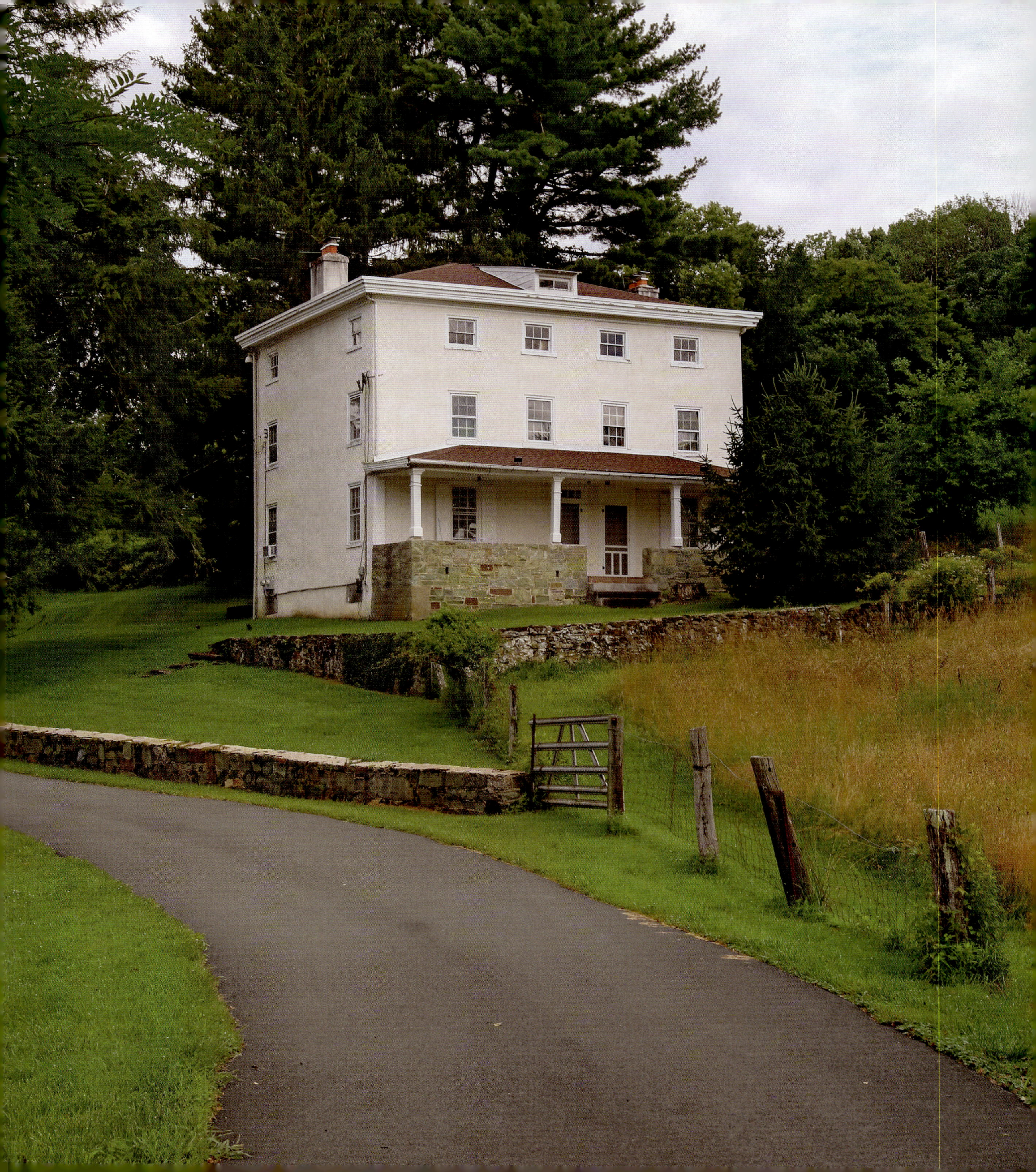

INVISIBLE ANXIETY

MICHAEL KILEY

The evocation of any mood or feeling through sound and music has everything to do with context. By working in a nonvisual form, sound designers and composers must embrace the fact that we cannot always control what else the listener is experiencing while consuming our work. Oftentimes the context in which our work is heard is a calculated part of the piece, but sometimes it is not. Our medium has the ability to be stored in a pocket or streamed over thin air. It exists everywhere. The environmental context that a listener inhabits has the power to completely alter the sensations that the music creates. Think of "Ode to Joy." Now think of "Ode to Joy" in the film *A Clockwork Orange* (1971). The feelings this music evokes are viscerally different because of this contextual relationship.

When I approach a new piece, the first thing I consider is if I have control over the context in which it will be experienced. That is why I often work in theater, where my sonic creation is in constant collaboration with other designers and can coalesce into a complete vision. I thus have more control over what I am making and the effect it will produce, because I know all the other environmental factors involved and have had input on how they will work together.

Sound can be the focus or it can be a layer. It can be quite a powerful layer *because* it is nonvisual. Sound artists have a special benefit: our medium is invisible, and therefore it is unpredictable. Because our work is temporal, we can create compositions that alter listeners' sense of time by literally slowing down or speeding up their heart rate. We can create illusions and give listeners a kind of dissonance of perception by manipulating their emotions. And though sound and music can summon joy, happiness, love, anger, and so on, I have found that aural work is perfectly suited to creating one feeling in particular: anxiety. After all, anxiety is largely the fear of the unknown, the invisible, the irrational. Nothing can create a sense of anxiety more than not understanding what is happening to you, and the medium of sound is the perfect tool to confuse and distort. Through the use of sonic dissonance (among other things), sound art deftly wields an invisible suggestion that everything is *not* OK.

In 2013 the Brandywine Museum of Art commissioned me to create a piece titled "Kuerner Sounds." It functioned as part of a tour of the Kuerner family farm, a place that served as inspiration for Andrew Wyeth and, I assume, his son Jamie as well. Supplied with headphones and an iPod, visitors were invited to experience the five-minute piece while wandering through the house and over the grounds. My goal was to alter listeners' headspace beyond that of a tourist or museumgoer, creating a mental atmosphere where they would open into a more emotional state. I find Andrew Wyeth's paintings and the farm itself to be highly emotive, but I understand that, as a tourist, it is easy to focus on the historical or factual aspects of a place. My job was to shake visitors out of that state of mind, providing a nondidactic way to experience this powerful dwelling.

To create the work, I began making binaural recordings of the farm. For those who don't know, binaural recordings are made with a special pair of microphones that record sound with the spatialization of human hearing, unlike a single microphone, which captures a monophonic signal. In other words, the mics—which sit in my ears like earbuds—record sound the way the human ear perceives it. I find that binaural recordings can open up the way a person listens by providing realistic spatialization and depth. I then made looped samples of the myriad existing sounds—insects buzzing, linoleum floors creaking, doors latching, birds chirping, pine cones crunching, water flowing—which I altered and composed into a sound bed from which a song emerged. I often develop tonalities, melodies, rhythmic ideas, and other compositional elements from the existing sounds in my site-specific works, and "Kuerner Sounds" was one of my first

← Kuerner Farm, Chadds Ford, Pennsylvania, 2023

attempts at this method. As I worked with the material, a hunch I had was deftly confirmed: Kuerner Farm is creepy.

From the first time I set foot on the property, I was struck with a sense of awe and anxiety. There is a special energy about the place—it felt almost like the ground was moving. A strange weight came over me. A dampness, a heaviness. The feeling was primitive and made me feel out of time. I began to wonder if that was why Andrew Wyeth kept returning to the farm over such a long period. Like this place, his paintings also feel out of time in some way. They feel both ancient and modern.

I therefore set out with the intent to create a sound piece that would make listeners feel as if they were transported through exis-

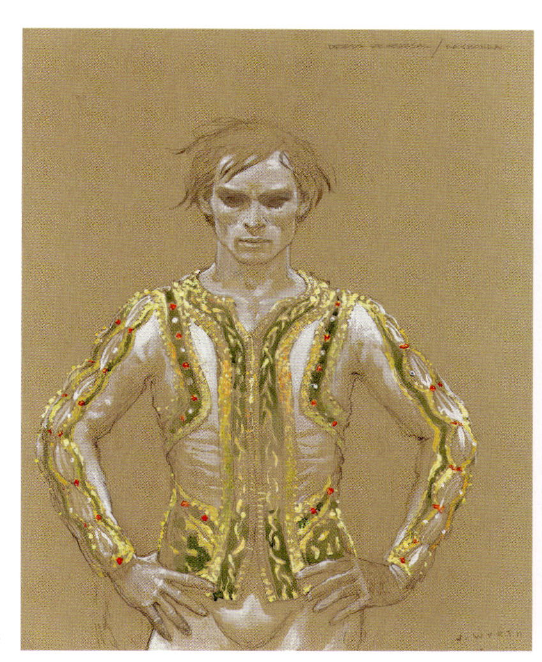

17

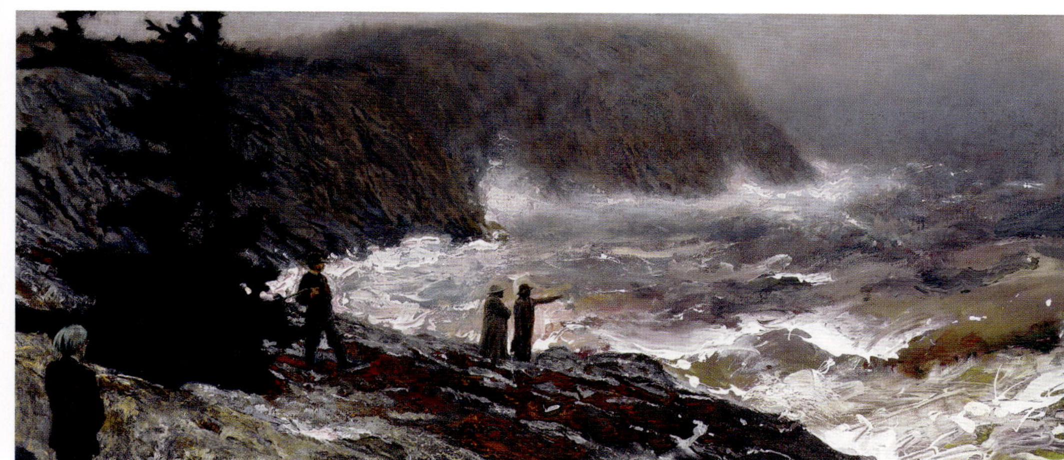

18

tential weight and anxiety to a strange nonlinear place. I wanted to honor the heavy emotions of Andrew Wyeth's work by creating something with a similar tone and texture. But I also wanted to portray the warmth and love he found there. For me, emotions such as fear, anxiety, and sadness are deeply coupled with their polar opposites: confidence, pleasure, and happiness. I find it difficult to express the dark side without also bringing in the light. There needs to be contrast. It is the coexistence of opposite emotions that causes things to vibrate, and I find that disorientation in artwork is always interesting.

That is also how I feel about the paintings of Jamie Wyeth. Multiple thoughts and emotions wrestle on the canvas. There is the grace of Nureyev but also the fierceness (fig. 17). This is the dissonance that excites and disquiets me. The first time I saw *Sea Watchers* (2009; fig. 18), I thought I was hallucinating when I noticed the figure of Warhol in the corner. It was like seeing a ghost, and each time I look at the work I still expect him not to be there. I know he will be, of course, but the haunting of that corner feels like he may disappear

17 Jamie Wyeth, *Portrait of Rudolf Nureyev—Dress Rehearsal / Raymonda*, 1977. Combined mediums, 20 × 16 in. Brandywine Museum of Art, Purchased with funds from the Robert J. Kleberg, Jr. and Helen C. Kleberg Foundation; the Roemer Foundation; the Margaret Dorrance Strawbridge Foundation of PA I, Inc.; and an anonymous donor, 2006. © The Wyeth Foundation, 2022

18 Jamie Wyeth, *Sea Watchers*, 2009. Oil on canvas, 24 × 53 in. Private collection

or travel to some other spot in the painting, or that someone *else* might be there in his stead. What a fantastic effect to create with a visual work. A distortion of perception in a static image.

Honesty can be more anxiety inducing than interpretation. I'm reminded of Jamie Wyeth's portrait of Helen Taussig (fig. 19) and how it was rejected when first viewed. Wyeth had honestly, at least in his mind, portrayed not only Helen's physiognomy but her intensity as well. The only problem was that those who had commissioned the portrait were not interested in her intensity. They wanted a representation of women in medicine as sweet, nurturing individuals. Perhaps they should have known that Wyeth often sees the depth and conflict in objects and people—if they had, they likely would have chosen some other painter to do the work. But I for one am grateful that history played out the way it did, and that we have this dynamic portrait of a wickedly intelligent woman whose contributions have saved countless lives, even if the work does make people gasp. The art world is all the better for it.

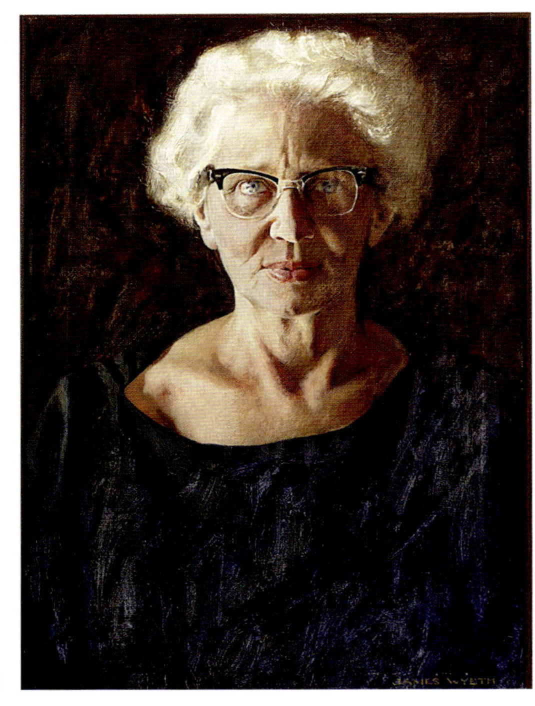

19

Now back to the farm and my attempt to represent a place with this type of honesty. As I mentioned, my site-specific work often establishes a tonality from existing sounds, which I morph and distort into eerie textures that you can't quite place. I am fascinated with turning recognizable sounds into the unrecognizable. I rarely want an audience to be thinking about the instrumentation of the music they are listening to. It is much more interesting if you react viscerally to sound, rather than saying to yourself, "That cello line is really nice." I try to take you out of an analytic mode of listening so that you stop evaluating and start feeling.

One of my most anxiety-producing sound designs was composed of nothing but the noises of fans and HVAC systems. Hums and drones can be incredibly spooky in the right context. This context happened to be Act II of *Ludic Proxy*, a play by Aya Ogawa about radiation and nuclear power. Act II takes place in Fukushima, Japan, during the earthquake of 2011. As the story progresses, the fan sounds begin to accumulate at such a level that you hardly notice. The act is broken up by a series of questions, during which the audience is polled for answers to determine the course of the play in real time. When each polling session occurs, the fan sounds go quiet. They pop on again each time the action resumes, growing louder and more present as we near the moment of the earthquake, which is of course a deafening series of sounds. By the time the earthquake hits, the stakes are already very high, and the audience is very tense, all because of the context of the play—and the sound of some fans.

That brings me to my favorite sound designer for cinema, Leslie Shatz, who has worked on many films, most notably Francis Ford Coppola's *Apocalypse Now* (1979) and *Bram Stoker's Dracula* (1992). When he and Coppola delivered *Dracula* to the studio, the executives loved the film but complained that the shots of the count's castle weren't scary enough (fig. 20). It was then Shatz's job to go back

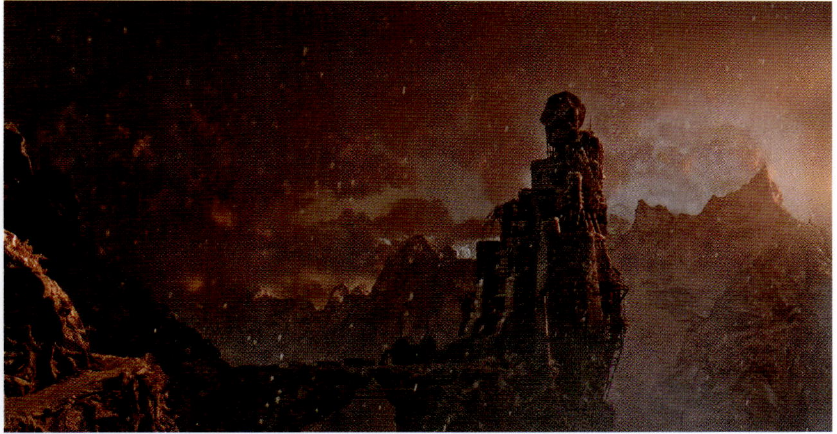

20

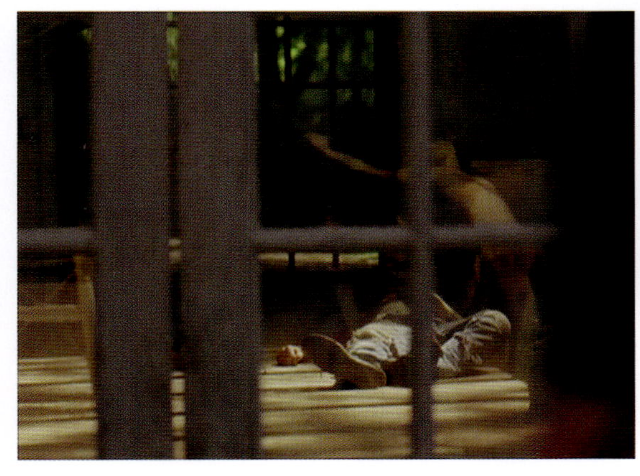

21

and make the static image of the castle scarier because, as he put it, "you can shut your eyes, but you can't shut your ears." Sound often does the heavy lifting when it comes to fright, fear, and tension.

Shatz created one of my favorite moments in film in Gus Van Sant's *Last Days* (2005), which is a loose abstraction of the final days of Nirvana frontman Kurt Cobain. Near the end of the movie, there is a long processional shot of the main character walking to the greenhouse where he will end his life (fig. 21). For this moment, Shatz chose an abstract composition by the composer Hildegard Westerkamp titled *Doors of Perception*. Recorded in 1989, this sound piece is made from recordings of doors opening and closing, church bells, automotive engines, and birds, among other sounds. On its own, it takes you on a journey that is almost narrative but not linear. Used in the context of the film to follow the antihero into the room where he will take his last breath, it creates a new narrative. It is disorienting, mostly because, until this point, the sound in the film has been relatively naturalistic. You, the viewer, know that something is horribly wrong. The sounds of doors opening and closing do not match the action of the film until they finally sync as the character enters the greenhouse, imparting a powerful feeling of dread. The camera holds a long shot of his face while the sound continues to clatter away, and we know that this person is lost forever.

19 Jamie Wyeth, *Portrait of Helen Taussig*, 1963. Oil on canvas, 24¾ × 15¾ in. The Johns Hopkins University Portrait Collection

20 Dracula's castle as seen in *Bram Stoker's Dracula* (1992), directed by Francis Ford Coppola

21 Michael Pitt as Blake in *Last Days* (2005), directed by Gus Van Sant

Assortments and arrangements of multiple sounds can certainly be unsettling, but perhaps the most ominous, anxiety-producing technique is the single tone. Just one note, held. Without other notes in play, the listener doesn't know what will come next. Will it be consonant or dissonant? Major or minor? Atonal? The tension is in the setup. The single brushstroke. Like the monochrome background of many of Jamie Wyeth's portraits, sitting there, allowing for the tension of the figure to emerge into the foreground. Just as N. C. Wyeth chose to illustrate the moments of *Treasure Island* before or after the action . . . the suspense is what is worthwhile.

I have begun more pieces than I can count with a single bass note, which is then repeated and added to. Yet sometimes I want

22

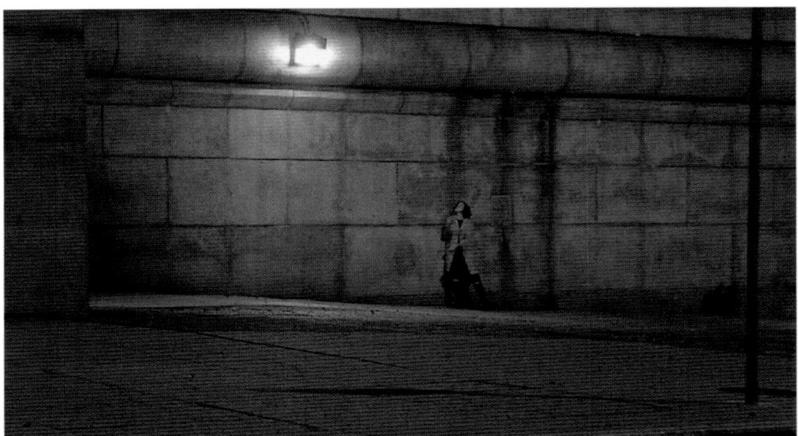

to commit to the tension right away, as I do in *Animina*, the soundwalk I created for the Race Street Pier in Philadelphia. I have composed several such geolocative pieces, which are delivered through a smartphone application, to control what you hear while traversing a specific area. These works are among my favorites because the context allows me to sculpt a journey for the listener that responds to a location as I see fit. For a brief moment, I get to soundtrack your life.

I grew obsessed with the walk from 2nd and Race down to the newly constructed Race Street Pier when it opened in 2012. As you walk toward the water, the base of the Benjamin Franklin Bridge towers over you (fig. 22). The scale of this structure makes anyone who stands next to it seem miniature, as though you are suddenly transported to Lilliput. It gives you a very real sense of dysmorphia. You then descend under the overpass of I-95 into a reverberant tunnel that hums with the traffic above. Once you emerge, the murky water of the Delaware awaits you at the end of the pier. No matter the time of day, the river is dark and foreboding. I couldn't resist making a piece that would guide you on this journey.

22 Pylon of the Benjamin Franklin Bridge

Animina begins with a loop made from the screeching brakes of the El train as it whooshes overhead. This found sound establishes a key of D major, which I developed into a melodic theme. I may be alone in this opinion, but I think major keys are great for creating dark-sounding pieces. Minor keys often sound too sad to be scary. The rhythms of *Animina* come from the space between tires as a car zooms over a highway, one section to the next, *ga-gunk*. I wanted to create an ominous sense of excitement as you descend under the bridge and emerge out of the tunnel toward your final destination: the river.

The piece is not entirely anxiety inducing, however. Contrasted with this suspenseful feeling are sections of calm and sweetness, and the overall message is that everything will be fine. But I felt I could not arrive at a sense of calm until I had produced a sense of uneasiness. Mostly I wanted to follow my goal of creating non-didactic ways of experiencing a place through sound. I intentionally play with your emotions and try to slow down or speed up your inner clock. If my sense of time has not been altered while I am experiencing a work of art, then I feel that it is not successful. If, while looking at a painting, I am marking my experience by the same temporal scale as when I'm eating breakfast, something is horribly wrong. I try to make you forget about time, to make you forget yourself for a while. That is why I love sound. It can truly transport you.

I say all of this knowing that feelings and emotions are personal. They are unique. There is no single experience that will cause every human being to feel the same thing. This is precisely why the work of Jamie Wyeth fascinates me. Not many people see spiders when they look at tree roots, or the seven deadly sins embodied by seagulls. It is his precise view of the world that shocks us into seeing things the way he does. My goal as a composer and sound designer is to create that same effect: to make you feel how I feel about a certain occurrence. To feel my point of view.

Transportive art changes the way you see things, for better or worse. It inspires change. It is the most powerful thing I have known.

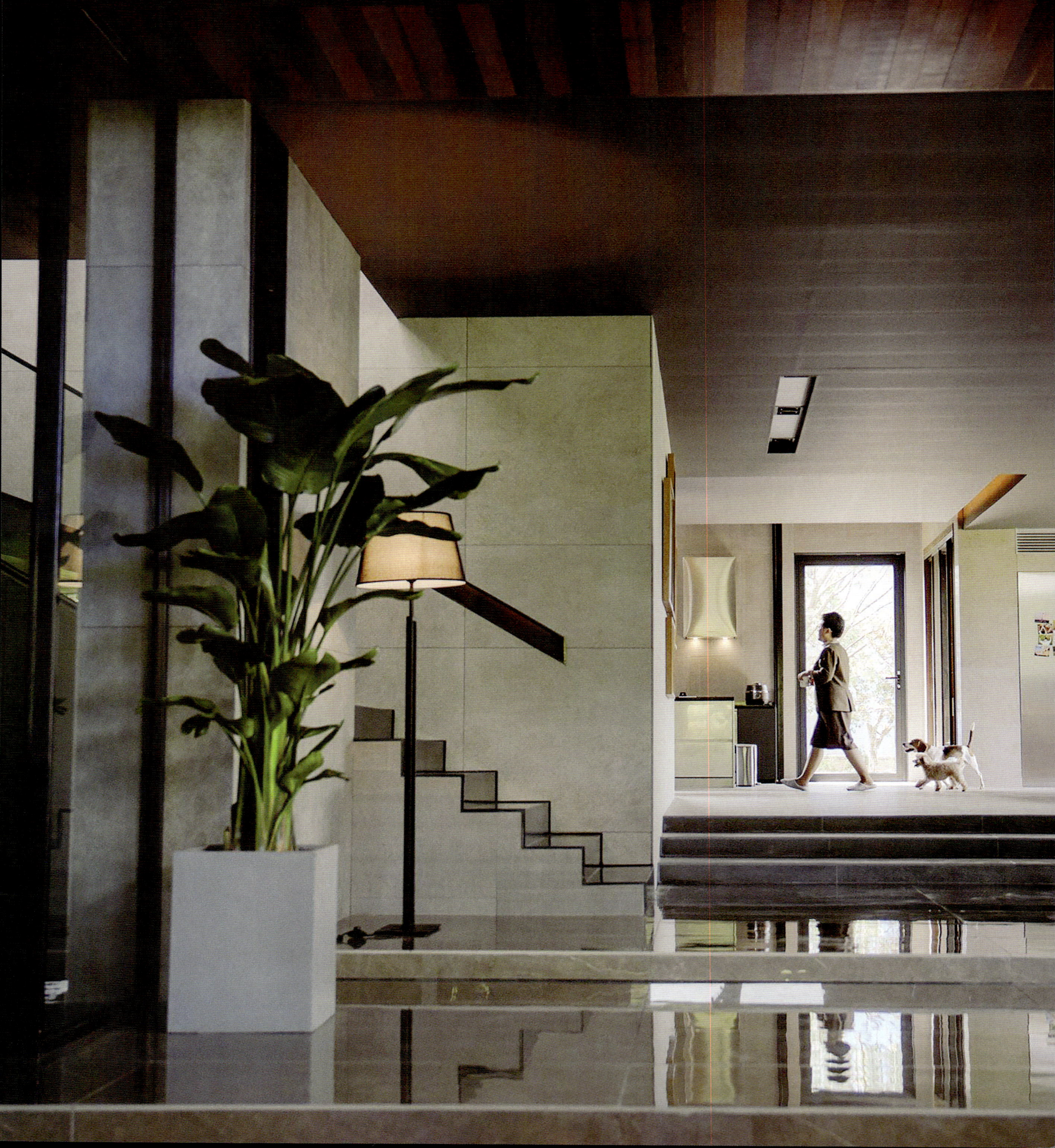

A BOMB UNDER THE TABLE: *MASTERS OF SUSPENSE AND TENSION IN CINEMA*

JOHN RUSK

I have an insatiable appetite for devouring film. In my formative years, I would often discover my mother watching old movies late at night on a black-and-white television. I was always amazed she knew every actor in every film and could articulate each emotional beat of the story. I inherited her passion. I studied French so I could watch Truffaut films without relying on subtitles. I traveled hours to special screenings of old Chaplin classics. I spent countless nights sequestered in decaying movie theaters with my feet stuck to the floor. I embarked on an implausible quest to follow that passion and pursue a career in filmmaking. In my fifty-year journey, I've had the good fortune to collaborate on cinematic classics with legendary directors and thousands of talented artists and actors.

All art has the potential to move us. Cinema, with its vast arsenal of elements, is uniquely suited to evoking potent emotional responses. The power of filmmaking is derived from melding aspects of other media and its ability to juxtapose images. This power can provoke tears of joy or jitter your popcorn right out of its bucket.

My focus here will be on film's unrivaled ability to unsettle an audience. I will avoid addressing television, although, granted, the distinction between television production and filmmaking has blurred over time. However, their delivery systems—sitting in a darkened room with a crowd of strangers as opposed to watching alone in your home—create different experiences. Imagine watching a slapstick comedy by yourself versus being among hundreds of laughing children. Or sitting in the deafening silence of a hushed theater, sensing that everyone is afraid to breathe until compelled to erupt in a collective involuntary gasp.

Unlike most other media, filmmaking blends visual art and performing art. It borrows techniques from painting and drawing and other two-dimensional media. The ability to manipulate light and simulate movement allows the medium to imitate three-dimensional art as well. It can employ sound, therefore incorporating the might of music and moving dialogue spoken by actors. Film is a powerful storytelling medium like literature and theater, but often it is grounded in a more realistic setting than what is experienced from the written page or on a stage.

Another aspect peculiar to film is the ability to manipulate time—not only in the sense of the actual amount of time it takes an audience to digest the content but also the altering of time through editing. Time can flash backward or forward to different points in the story. Motion can be accelerated or slowed or even frozen. Irrelevant passages of time can be eliminated from the story. Alfred Hitchcock remarked that drama is simply "life with the dull bits cut out." Editing to juxtapose images and scenes is another powerful storytelling tool for filmmakers. We, the viewers, must synthesize and respond to the relationship between those images.

In this age of commercials and incessant online content, today's audiences have grown more visually literate than previous generations. We are constantly bombarded with rapid-fire images. An emotional story with a beginning, middle, and end can now be told in fifteen seconds. The average shot length has diminished from twelve seconds to fewer than three. A film from the early days of cinema seems slow and plodding. Contemporary viewers have learned how to digest content much more rapidly.

There is a language of film, with its own grammar and syntax. Like other languages, it is assimilated over time. Viewers must interpret the thousands of frames hurtling past their eyes and construe meaning based on years of consuming content. As a result, we have grown to accept many of the conventions of the cinema, such as the "fade-up" to signify a new beginning and the "fade to black" to indicate the end of a scene. When one scene dissolves into another, we interpret this dissolve as a change in time or place.

← The Park mansion in *Parasite* (2019), directed by Bong Joon-ho

These and other conventions have been learned through previous watching experiences. When a film challenges these universally accepted conventions, it unsettles its audience.

Let's examine several films from different eras to understand how each director has artfully employed techniques and, occasionally, defied conventions to elicit viewers' emotions. Fritz Lang pioneered German expressionist cinema in the 1920s and early '30s, prior to fleeing to the United States when the Nazi regime began gaining power. In *M* (1931), his first sound film, Lang tells the story of serial killer Hans Beckert, who preys on young children. *M* is based on a real-life murderer who terrorized Düsseldorf families in the 1920s.

23 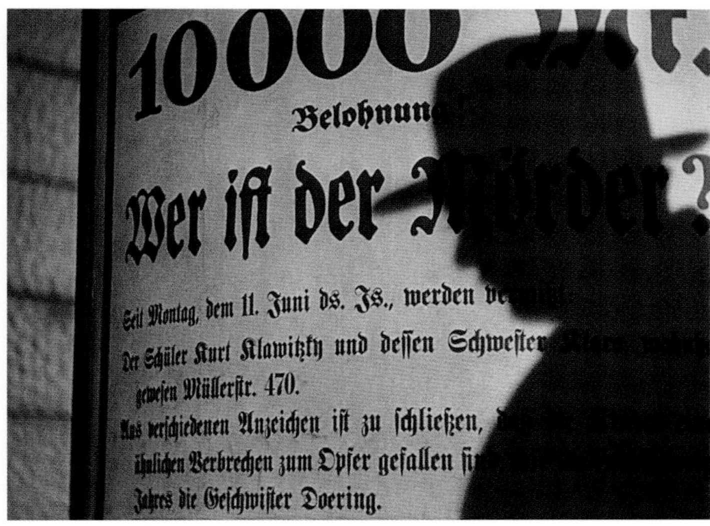

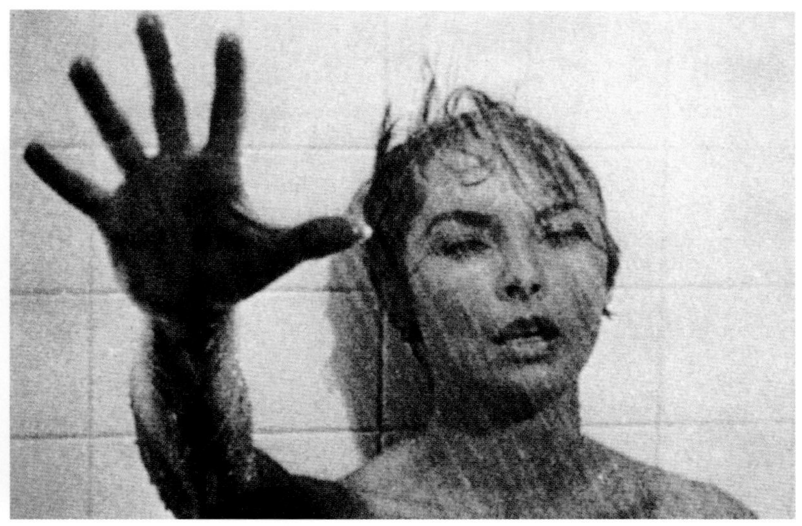 24

Lang's techniques in *M* are masterful. As the film opens, we follow young Elsie Beckmann dribbling her ball on the sidewalk as she walks home from school. She bounces the ball on a kiosk, and we see a reward poster soliciting information about the killer. Elsie is approached by a man we see only in shadow but hear his voice as he gently captivates the girl (fig. 23). This nice man buys Elsie a balloon.

Lang skillfully juxtaposes a series of images and sounds to suggest what transpires next: Elsie's mother is reminded by an unrelenting cuckoo clock that her daughter is late coming home. What begins as joyful anticipation quickly transforms into panicked worry. Her calls for Elsie echo down the empty stairwell of their apartment building. The annoying clock chimes again. The woman continues to watch the clock, awaiting her daughter's arrival. We see Elsie's empty place setting at the table and the silent attic where her laundry is hung to dry. Finally, we see an unattended ball rolling to a stop in a lonely park and the balloon drifting like a spirit toward the heavens. We

23 Peter Lorre as serial killer Hans Beckert in *M* (1931), directed by Fritz Lang
24 Janet Leigh as Marion Crane in *Psycho* (1960), directed by Alfred Hitchcock

connect the dots to paint the chilling portrait of a madman while never seeing his face. Lang went on to make dozens of films in Hollywood, but few approached the quality of his early German classics.

Alfred Hitchcock is regarded as the "Master of Suspense." When he directed his legendary film *Psycho* (1960), he was at the peak of his popularity. Renowned for its landmark shower scene, *Psycho* is much more than those three minutes of terror (fig. 24). Hitchcock defies convention by eliminating his protagonist midway through the story.

The film appears to be about Marion Crane, who escapes from Phoenix with a large sum of money embezzled from her boss. We are led to believe that she is fleeing to California to meet Sam, with whom she is having an affair. Marion's story turns out to be a MacGuffin—a plot device designed to engage the viewer. A MacGuffin is a thread pulling the audience through the storyline but is not the actual plot. The quest to find the meaning of "Rosebud" in the Orson Welles film *Citizen Kane* (1941) is a quintessential MacGuffin. There is no payoff to understanding the meaning of Kane's last word, but it is the vehicle on which the audience journeys through the narrative. In *Psycho*, we believe that we are watching a drama about Marion, but then she decides to take a shower and suddenly we are thrust into a completely different story. The stolen money is inconsequential. We are left uncomfortable watching a tale that has taken a sharp left turn.

Hitchcock believed the key to attaining suspense was to give his audience more information than his characters possess, a recurring device in many of his films. One famous Hitchcock anecdote involves four characters sitting around a table talking about something trivial. The audience is aware that a bomb has been planted under the table and will explode in five minutes. We want desperately to warn the characters, but we are powerless to act. The suspense is derived from the audience anticipating the outcome while the characters are oblivious to the impending threat. Hitchcock desired to "always make the audience suffer as much as possible."

Like Hitchcock, the Australian director Peter Weir is an unparalleled storyteller. His films reflect the recurring theme of culture clashes: the gritty Philly cop harboring within the puritanical solemnity of an Amish community in *Witness* (1985) or a rogue teacher bucking traditional values of a staid and stodgy boys' academy in the late 1950s in *Dead Poets Society* (1989). I had the great fortune to work with Weir on three of his films. Not only is he one of the most brilliant people I've met in the business, but he also may be the most brilliant person I've ever encountered. A scholar of human behavior and emotion, Weir is an ardent believer in the power of music. He would often play it on the set to create the right tone for the actors and crew. He also masterfully uses music to dramatically amplify the tension in his films.

In Weir's film *Gallipoli* (1981), the music itself becomes a dramatic harbinger. The movie chronicles the plight of two young athletes from different backgrounds as they are swept into the Australian army during World War I and deployed to the ill-fated campaign on the Gallipoli Peninsula in Turkey. The somber foreboding of Tomaso Albinoni's Adagio in G Minor repeatedly signals that the worst is approaching. To this day, I'm incapable of listening to the adagio without conjuring up images of the tragic deaths of thousands of young Aussie soldiers. A debilitating pall is rekindled from the indelible impression left by a film I first watched decades ago. In sharp contrast, Weir uses contemporary electronic music during action scenes, which evokes strikingly different emotions from those called forth by the baroque classical piece. The soundtrack to *Gallipoli* also effectively incorporates diegetic music—music sourced from within the scene. As a diversion, our two heroes sneak into a celebration and joyfully dance with some nurses to light entertaining music. Later we find their commanding officer in his tent, privately listening to (and then singing along with) a Bizet opera on his phonograph prior to sending his troops into a certain massacre.

25

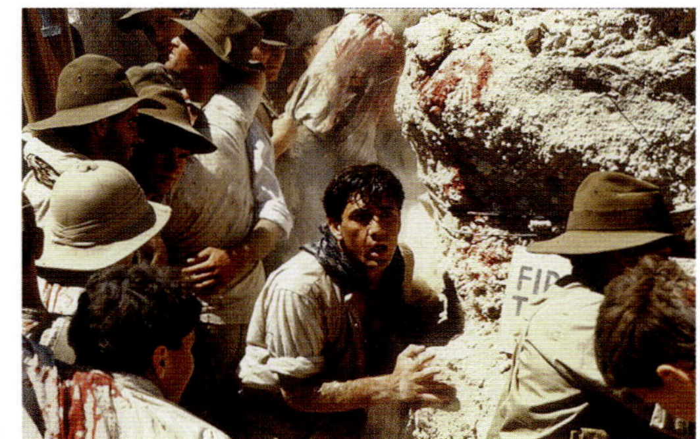

In addition to leaning into the powerful role of music, Weir juxtaposes sound and image to elevate the effect of a scene. In one brief battle sequence, rather than showing the violence of human versus human, Weir uses the cacophony of the battle over the reaction of soldiers who can only hear the results of the distant melee. The character of Frank, played by Mel Gibson, listens to the artillery and the familiar whistle signaling the infantry charge (fig. 25). He hears the relentless machine-gun fire of the Turks defending their homeland. We don't see the Australian soldiers as they are gunned down, but we hear their horrendous screams and witness the terror reflected upon the faces of those who are about to confront the same fate. After the battle, when Frank discovers one of his mates gravely wounded, the haunting strings of Albinoni's adagio begin again. We don't need to see what happens next. Instantly we know. Weir has conditioned us. He skillfully elicits a visceral response for us to experience the impending doom of his characters. Weir's powerful storytelling techniques permeate all his films.

25 Mel Gibson as Frank Dunne in *Gallipoli* (1981), directed by Peter Weir

"I see dead people." This whispered confession reverberated across the globe in 1999 thanks to a quiet film by a young unknown filmmaker from Pennsylvania. That year's second-highest-grossing movie, *The Sixth Sense*, became a cultural phenomenon and M. Night Shyamalan was catapulted into the limelight. I have collaborated with this brilliant filmmaker on twelve of his films. Like Hitchcock, he meticulously storyboards every shot and designs the movie before he ever arrives on set. He is a master of pace and tone. His lingering shots defy today's quick-cutting conventions, and his techniques to create tension have solidified him as a highly respected artist.

Early in *The Sixth Sense*, we meet psychologist Malcolm Crowe, who is confronted by a disturbed patient from his past

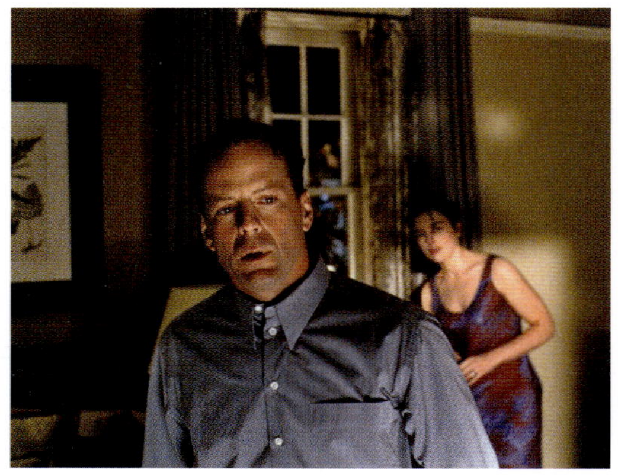

26

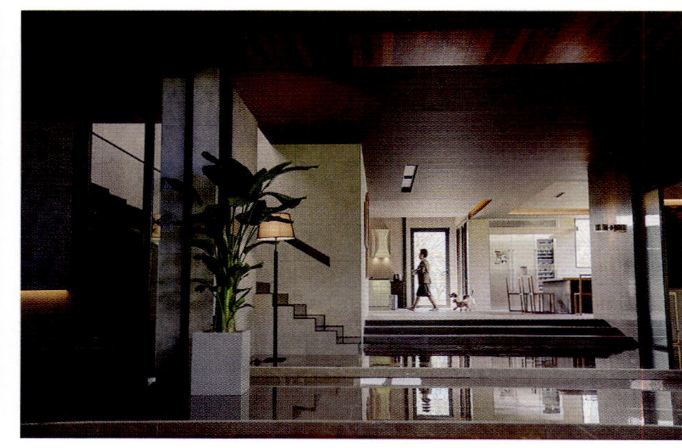

27

(fig. 26). Malcolm struggles to remember him. The camera slowly pans past the troubled young man from right to left, and when intercutting back to Malcolm it pans past him in the opposite direction. Traditional scene coverage is abandoned; we become uneasy. While the audience struggles with this disconcerting scene, Shyamalan shocks us with a pivotal plot point. A trademark of his films, the slow and deliberate unfolding of events builds tension and forces the audience to decipher where the story is going.

Later in the movie, we find Malcolm joining his wife, Anna, at an ornate restaurant. She is seated alone, and he apologizes for arriving late for their date. She ignores him when he sits down. She can't even look at him while he describes the problems he's encountered with a new patient. When the waiter brings the check, Malcolm tries to grab it, but Anna snatches it first. She whispers, "Happy anniversary," and leaves abruptly. The scene was filmed in one long languid shot. Again, Shyamalan shunned conventional coverage of close-ups of each character. We feel like we are at the table with the couple, but we don't understand the disconnect between them. To witness this unraveling between husband and wife is disturbing. It's

26 Bruce Willis as psychologist Dr. Malcolm Crowe and Olivia Williams as his wife, Anna, in *The Sixth Sense* (1999), directed by M. Night Shyamalan

27 The Park mansion in *Parasite* (2019), directed by Bong Joon-ho

not until the end of the film that we learn why Anna is unable to make eye contact with her husband.

Shyamalan captures subtle feelings throughout the film while keeping the audience engaged. He ultimately jolts us with a twist no one predicted. And with that, *The Sixth Sense* became an instant classic.

In 2020, the unlikely winner of numerous major awards was the South Korean black comedy *Parasite*, directed by Bong Joon-ho. The dissonance between haves and have-nots is at the heart of *Parasite*. In his own version of a visual canvas, Bong uses lighting and composition to contrast class inequities. The Parks live in a modern, spacious home with large expanses of beautiful windows through which daylight streams in (fig. 27). The Kims live in a dingy basement apartment allowing only a limited amount of light to pass through one small street-level window looking onto an alley. At night, their apartment is lit by the hideous green cast of brooding fluorescent lights. The Park mansion, meanwhile, is illuminated luxuriously with built-in lighting.

Stairs and elevations are also key compositional elements. The Kim family lives belowground and must travel up stairways to get to the rest of the city. When their son travels to the Parks' for a job interview, he must climb uphill to reach their house. Similarly, there is an underground compartment hidden beneath the Parks' house. To get there, they must descend a long stairway.

Toward the end of this chilling movie, the Kim family infiltrates the Park house and they are forced to hide under a living room coffee table to avoid being caught. The Parks decide to spend the night in the same room, and an entire sequence must play out with the Kim family hidden under the table. Hitchcock would be proud.

Movies have become an amalgamation of art and commerce. Producers produce to generate money; directors direct to generate emotional responses. They enlist the multifaceted elements of film to implant visceral feelings deep into our being. They prey upon our eyes and ears to defy the conventional language of cinema, thereby unsettling our subconscious. We are unaware that we are being manipulated. As the late French director Jean-Luc Godard famously theorized, "At the cinema, we do not think—we are thought." I believe Hitchcock would disagree. After all, a bomb might be planted under your seat.

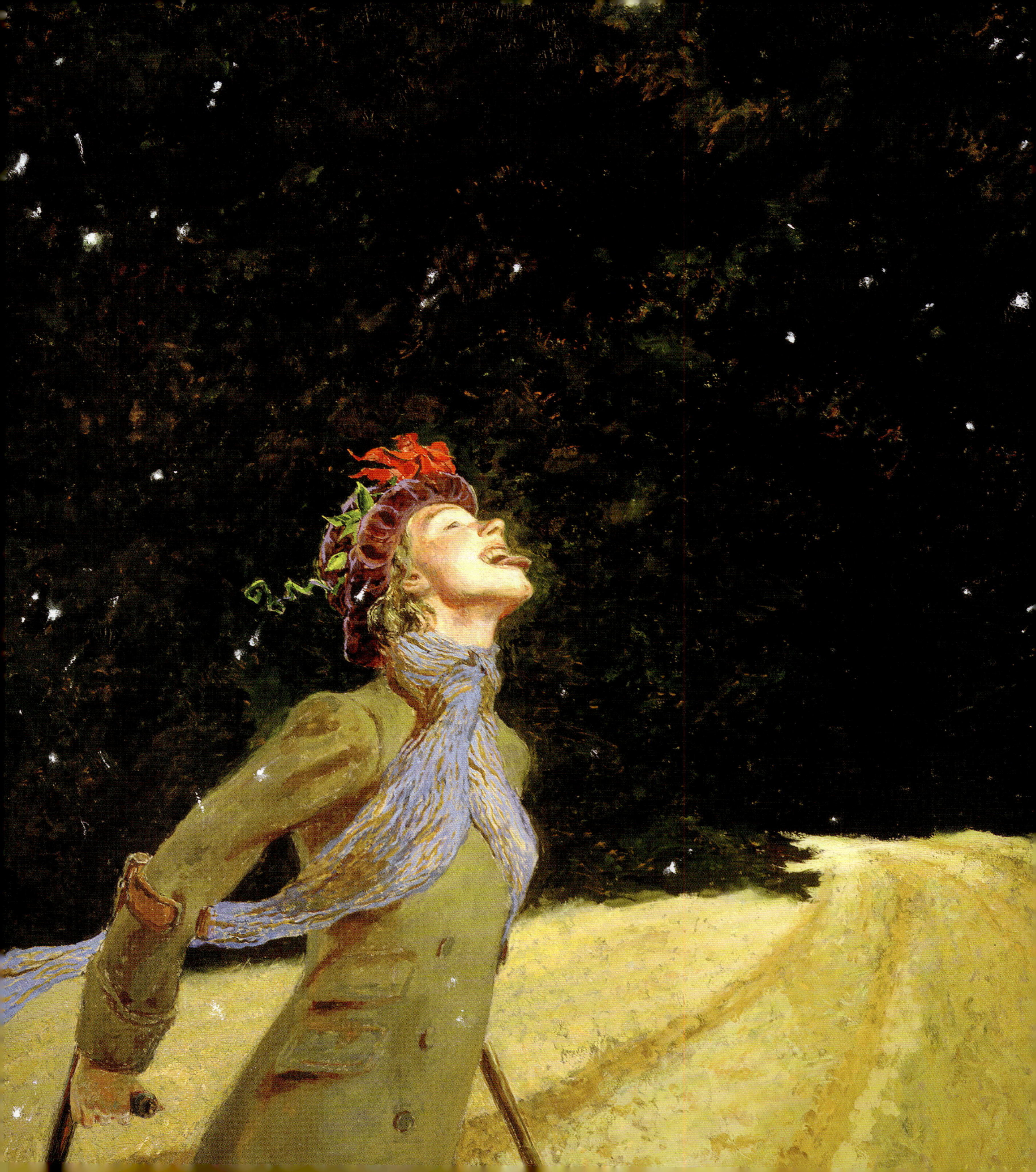

SOURCING THE CRUX

RENA BUTLER

Interestingly enough, Jamie Wyeth was a new name to me. His father, Andrew, I knew well from the art history books I had read in high school. His famous painting *Christina's World* (1948; fig. 1): the single female figure, yearning yet isolated and distanced from the traditional values that the home represents, expelled from the familiar and wanting something more, something else. . . . I can relate.

Works by African American artists have been largely underrepresented in the American art world, so I've always found relating to white subjects in the visual arts to be a challenge. When asked to find connections between my choreographic work and Jamie Wyeth's paintings, I had to dig deep, and the darkness that his work evokes speaks volumes.

It is difficult to explain just how dehumanizing the Black struggle was and still is—especially in the United States—when Black culture has been overlooked as well as appropriated since the birth of this country. I won't take this space to detail all of the violent physical, psychological, and emotional effects this mistreatment has wreaked on Black people. Instead, I will dive into how to churn personal disparity into artmaking and choreography, finding enlightenment through the most extreme and unsuspecting pathways of perspective.

Starting with the familiar: Edgar Allan Poe's story "The Tell-Tale Heart." This was the first piece of literature that made me feel seen as a thirteen-year-old girl. Ironically, I felt most seen by the elderly man's "Evil Eye," as the narrator puts it, and I connected to the narrator's obsession with wanting to destroy the Eye. Reimagining the narrative, I saw the Eye as representing society's perspective of the Black female being as monolithic, less human, and the most "othered" of any of her counterparts. The constant guilt that the narrator feels after murdering the old man with the Evil Eye is like the feverish desperation of trying to eradicate this particular trope, over and over again.

But what is the other, exactly? I have mulled over this question for years, trying to understand my relationship to the world as I appear when I step outside my front door every morning. In phenomenology, it is the individual who is perceived by the homogenized group as not fitting in or belonging. The group sees itself as the norm and passes judgment on those who do not meet those standards. In my own life, my artistry has been a way for me to converse with this definition and society's perception of who I am, as any artist may do. Artists create dialogues with something, whether it be themselves, a passage, specific ideologies, or the world. This was my way into Jamie Wyeth's work: understanding the conversation between our two worlds and how they could in fact respond to each other. Abstracted and reimagined, his paintings allowed me to find many a connection. There is a rich fabric of differences and nuances to explore in my work as a contemporary surrealist choreographer encountering Wyeth's work as a contemporary realist painter.

For instance, in Wyeth's painting *Julia on the Swing* (1999; pl. 27), the juxtaposition of shading is brilliant. The contrast between the light and shadow is drastic, marrying something seemingly content with something shaded and dark. The work brings a deep sense of anxiety, evocative of the way a person who is constantly labeled as the other in society may feel in homogenized spaces, constantly swinging in and out of light and shadow. A choreographic work of mine titled *This, That, and the Third* (fig. 33) is reminiscent of this painting. Commissioned by the Princess Grace Foundation and performed by Hubbard Street Dance Chicago in 2019, it was inspired by navigating an alien experience within homogenized spaces and how we come about intersectionality. I often feel the push and pull of switching my vernacular—whether language, natural movement, or simply self-expression—to fit into something "normal." I have code-switched my

← Jamie Wyeth, *Catching Snowflakes*, 2004. Detail

way through life, trying to make myself more palatable to society. And so *Julia on the Swing* elicited this curiosity in me about whether we choose to sterilize our personalities, or if we are in fact developing a multifaceted version of ourselves—the constant swing between the light and the dark.

To accomplish this effect with choreography, I was compelled to create a world around juxtaposition and opposing extremes. I continually jump-cut musical genres so that everyone could gain a sense of what it feels like to be the other while navigating a continuous, shifting landscape—similar to the way French director Jean-Luc Godard does in his films. My longtime collaborator and composer Darryl J. Hoffman unified the varying tracks with an original score, and we were granted permission by Chance the Rapper to use his tracks in the work. I wanted to incorporate rap music because of the stigma that surrounds it: that it's too aggressive, vulgar, or violent when in fact it is poetry in motion, set to a percussive beat. Rap artists use literary devices such as alliteration, hyperbole, and metaphor, and it's important to portray those connections and to demystify the trope.

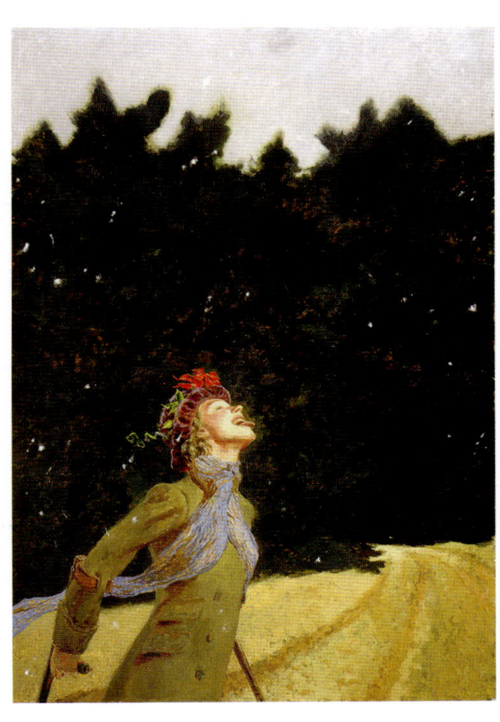

28

Another question I asked myself while creating *This, That, and the Third* was how to pose opposition in the score while celebrating the diversity in what we hear. Within the work is an excerpted duet that embodies this push and pull between an Asian American cisgender woman and a white American cisgender man. They are lit in opposing temperatures—one side of the stage is a warm color, the other side is a cool color—suggestive of their opposing worlds. They aggressively partner with each other to lift the vernacular barriers that separate them, similar to the way sumo wrestlers battle, and yet in the end they find themselves unsuccessful in understanding each other because of the constant rebounding off the other's body. In another excerpt, six dancers find themselves in separate boxes defined by white light. They gyrate and dance aggressively to a bombastic beat, attempting to break out of their confines. The music acts as the aggressor here, pummeling the dancers as they try to find their way into a space that is undefined by white light, a place they are able to move in freely.

Another of Wyeth's works that fascinates me is *Catching Snowflakes* (2004; fig. 28). Perhaps it is the immediate action of trying to capture as many particles in the air that can in an instant melt away in your mouth. The expression on the subject's face is excitable, and the intended consistency is all too familiar. When considering this painting, I found parallels to an excerpt in a choreographic film of mine, *The Under Way (working title)*, which premiered with the

28 Jamie Wyeth, *Catching Snowflakes*, 2004. Gouache and watercolor on toned rag board, 40 × 28 in. The Phyllis and Jamie Wyeth Collection

Philadelphia-based company BalletX in the fall of 2020. Coming out of a summer engulfed in a slew of pandemics, from COVID-19 to Black Lives Matter, I made a response to the psychological remnants of the Underground Railroad, filtered through Plato's Allegory of the Cave, and how it affects our livelihood today. It poses questions: In which ways are we still running? Are we running away, or are we running toward our personal liberations?

The particular excerpt I'm referring to is a movement phrase (a series of movements) in which a woman is dancing while silhouetted and strung up with LED Christmas lights. As the movement phrase continues, one can start to hear and see the names of victims of police brutality interwoven with the names of constellations.

29

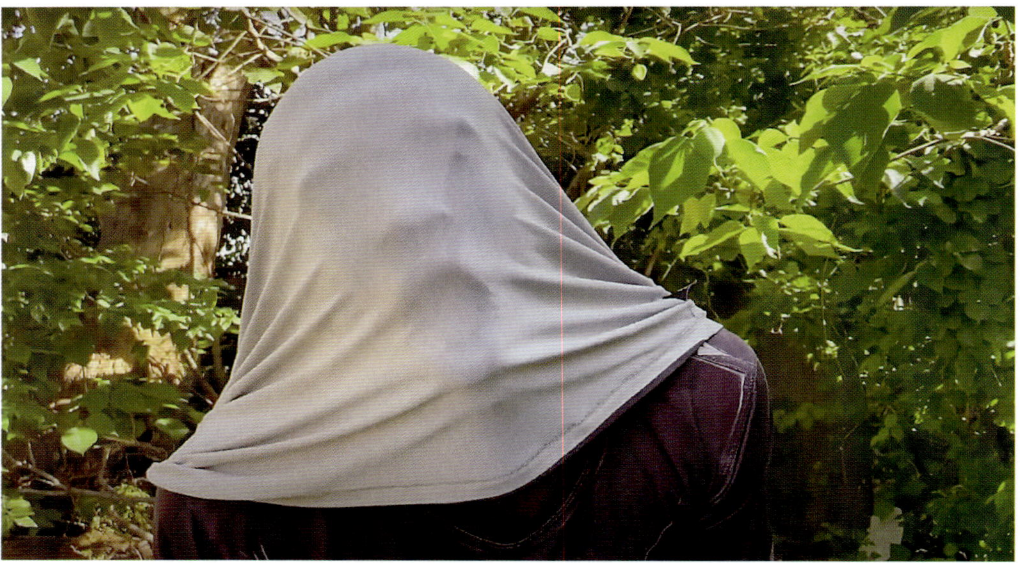

These accumulate from one name to more than a hundred, akin to how a snowfall begins. We try to catch each name, each snowflake, with urgency, just to get a grip on where we presently are—confirming what is tangible, what is real. In the instance of this excerpt, we are searching for that North Star to guide us. But those names or the advocacy behind movements supporting Black lives evaporate into thin air or are forgotten all too quickly.

In the painting *Other Voices, Study #1* (1995; pl. 2), I find that the inaction is most entrancing. The title spooks me in ways that transcend the image. Here Wyeth paints a figure leaning in to hear what is behind the door. The conversation between the figure and whatever is on the other side is the motion that keeps the viewer questioning the world beyond the canvas. *The Under Way (working title)* contains an excerpt that speaks to *Other Voices*. It begins with one Black male dancer hearing indistinguishable rhythmic breaths that are gasping for air, only to hear a few moments later that infamous phrase "I can't breathe." The dancer is then captured with his own T-shirt by another Black male dancer (fig. 29). The excerpt then develops into a wild ride of inner psychosis, which is conveyed through flippant images and pirouettes, jutted elbows and ghastly facial expressions.

It is important to note, while watching this four-minute excerpt, the inner dialogue that occurs in Black people when they are challenged by racial happenings and insults. This interior conflict is suggestive of what dehumanization may feel like and look like within the film. You see distorted images backed with fervent momentum as the two Black men run in place while the landscape continually

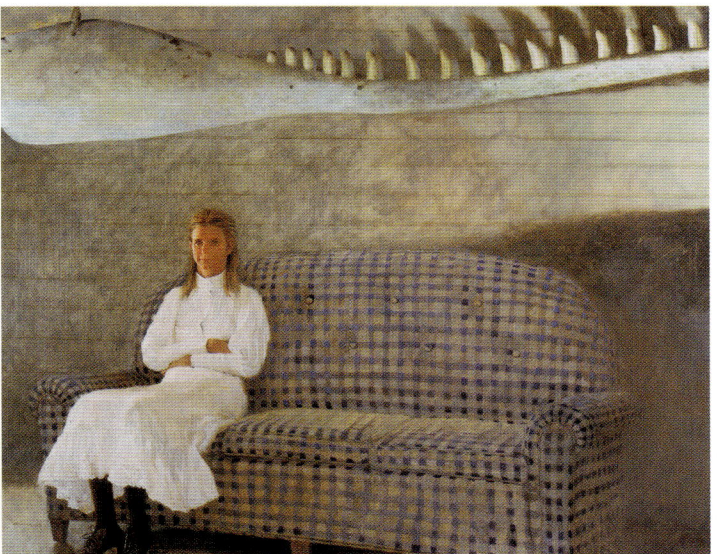
30

shifts from inside their homes, within a forest landscape, in front of a statue of Frank Rizzo. That same statue, of a Philadelphia police commissioner notorious for brutalizing Black people while serving his term, was torn down during the Black Lives Matter riots just days after this scene was filmed. At the end of the excerpt, the male dancer is uncaptured/released from his T-shirt, as if to insinuate the inner turmoil that comes from being Black and how seemingly composed we are expected to be as a survival mechanism in society. This excerpt could very well be the voices on the other side of that door—the inner voices that keep us suspended and arrested in curiosity, fear, and confusion. The inaction in fact contains the most action, though it is not visible or recognizable to the naked eye.

As the examples I've described indicate, when viewing any painting, the first thing I look for is the narrative, whether literal or abstract. It is a joy to imagine the personal stories behind the colors,

29 *The Under Way (working title)* (2020), choreographed by Rena Butler
30 Jamie Wyeth, *Whale*, 1978. Oil on canvas, 36 × 46 in. The Phyllis and Jamie Wyeth Collection

the expressions of the figures, or the brushstrokes and textures in the work as a whole. Even if the mark is missed, it is quite amazing to imagine the meaning the work represents. In *Whale* (1978; fig. 30), Wyeth presents a figure who sits as erect as the spine above her, her direct gaze challenging the viewer and leaving us completely unsettled. It even seems as though the spine is the textured image of her existential thoughts. We are left to wonder what sends her to such lengths in imagining thoughts that produce these twisted images. The elegant curvature of the bones suggests her contempt as well as the toughness of her feelings about the very thing she could be thinking of. There is an intimate yet disconnected dialogue here, and we are left to guess what it could be.

A three-minute excerpt in *The Under Way (working title)* has a similar disjointed connection to what we as viewers question in our own perceptions. Here you see two dancers, one female and one male, using all four walls of their living room as they engage in a duet about a power struggle. During the pandemic, the safest places to film were in the dancers' homes, and so we made do with what was available. The dancers and I adapted the movement to fit within the structure of the home, slamming the choreography against the wall, using the island in the middle of the kitchen and living room as a barrier between them. I wanted to curve and spiral the trajectory of the choreography, architecturally in space and body. The most effective tool was editing the scene to distort the viewer's perception by constantly rotating the image from right side up to upside down. Doing so prompts us to question what our realities actually are: if we are seeing what is before us or distorting what it is to fit into the comfort of our worlds. On reflection, it is disturbing to know that perhaps we are settled in the comfort of our own distorted realities, not seeing the world for what it truly is and how that distortion is projected and attached to us. Which images define our darkest thoughts?

Wyeth's *Pot* (1969; fig. 31) is another work that finds a parallel in an excerpt from *The Under Way (working title)*. In connecting these two works, we see that the expression of the single figure is complacent, not knowing what grim circumstances await them or what lies beyond the barriers or structures they find themselves in. In Wyeth's painting, a duck is in a cast-iron pot that encompasses it circularly. Only the viewer knows that what comes next is a lit stove and the duck's demise. In the excerpt, a white male figure dances in his living room as the televised funeral of George Floyd plays on the screen. The scene begins with the dancer on the couch, staring blankly, devoid of emotion. As he flips backward and turns to use his living room furniture in unconventional ways, he lists the everyday activities he has the privilege of doing compared to his Black counterparts. He is in fact also caged in his living space and in his own pot of soon-to-be boiled water—a cooked duck. But he recognizes that once he is free, he'll still be able to do as he pleases, without his actions being a threat to his existence.

In fact, the living room is a metaphor for the cave in Plato's allegory. The figure is indeed rummaging in a vicious cycle of the same repetitive thoughts that violently overwhelm him. He is eventually

31
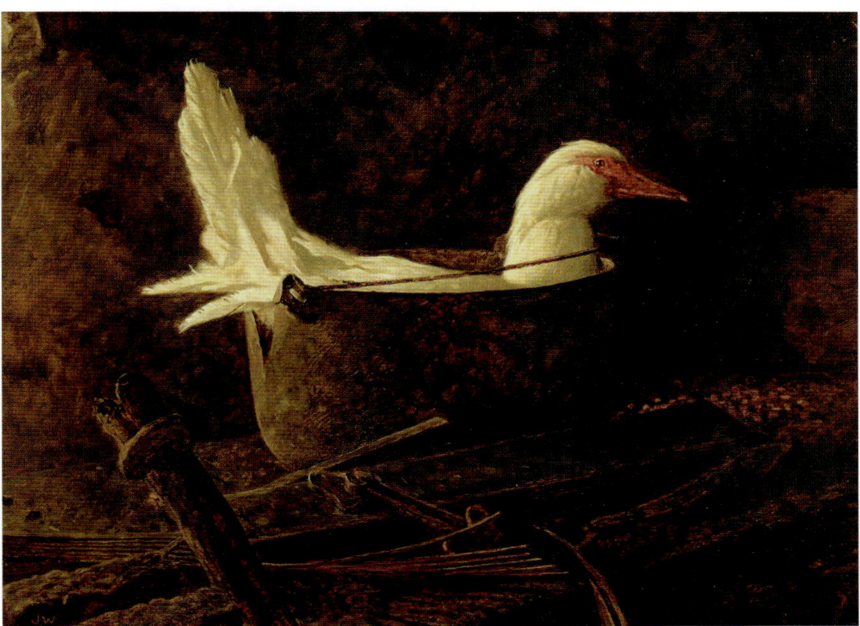

32
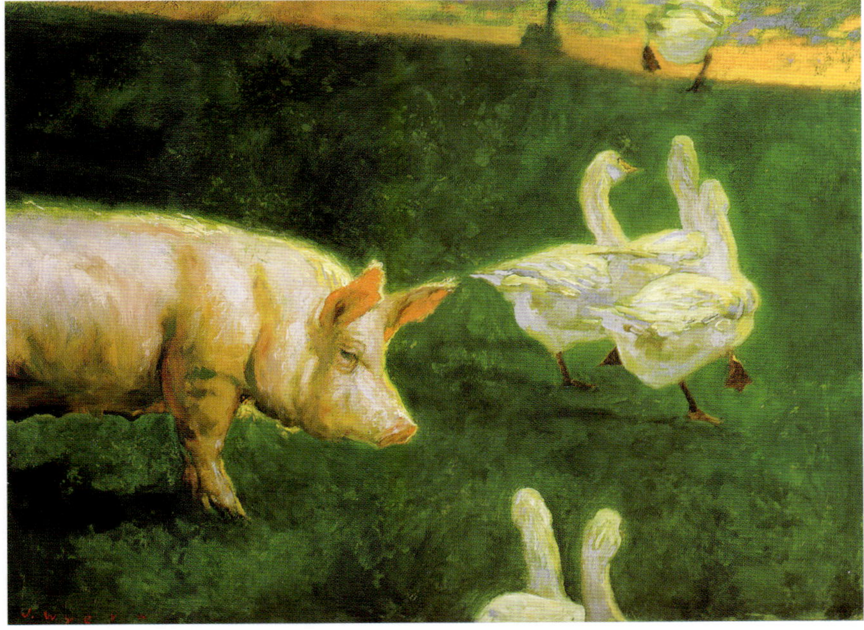

31 Jamie Wyeth, *Pot*, 1969. Oil on gessoed panel, 18 × 24 in. Private collection
32 Jamie Wyeth, *And Then into the Sunset*, 2007. Oil on board, 17 × 23 in. Private collection

overcome by the scenario and decides to exit into an effervescent light. The light is hopeful, but hopeful for what? We don't know, and the viewer is left questioning whether the light is liberating with a sense of onward progression or lighting the figure's way into another cave offering a similar demise. The light is the image of enlightenment. The irony that both these works present is the connection I find between them: being caged by your own freedom. The difference between the two experiences could very well be the realizations the figures find with action versus inaction.

And Then into the Sunset (2007; fig. 32) is a lovely work. Call me sentimental, but I especially admire the brightness of light that Wyeth creates. Perhaps that is unsettling for some—ironic, isn't it?

33 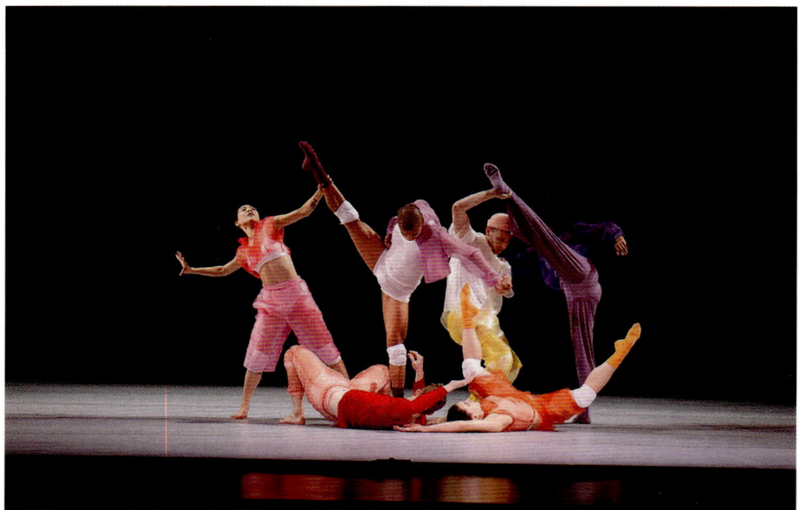

You may see this as a simple image, but for me the togetherness and serenity this painting holds are immensely comforting. There is a sense of collective construction and hope that I am especially drawn to. Again, an excerpt from *This, That, and the Third* can be called in for comparison.

"House Divided" (fig. 33) is a study of six dancers building six houses that keep falling apart because of one person's unwillingness to hold their weight or frame within the structure. I examined Abraham Lincoln's "A House Divided" speech from the Republican State Convention of 1858 in Illinois and tried to modernize the language to understand if it still held weight in 2019. I divided the speech into four parts and asked some of the dancers to translate the text into their native language. It was a diverse cast, so we translated from English into Spanish, Mandarin, Arabic, and back to English. This gave each audience member the experience of what it's like to feel like the other in space. When something is unrecognizable to you but home

33 "House Divided," excerpt from *This, That, and the Third* (2019), choreographed by Rena Butler

to someone else, how do you relate? Do you accept it or reject it? All the while, the meaning of Lincoln's speech is about coming together to find commonality, hope, and vision—reimagining and innovating our futures based on what wasn't working before. In this excerpt are visual and audible examples of construction, deconstruction, and reconstruction. The focus is on the work of building a hopeful, inclusive future together, the same way the pig and the swan can exist and walk together into the light.

~ ~ ~ ~ ~ ~

It is fascinating for me to recognize coincidence, and life has a brilliant way of presenting unexpected connections unto us. Yet the question remains: Is the coincidence something we are desperately searching for in order to find connectivity between us, or is it simply a matter of intersectionality? And when seeking connections out, what is the disturbance that is unearthed, the obsession that is lamented until activated by spurious thoughts?

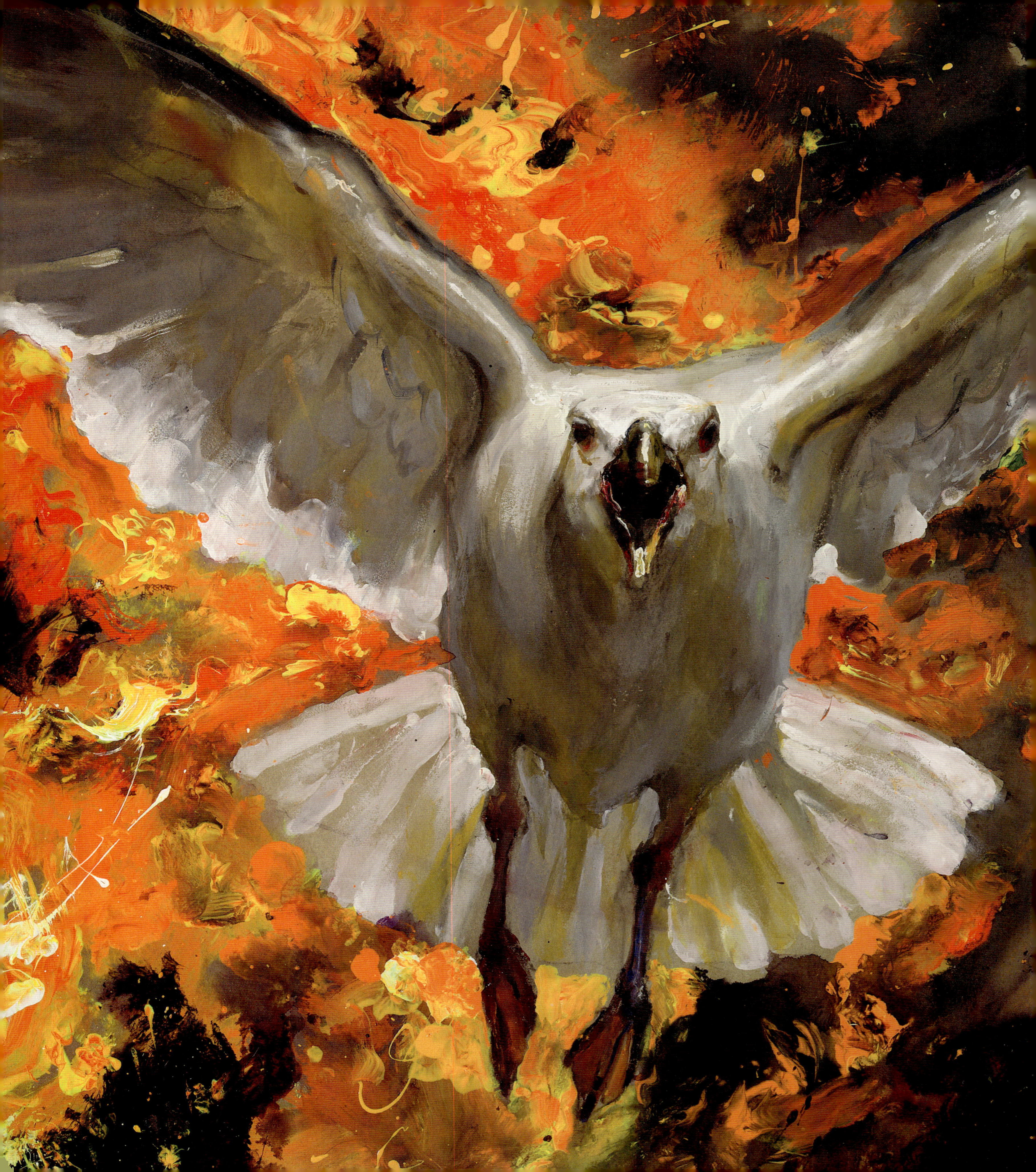

PAINTING WITH SOUND

JENNIFER MARGARET BARKER

In choosing titles for my musical compositions, I am most excited when I settle upon one word: *Kaitiaki*, *Ealasaid*, *Nollaig*, *Geodha*, *Chincoteague*, *Moana*, *BuMian*, *Dumgoyne*, *Effigies*, *Nyvaigs*, *Earthtones*, and a future one, *Inchcailloch*. That explains why *Unsettled*, the title of this book and the exhibition that inspired it, resonates greatly with me. It conjures up two other words that I have come to associate with Jamie Wyeth's work. *Obsessed*: a word that trumpets forth in marcato and crescendo on many an occasion from Wyeth's lips. *Detail*: a word that gently tumbles from the lips of curators, scholars, and Wyeth himself on so regular an occasion that it becomes a motif.

In terms of my own work, three words have become synonymous with my compositions. The first is *haunting*. Multiple reviewers have favored this word, with a *Gramophone* review declaring my composition to be "the most haunting" on a CD recording of works for clarinet.[1] The second word is *evocative*, followed closely by the third, *poignant*. Of course, the definition for *haunting* as an adjective can include the words *evocative* and *poignant*, and so an impression of the nature and oftentimes the mood of my compositions evolves through three single words.

The mood of a new piece is one of the first decisions a composer must make. I regularly remind my students that their choice of instruments and voices will determine the nature of a composition. The opposite approach, wherein the composer selects instruments in order to create a particular mood, also applies. Choosing to pair a flute with a vibraphone will create a very different piece from one that pairs a clarinet with a marimba. Wind, string, brass, metal, wood, skin, plucked and struck, combine with high, middle, and low ranges, bright and dark characters, and varying degrees of fluidity, versatility, virtuosity, warmth, dynamic range, overtones, and resonance to provide a cornucopia of colors and textures that can more than compete with an artist's palette. This range of possible combinations is one of the main reasons that I have chosen to spend my life's work in the world of contemporary classical music. Color and texture are central to my creativity, not only as a composer but also as a pianist, a seamstress, a crafter, a gardener, and a video editor. They, and where appropriate my sense of touch, are the essence of all of my creative activities, the driving force behind my creations.

34

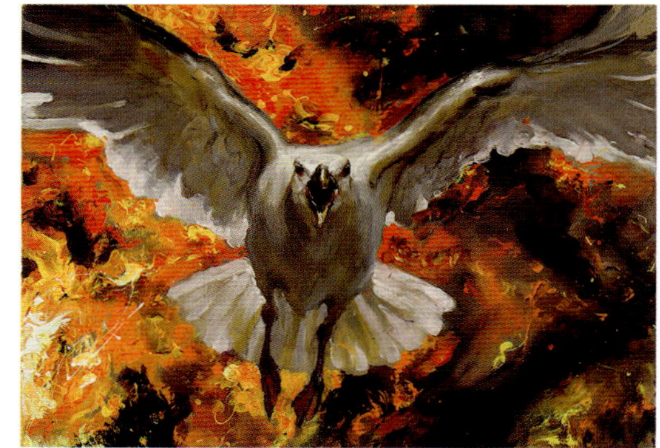

For me, the most visually satisfying painting medium is oil. I adore the textured look of oils and often dream of a second life working on large canvases while covered from head to toe in paint. My gardening hours are spent hunkered down on my knees with fingers dug deep into dark wet soil. So, in many respects I can understand this affinity with oil paint on a tactile level as well as a textural level. However, having received less than a year of formal training as a painter in my youth, I approach works of art with an untrained eye, searching for connection through color, texture, mood, light, or subject matter.

It is with these thoughts in mind that I return to the word *unsettled*. How does one create an unsettled mood in art, and how does that approach compare to creating the same mood in music?

Let's start with Wyeth's *Carney Gull #3* (fig. 34), a most striking painting and one that I return to time after time. On a certain level it almost terrifies me, but on another I find it stunningly beautiful in terms of color, balance, and movement. Having created a sanctuary for birds in my garden, I love watching the activities of our resident sparrows, wrens, cardinals, juncos, chickadees, woodpeckers, catbirds, doves, hummingbirds, and jays. We even have an annual winter resident in a red-shouldered hawk. From time to time, however, our haven of birdsong is disrupted or silenced by a murder of crows that stake their claim loudly and aggressively. Add to this the fact that my native country is Scotland, where seagulls reign supreme on the coast, to the point of swiping ice cream cones from the hands of children.

← Jamie Wyeth, *Carney Gull #3*, 2009. Detail

34 Jamie Wyeth, *Carney Gull #3*, 2009, Combined mediums on paper, 34½ × 48 in. Crystal Bridges Museum of American Art, Bentonville, Arkansas, 2009.12

And so my appreciation of the manner in which Wyeth chose to present this particular creature is fully understandable. To my amateur eyes, the unsettling drama present in this painting is a result of the artist's decision to paint the gull head-on, with wings outstretched, beak open, and neck projecting toward the viewer. The bird's strength is apparent in the foreground muscles of its wings as well as in its body. I can feel the power and potential impact of those wings to the point where, when viewing this painting, I feel almost compelled to lift my arm in an act of protection across the front of my head.

One particular element that I love in this painting is the intense relationship between figure and ground. The rich, vibrant hues of the somewhat abstract background stand in startling contrast with the neutrals of the realistically portrayed gull, swirling across the canvas in an intense Dante's inferno of yellows and oranges to blacks and grays. One envisions a foreboding darkness within striking distance were the yellows and oranges to be peeled away. In every aspect, it is an unsettling scene, yet one so utterly compelling too.

If I were to paint this image in music, I would be obligated to score it for symphony orchestra. Wyeth may have painted a solo gull, but the force of the painting necessitates an eighty-member musical ensemble. Supported by a foundation of blaring low brass vying for attention amid a cacophony of skinned percussion, the richness of the color and depth in the background warrant the use of the entire gamut of orchestral instruments, from piccolo to contrabassoon. Screaming high winds flying alongside marcato strings and triple-tonguing trumpets would bring the full force of the gull's wings and beak down upon the listener. But instrumental color is just one of many layers within a musical composition.

In each period since the Middle Ages, classical composers have used different compositional techniques to create a variety of moods, building upon or diverging from the craft of their forebears. Today, the range of compositional tools at the disposal of the classical composer is more expansive than ever. Stravinsky, Debussy, Schönberg, Bartók, and many more composers of the early twentieth century pursued and forged new compositional aesthetics, techniques, and structures beyond those of the late Romantic period. Throughout the century these new approaches were developed further or challenged by composers such as Britten, Orff, Hindemith, Cage, Nono, Stockhausen, Ligeti, Carter, Babbitt, Crumb, and Glass. Harmony, rhythm, and form found constantly changing or evolving avenues and identities throughout a century of experimentation and development.

Consequently, born out of this period of extensive experimentation, composers in the second decade of the twenty-first century have a myriad of styles, techniques, approaches, and philosophies upon which they can draw in forging their own artistic styles. A musical representation of the unsettled nature of *Carney Gull #3* could therefore draw upon constantly changing time signatures,

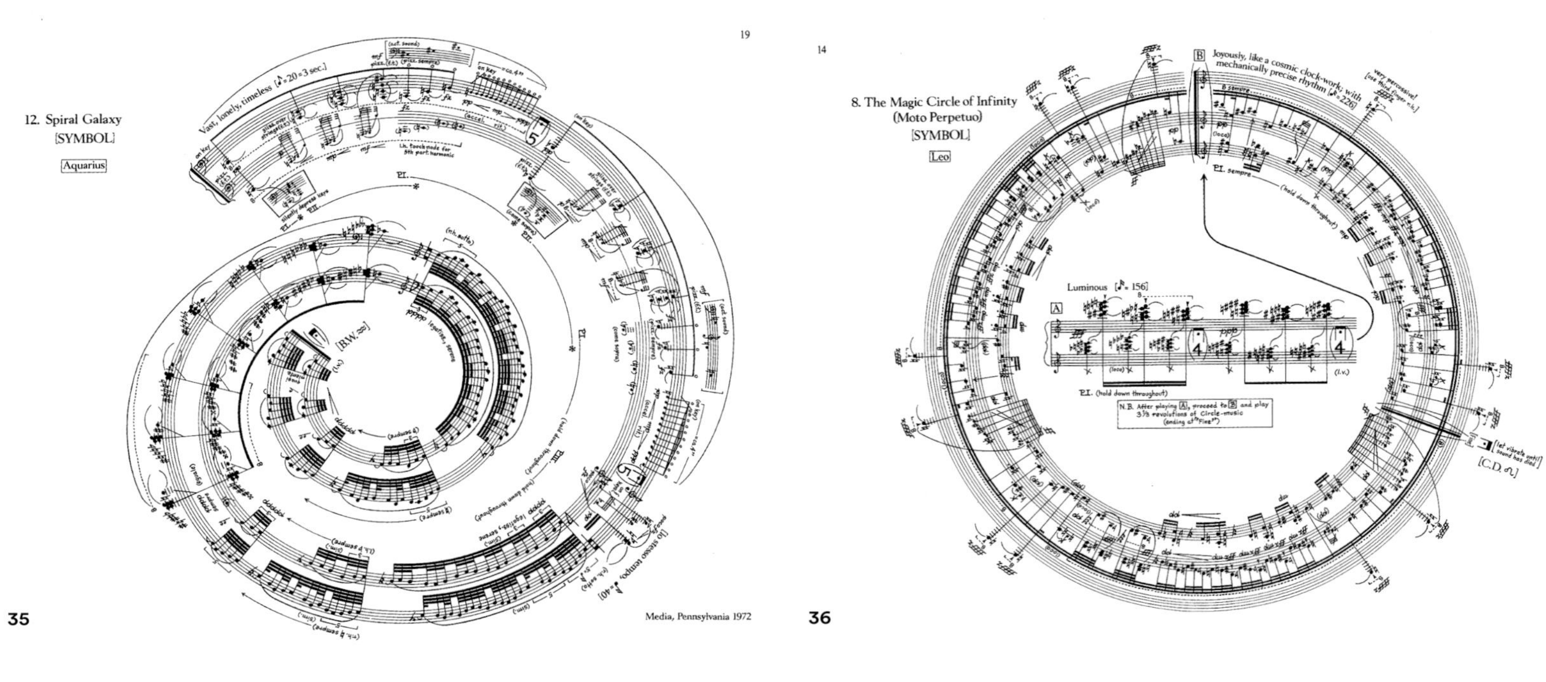

35

36

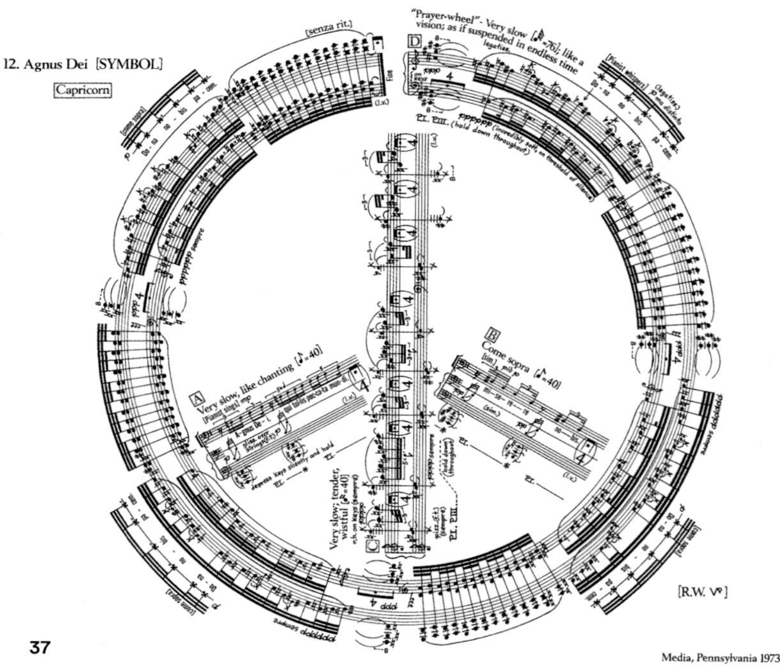

37

swirling polyrhythms, angular motivic material, unresolving dissonance, instrumental extended techniques, unbalanced structure, and extremes of range. Combined with the aforementioned orchestration, the composer could, in effect, create a work so rich in color and texture but, at the same time, so unnerving as to lift the hairs on the back of your neck, rendering an audience unnerved, uncomfortable, and unsettled throughout the performance.

In viewing and studying the art of Jamie Wyeth, I regularly find myself comparing his oeuvre and work ethic to those of George Crumb (1929–2022), the American composer and my former composition professor. Both artists spent their lives getting up at dawn to work on their art. Even in his nineties, Crumb composed every morning from 6:00 a.m. to midday. Both took time and care to perfect even the smallest of details, in Crumb's case not only in his music but also in his hand-drawn scores (figs. 35, 36, 37). The words *obsession* and *detail* apply to Crumb as much as they do to Wyeth.

The creation of a mood also appears to be as central to Wyeth's work as it is to Crumb's. The composer's *Black Angels* (1970) and *A Haunted Landscape* (1984) present more than just an unsettled mood. Crumb describes *Black Angels*, which was completed on Friday the thirteenth of March 1970, as being "conceived as a kind of parable on our troubled contemporary world. The numerous quasi-programmatic allusions in the work are therefore symbolic, although the essential polarity—God versus Devil—implies more than a purely metaphysical reality. The image of the 'black angel' was a conventional device used by early painters to symbolize the fallen angel."[2] So, how does Crumb create such an unsettling mood?

There are numerous musical and even nonmusical elements, too many to discuss here. However, a few overarching elements can be summarized: the individual amplification of each instrument in the string quartet, the startling jumps from loud and intense material to canyons of calm stasis, the performers shouting as they play, unnerving numerology, eerie musical quotes from the classical canon, and extended string techniques. Layer upon layer, from the micro to the macro, this work keeps the listener on edge from beginning to end via "the unexpected." No virgin listener can anticipate the next turn or when it is going to happen. It is a profound work that ushered in new sounds and textures, bringing with it an even closer relationship between music and emotion. *Black Angels* is an icon of the twentieth century and, on a lighter note, an excellent choice to awaken students and challenge them at the start of an 8:00 a.m. undergraduate theory class!

35 George Crumb, *Spiral Galaxy* from *Makrokosmos, Vol. I*, 1973
36 George Crumb, *The Magic Circle of Infinity (Moto Perpetuo)* from *Makrokosmos, Vol. I*, 1973
37 George Crumb, *Agnus Dei* from *Makrokosmos, Vol. II*, 1973

Intentional or not, Wyeth's *Orchard* (1967, private collection) brings me to the same state of emotion. Where Wyeth's angular, graceless, barren trees in monochrome initiate an otherworldly state of bleakness and despair, Crumb's amplification of the strings disconnects my emotions from expected warmth and natural resonance, thereby bringing me to that same otherworldly state. The consuming darkness of Wyeth's *Consommé* (2013; pl. 11) also evokes thoughts of *Black Angels*. The painting's blues are so dark as to be almost indistinguishable from the blacks. Together they create an almost hidden cave of camouflage for the figure of Andy Warhol. It always takes me several seconds to find and focus on Warhol, at which point my feeling of tenseness releases into calm contemplation. Warhol may only be sitting down to enjoy some soup, but my senses view the seated figure, ignored by those standing around him, as of another world where life is focused solely on thoughts. In their own way, the upright figures in stark contrast to the sole seated man, the dark palette with the occasional spark of light, the contrast of emotions evoked by this image—each of these elements reminds me of the structural and emotional contrasts present in *Black Angels*.

Creating an unsettling mood is something that, to date, I have reserved for sections of my works rather than an entire composition. The one example where I sought to create an extended unsettling and subsequent otherworldly mood is *Naibh Beags/Nyvaigs* (1997). During my youth I spent many summers at my grandparents' house in the Ayrshire town of Largs, Scotland, and each time I visited I was drawn to the replica of a Viking ship that sat atop a grassy knoll down by the seafront. I loved the shape of the ship and, even more, the fact that it was made entirely from wood. Upon receiving a commission for a chamber work that included alto saxophone from the American saxophonist James Richmond, I searched for a subject inspired by the metallic quality and extremes of dynamics characteristic of that instrument. Finally, I chose to address the struggles of the eleventh- and twelfth-century Scots against the Vikings, with particular emphasis on a legend from the battle of 1156, which preceded the victorious Battle of Largs in 1263. Having failed to defeat the large, powerful *drakkar* ships, the Scots invented a midship rudder for their *naibh beags* (Scottish Gaelic for "little ships"), which allowed them to outmaneuver the invading vessels, whose starboard-mounted rudder was not much more than a steering oar. As the Vikings retreated up the East Kyle, they burned their dead on the Burnt Isles in the Kyles of Bute. Legend states that this is why little grows on those isles today, which are inhabited only by gulls and the souls of the Viking dead.

In composing *Naibh Beags/Nyvaigs*, I sought to create an atmosphere of mounting aggression and violence followed by a sense of otherworldly sorrow and loss, a musical journey that was as unsettling as it was haunting and poignant. To the chamber ensemble I added flute (one performer playing three different flutes: alto flute, C flute, piccolo) and soprano voice, not only because of their association with Celtic folk music but also for the extended range and diversity of color provided by the flutes and the soulfulness of a wordless voice. I then added piano and three multi-percussionists, which supplied a legion of percussive colors and textures, from startling metallic hits to reverberating, highly resonant ethereal soundscapes. To evoke the unsettling soundscape of ships rowing into battle, I created irregular, jolting phrases that grow in drive and intensity until the culminating phrase releases in a wash of metallic sound. To muster the awkward and cumbersome movements of heavy oars fighting to maneuver within chaos, I devised circular, descending waves punctuated by large, ungainly final hits by the piano on nonregular beats within constantly changing time signatures. I composed ever-increasing dissonant, angular, ugly motivic lines and trills for the saxophone, C flute, and subsequent piccolo, which drive higher and higher, louder and louder, until each instrument reaches the upper limit of its range while fighting for dominance within the texture.

On top of this dueling fray I added multiple layers of metallic, wood, and skin percussion in quickly shifting ranges and irregular rhythmic punches: the clash of metal swords, the pounding of shields, the ramming of wood upon wood . . . the sheer ugliness of violence. Finally, I dropped the soprano notes to the bottom of the singer's tessitura, rendering her inaudible, an effect that has managed to unnerve at least one conductor as well as many performers and audience members. Witnessing a vocalist mouth syllables while being unable to hear the resultant pitches amid the all-encompassing din is, I have discovered, one of the most disconcerting and uncomfortable experiences for most people. Nothing in this section is beautiful or heartwarming. It feels awkward and, to this day, makes me uncomfortable. I shift in my seat every time I listen to it, asking myself why I did not write material that "sounded better" all while reminding myself that unsettling and disconcerting were exactly what I was trying to accomplish.

When looking at Wyeth's *Buzz Saw* (1969, pl. 71), those same uncomfortable feelings arise in my stomach. All one can see is rusty metal with menacing, even frightening, teeth. A glimmer of light and refuge peaks over the top right-hand corner of the blade, but to no avail. The saw is so large, so dark, and so rigid that it becomes overwhelming, just like the ancient *drakkars*. Where I used unbalanced structure, irregular rhythms, screaming dissonance, and clashing instrumental textures, Wyeth has used overwhelming size, extreme contrast of light and dark, and an impenetrable rusted texture in the central mass, which magnifies the disconcerting uniformity and terror of the saw's outlying teeth.

Much less unsettling, and actually quite comical, is *Farm Talk* (2016; pl. 52). The painting's two skulls should be extremely disconcerting, but to me they look like a pair of old smiling pals catching up on the local gossip: little and large having a good old natter. Black comedy is a genre that I have come to appreciate more as I have grown older. Humor is an element that I have only recently started to incorporate into my compositions. In 2015 the Scottish trio Vocali3e presented me with four Robert Burns poems to set to music as a song cycle titled *A Lassie's Love*. The fourth poem was "What Can a Young Lassie Do wi' an Auld Man." As you might imagine, the poem humorously relays the complaints of a young woman who married an old man, but in the last verse she announces that she will take her aunt's advice to "cross him an' wrack him, until I heartbreak him,"[3] after which she plans to use his money to buy herself a new pan. At this point in the poem one cannot help but laugh while simultaneously feeling shock at the fate of her seemingly doomed husband.

Two of the reasons that Burns's poetry transcribes so well into music are the natural lilt in the lines and the ease with which the Scottish words roll off the tongue in musical ebb and flow. As with many of his poems, the rhythm of the lines falls beautifully into a 6/8 time signature, like the song "Greensleeves." In an earlier generation, this poem would have been set in 6/8, but today the time signature of 7/8 is a well-heeled possibility. While usually conducted in a 3 + 2 + 2 or 2 + 2 + 3 pattern, the simple extra beat (6 + 1) provided me with a light, swift harrumph for the young lassie and an unstable comical limp for the old man. Add to that moments of pure theater, uncomfortable breaks of silence, a jaunty piano accompaniment interspersed with declamatory flute lines and the result is a humorous, expressionistic song with a dark underbelly.

My process for creating an unsettling mood in *Naibh Beags/Nyvaigs* and *A Lassie's Love* presents two ends of the spectrum within my portfolio. A further ten of my compositions approach the creation of an unsettling mood, whether otherworldly, disconcerting, or eerie, in their own way, just as we see in many of Wyeth's paintings. According to one writer, Wyeth "fashions himself a 'boring' person who simply paints, day after day, the things he loves."[4] For that I am extremely grateful, for in merely painting those things that he loves as he sees them, he captures the essence of the human spirit through an infinite range of moods.

I am also grateful for this intense period dedicated to the study and absorption of Jamie Wyeth's work. It has been a great time of affirmation for me. In making new discoveries with each viewing and comparing those discoveries to elements in my own work, I have affirmed the characteristics and qualities that embody my compositional voice. I stated at the beginning that color and texture are central to my creativity. That is true, but color and texture are merely the tools by which I am able to create mood, and mood is the primary element through which I create the emotion inherent to each composition. Mood and emotion are two halves of one whole: a whole upon which my compositional voice is built and the sole reason for my practice of the art form.

Notes

1 Laurence Vittes, "Christopher Nichols: Almost All-American—21st-Century Works for Clarinet," *Gramophone* (December 2019), https://www.gramophone.co.uk/review/christopher-nichols-almost-all-american-21st-century-works-for-clarinet.

2 George Crumb, *Black Angels*, Nonesuch Records Inc., June 21, 1990, compact disc, liner notes.

3 "Complete Works," Burns Country, http://www.robertburns.org/works/323.shtml.

4 Mark Nardone, "The Ultimate Jamie Wyeth Retrospective," *Main Line Today*, December 19, 2014, https://mainlinetoday.com/life-style/the-ultimate-jamie-wyeth-retrospective/.

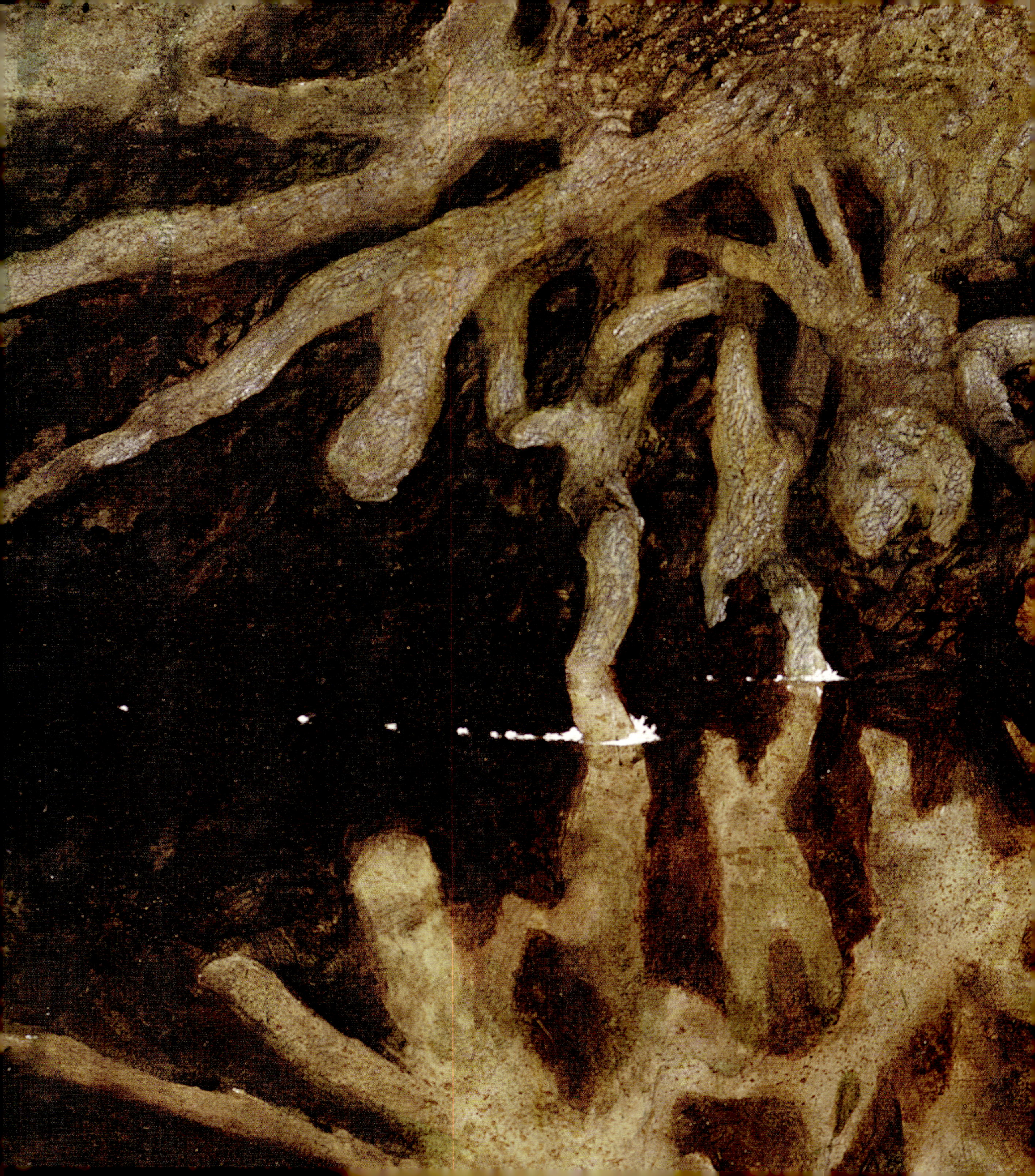

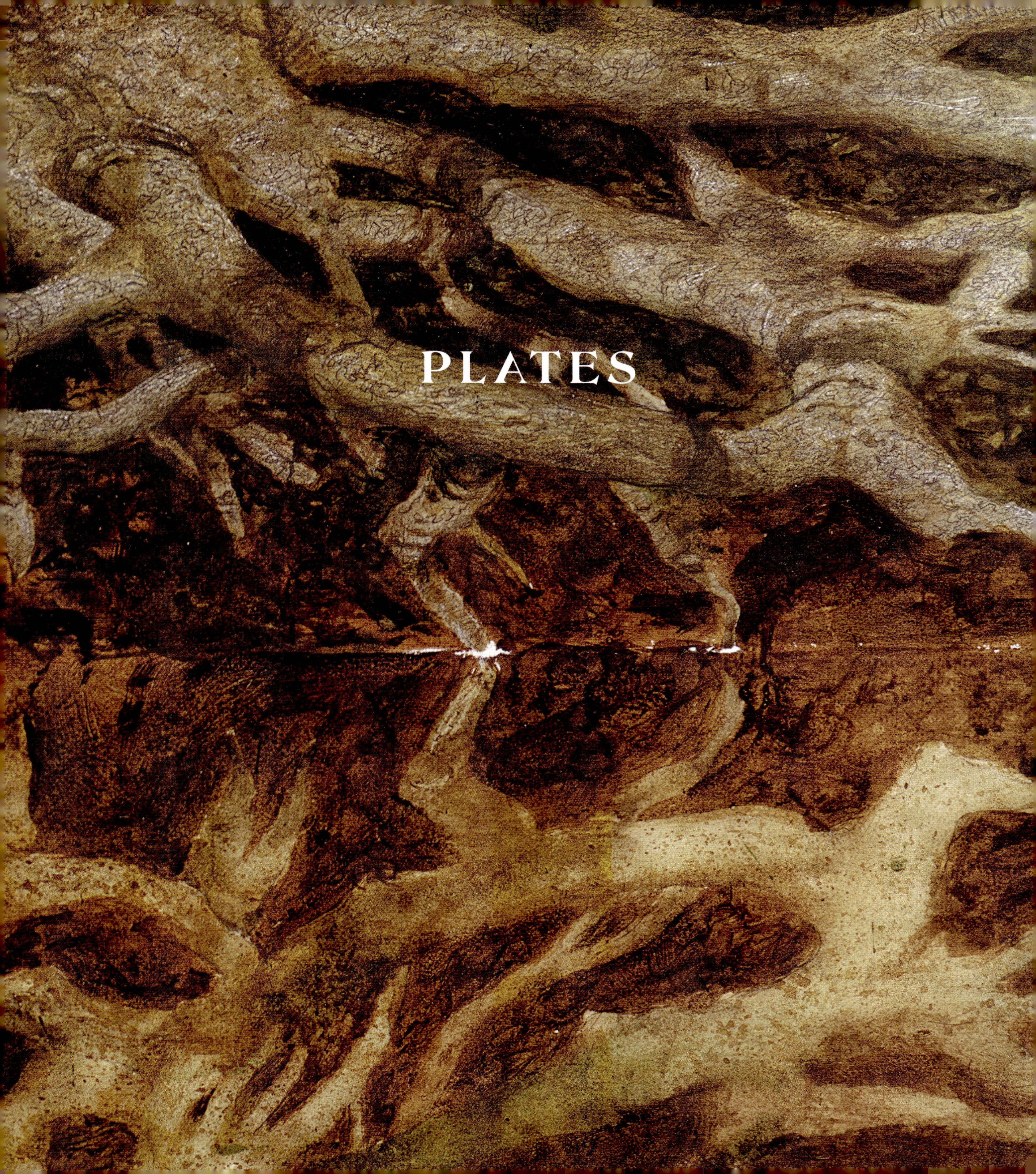

PLATES

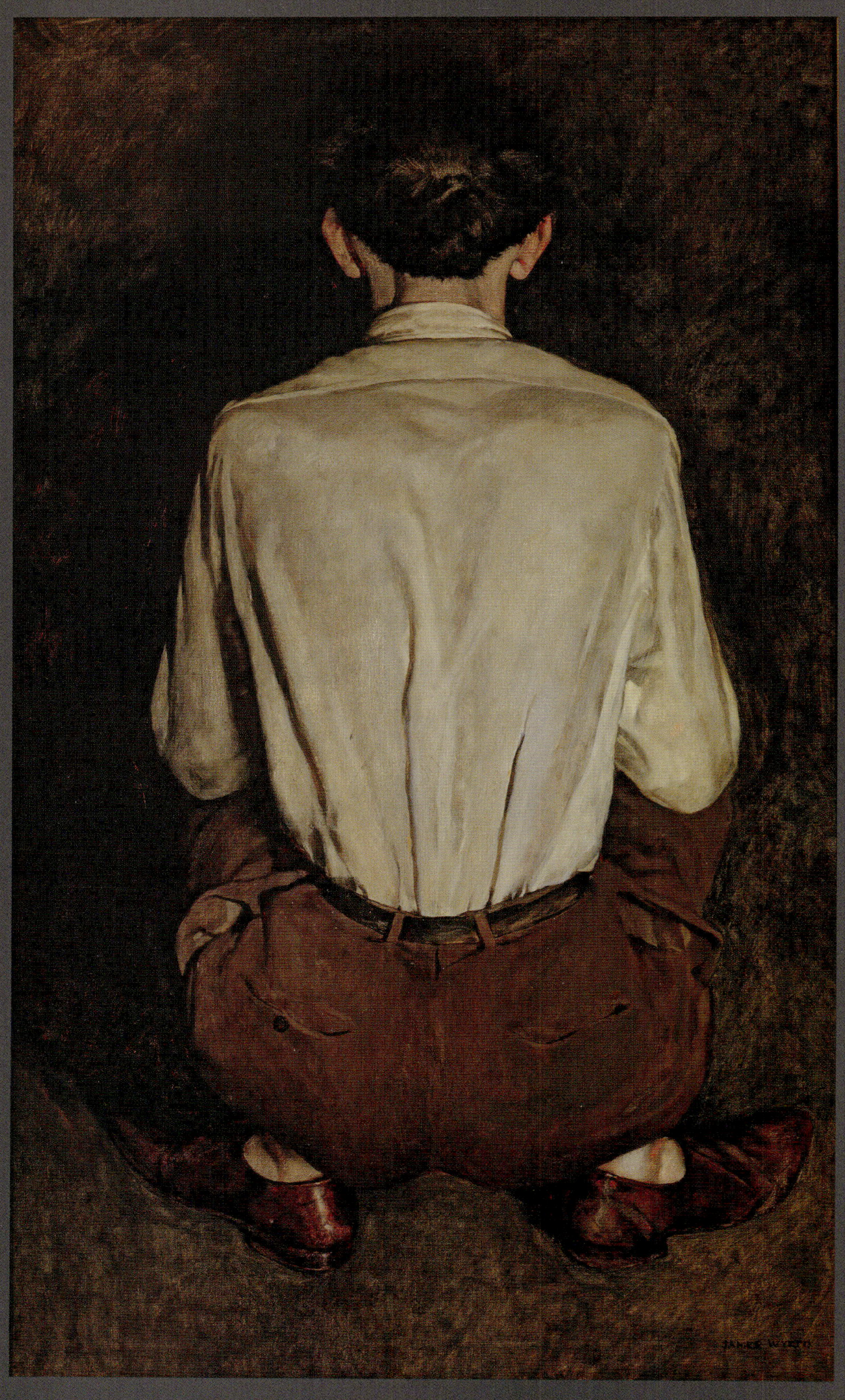

PLATE 1
Record Player, 1964

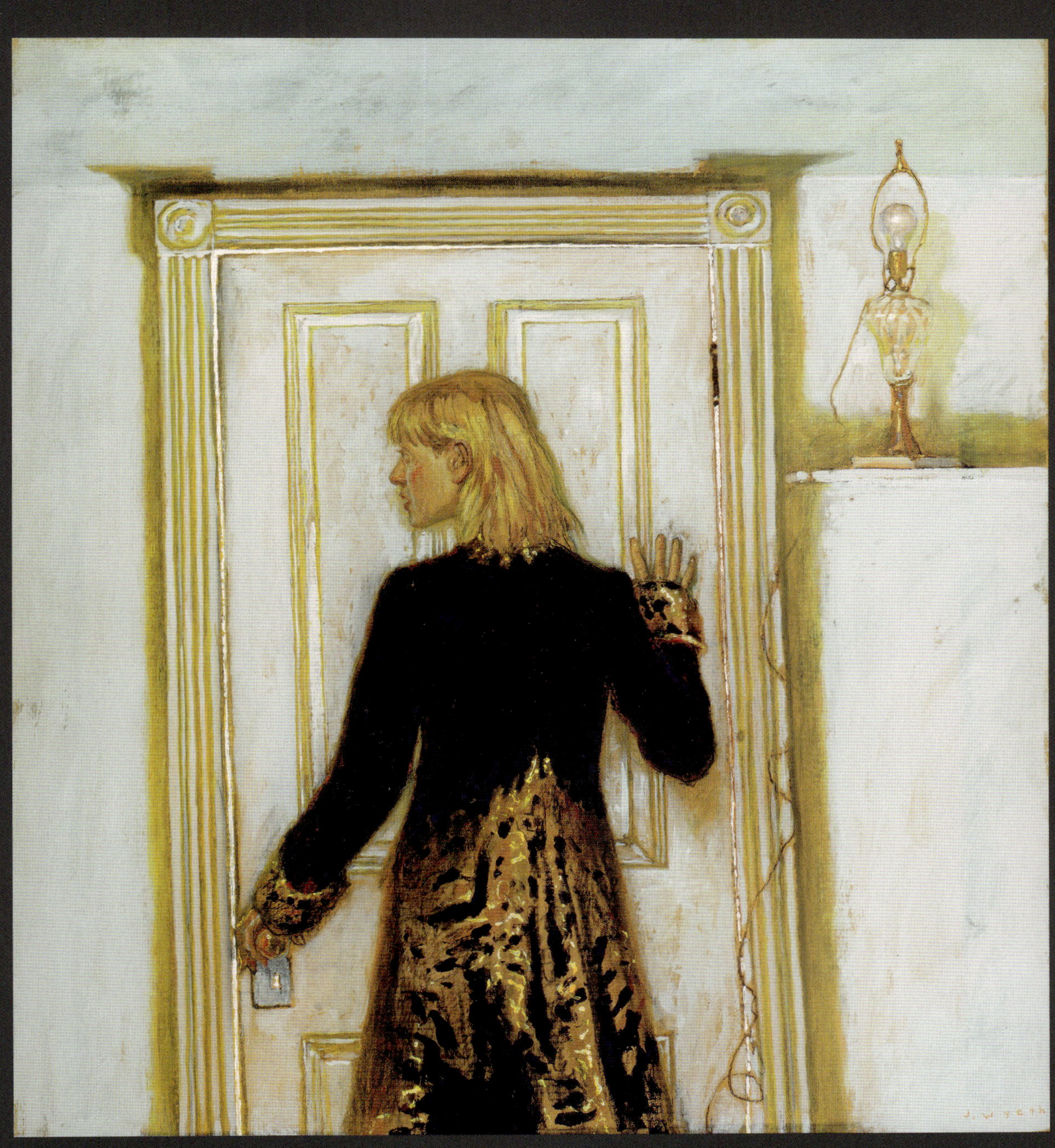

PLATE 2
oices, Study #1, 1995

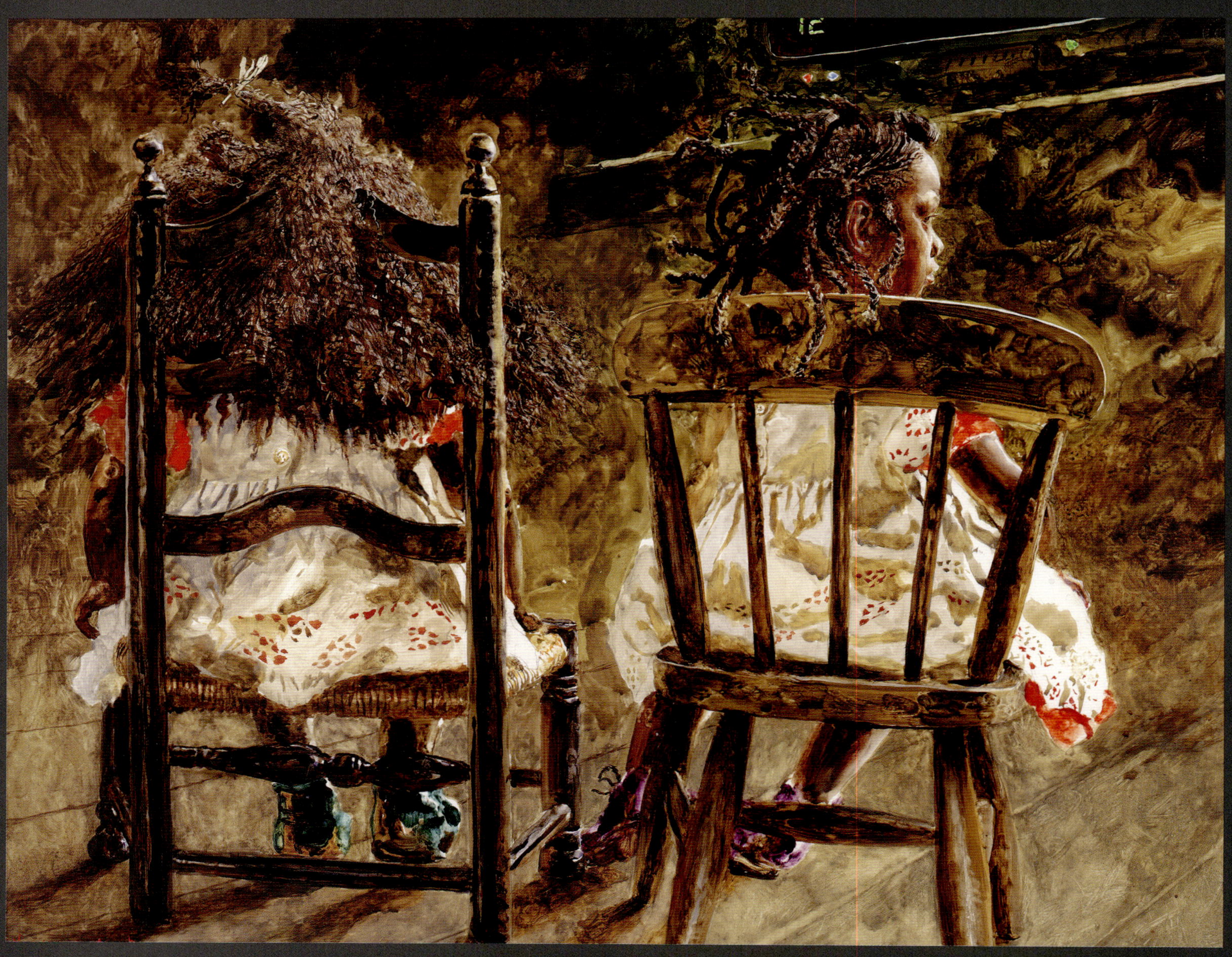

PLATE 3
Channel 12, 1992

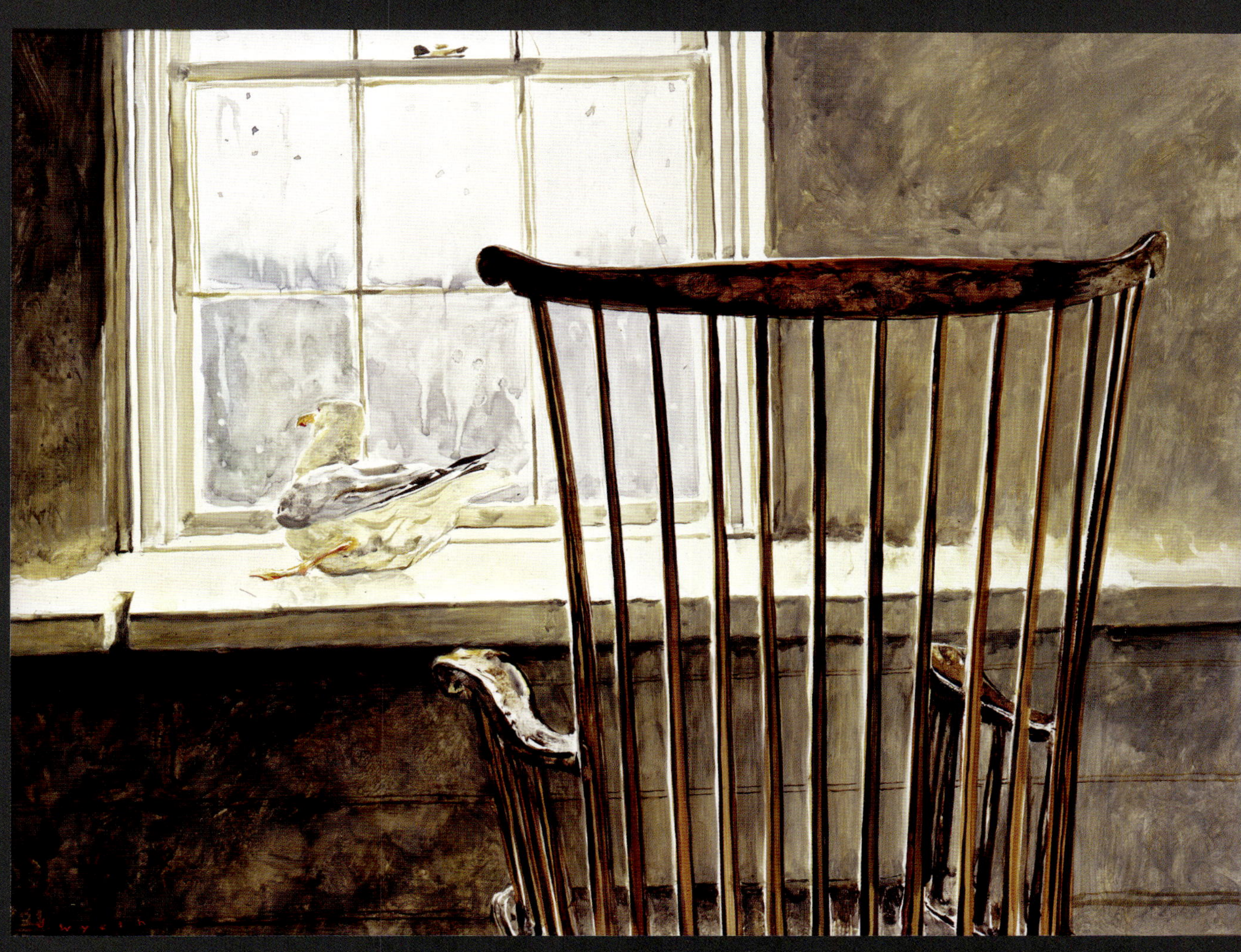

PLATE 4
Gull and Windsor, 1993

PLATE 5
Dead Cat Museum, Monhegan Island, 1999

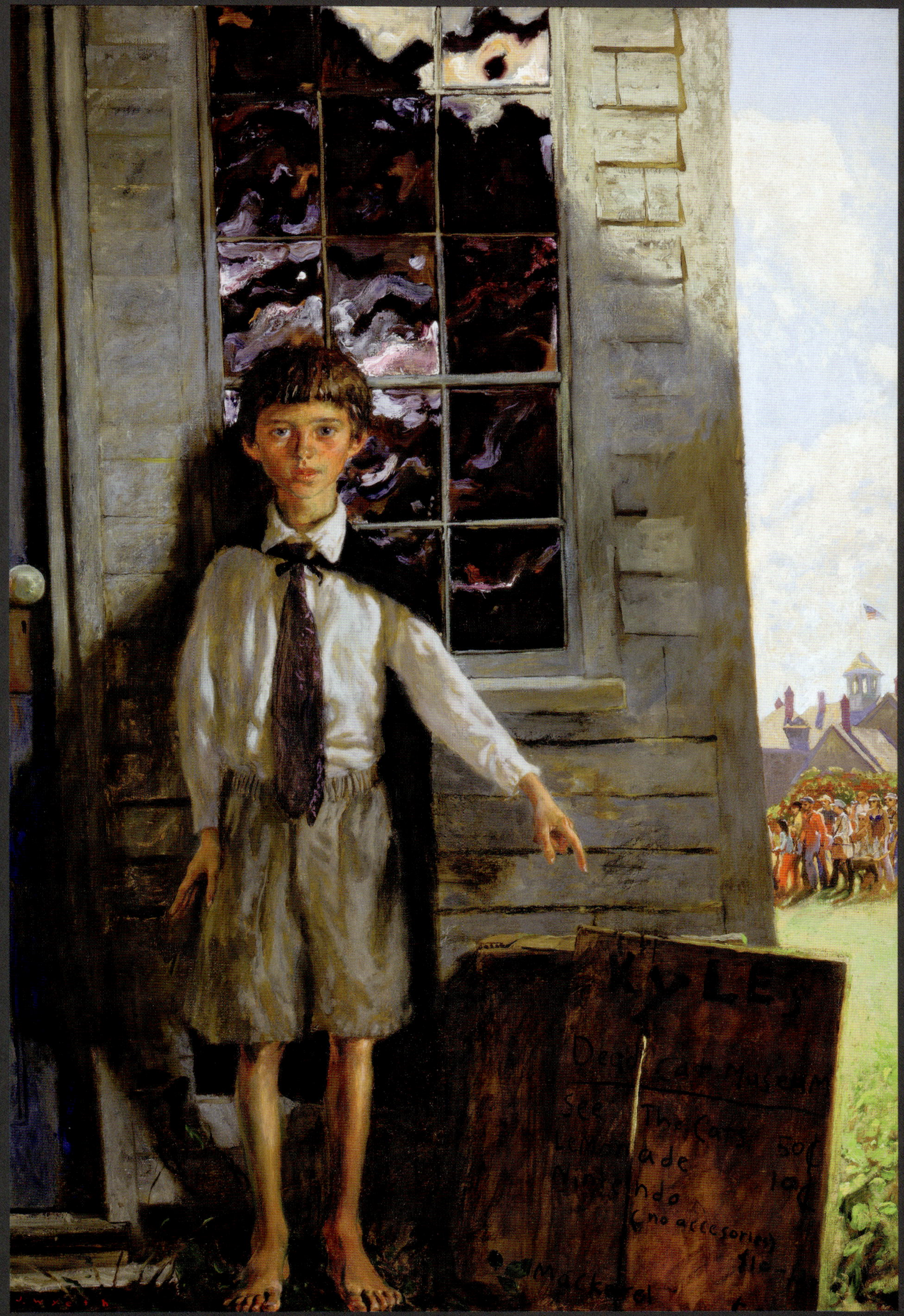
KYLES
Dead Cat Museum
See The Cats 50¢
(no accesories)
Mackerel

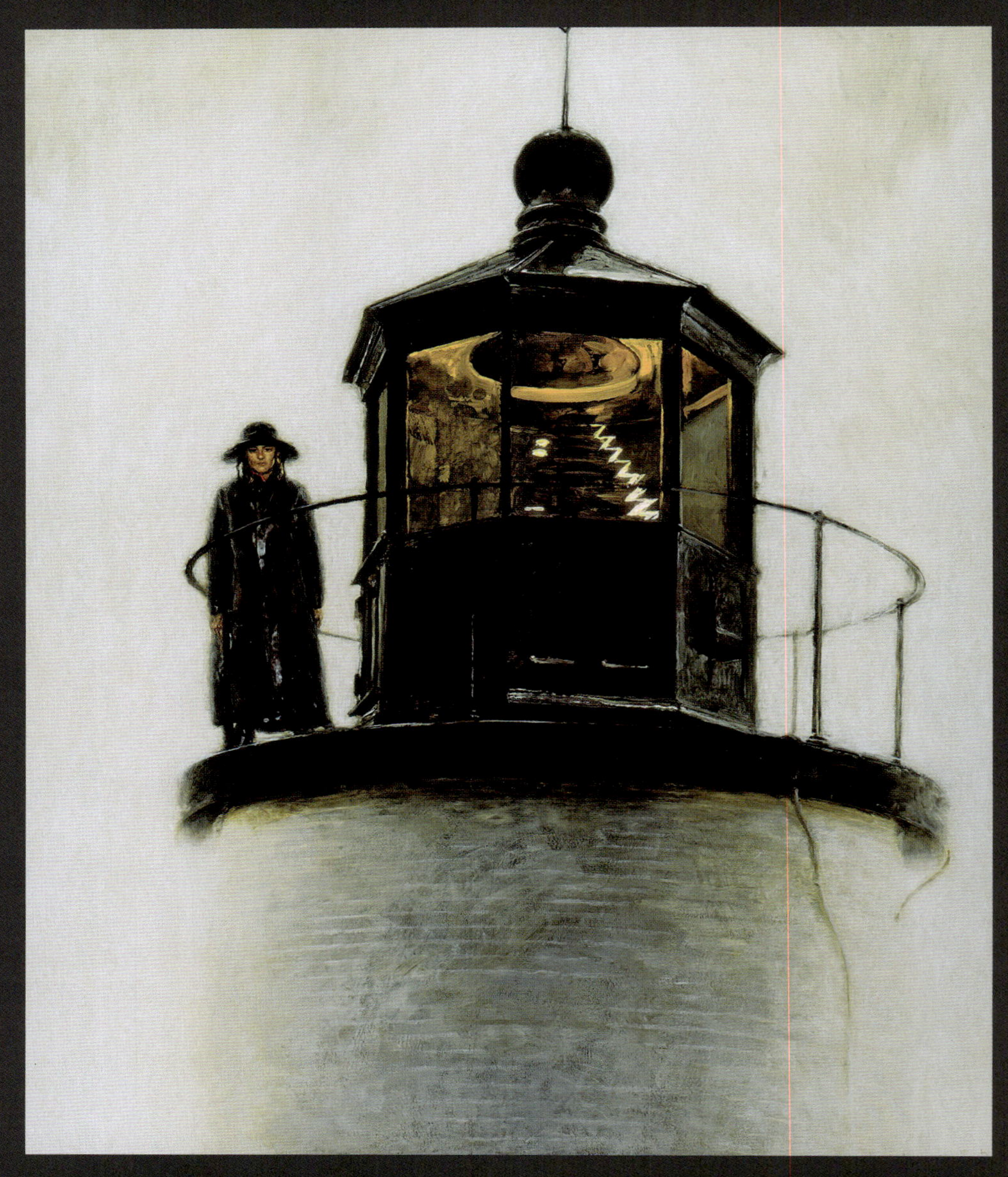

PLATE 6
Light Station, 1992

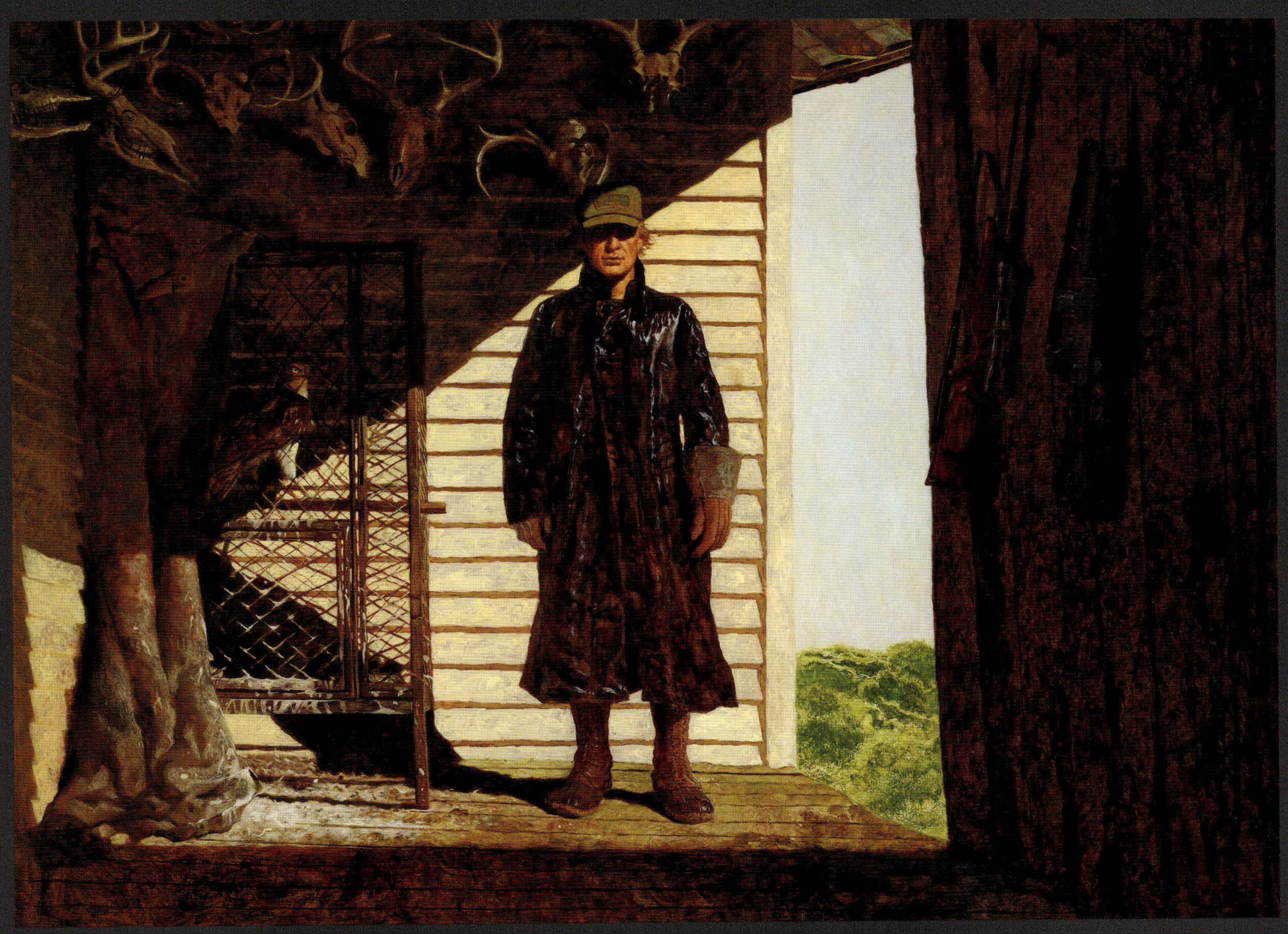

PLATE 7
Bean Boots, 1985

PLATE 8
Cat Bates of Monhegan, 1995

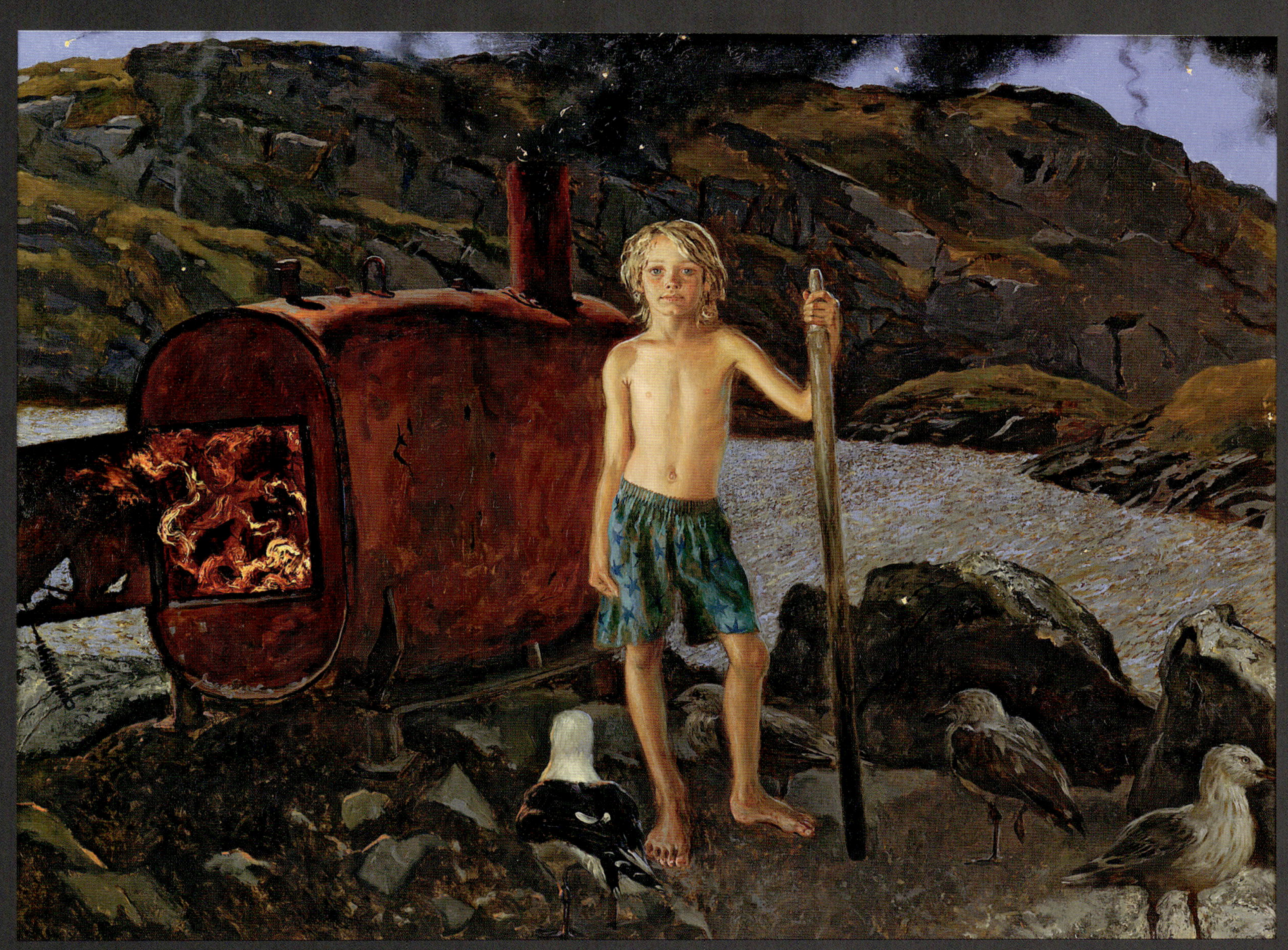

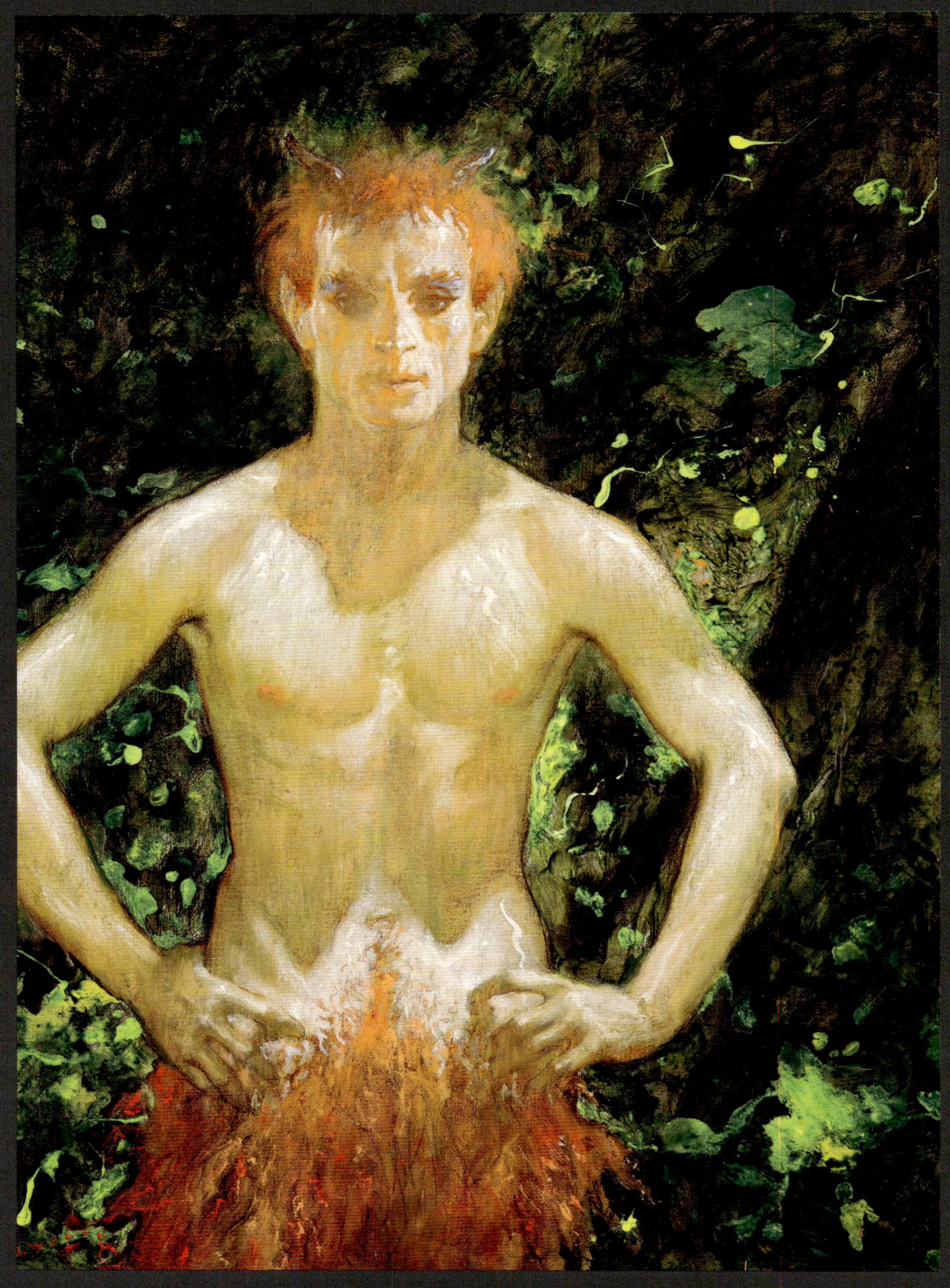

PLATE 9
The Faune, 1977/2002

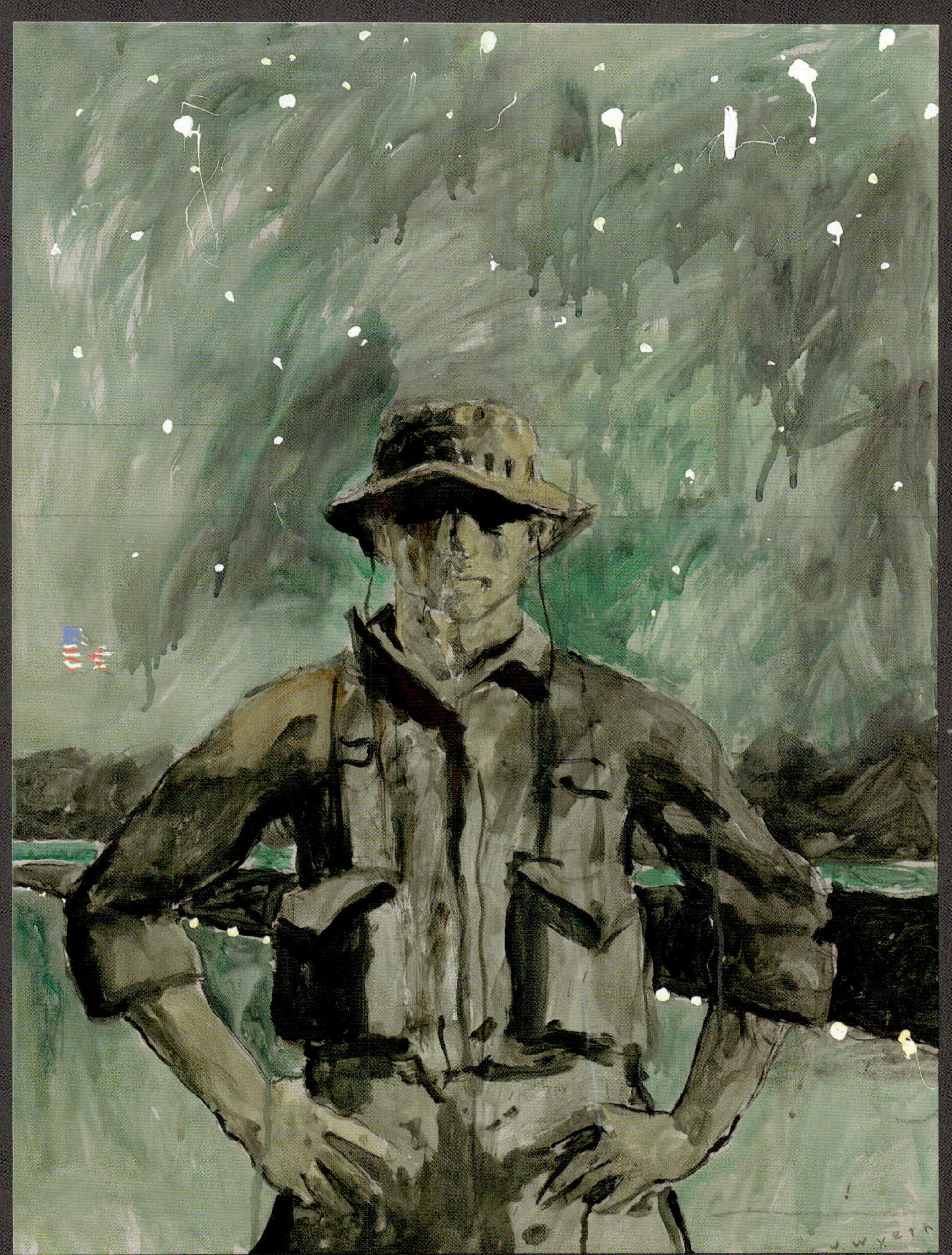

TE 10
Study II, 2002

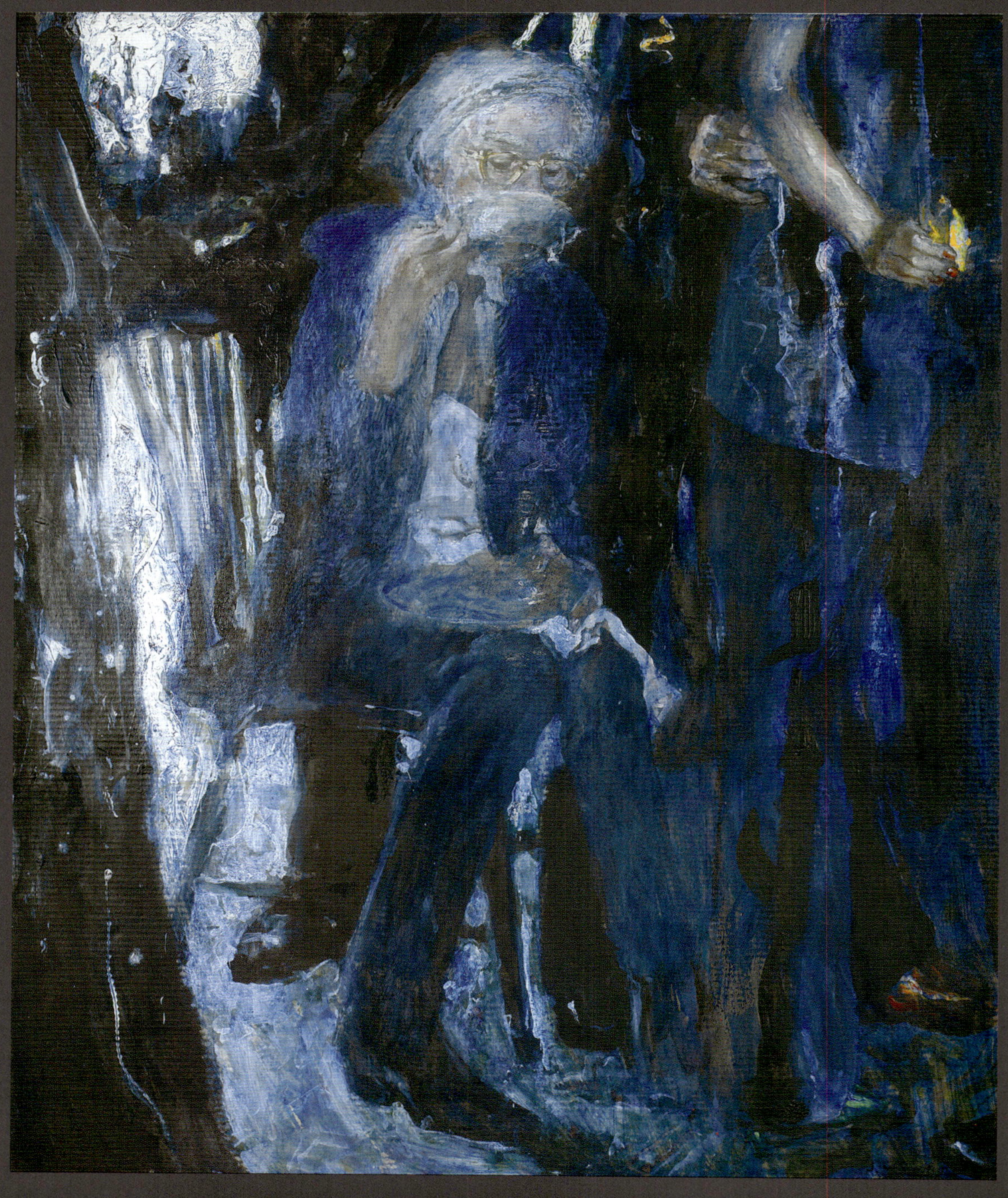

PLATE 11
Consommé, 2013

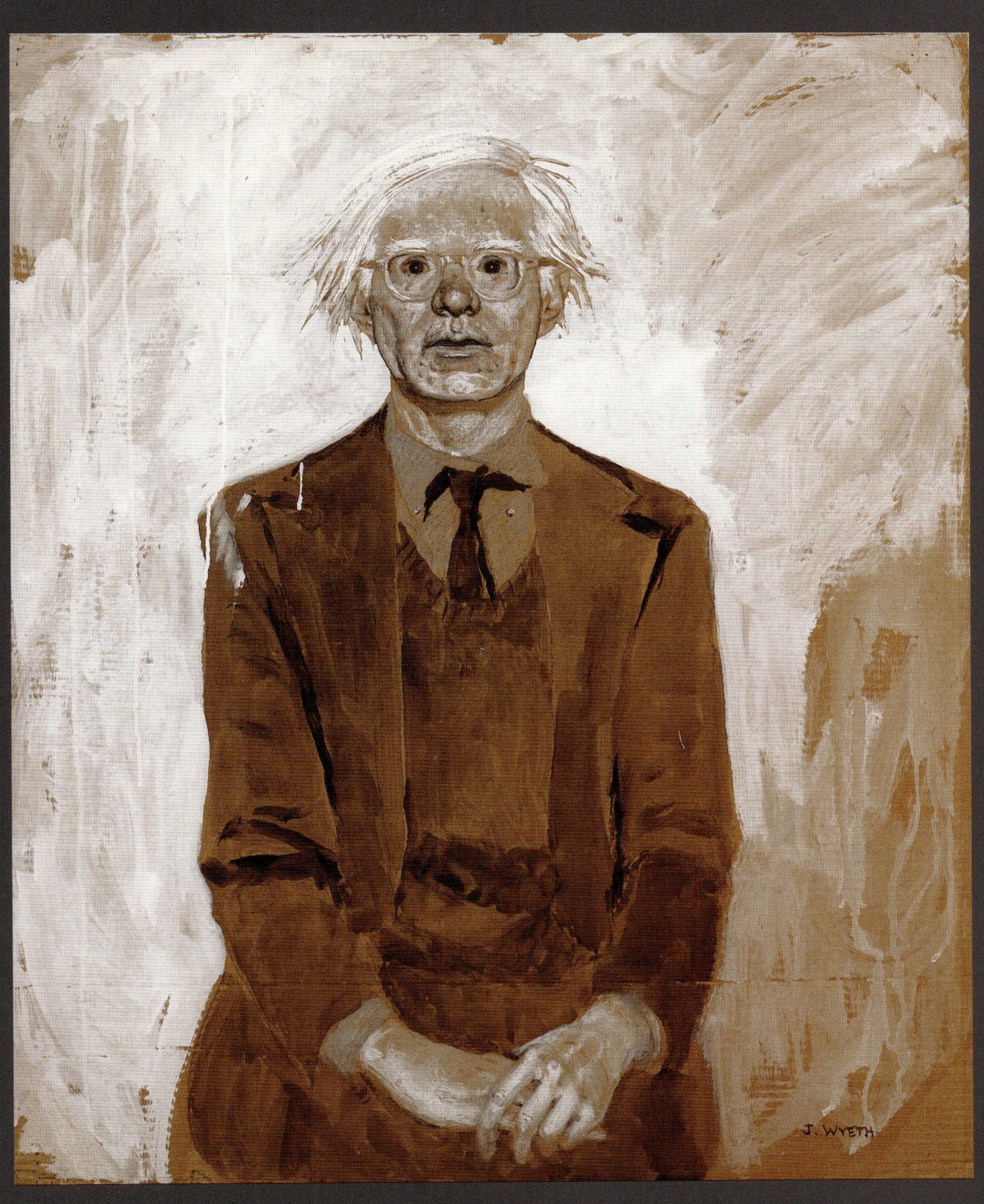

PLATE 12
Andy Warhol on White (Andy Warhol Study), 1976

PLATE 13

First in the Screen Door Sequence, 2015

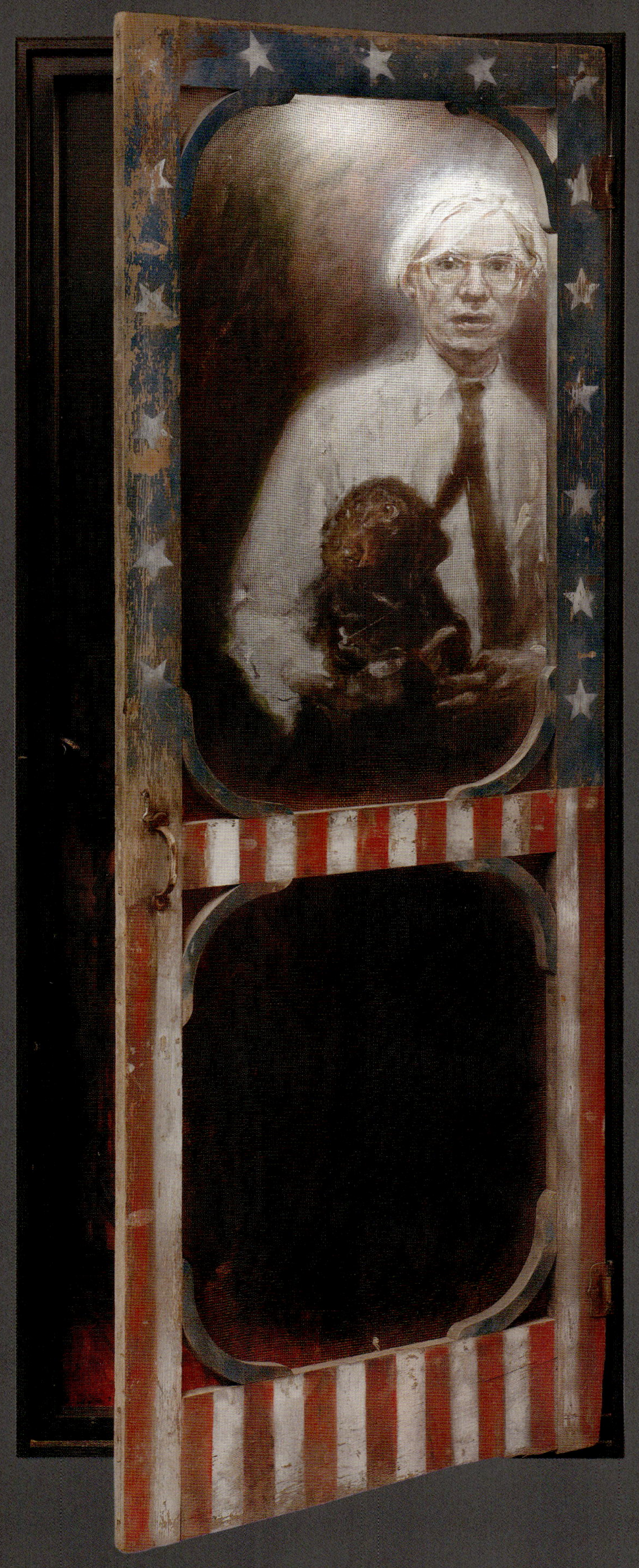

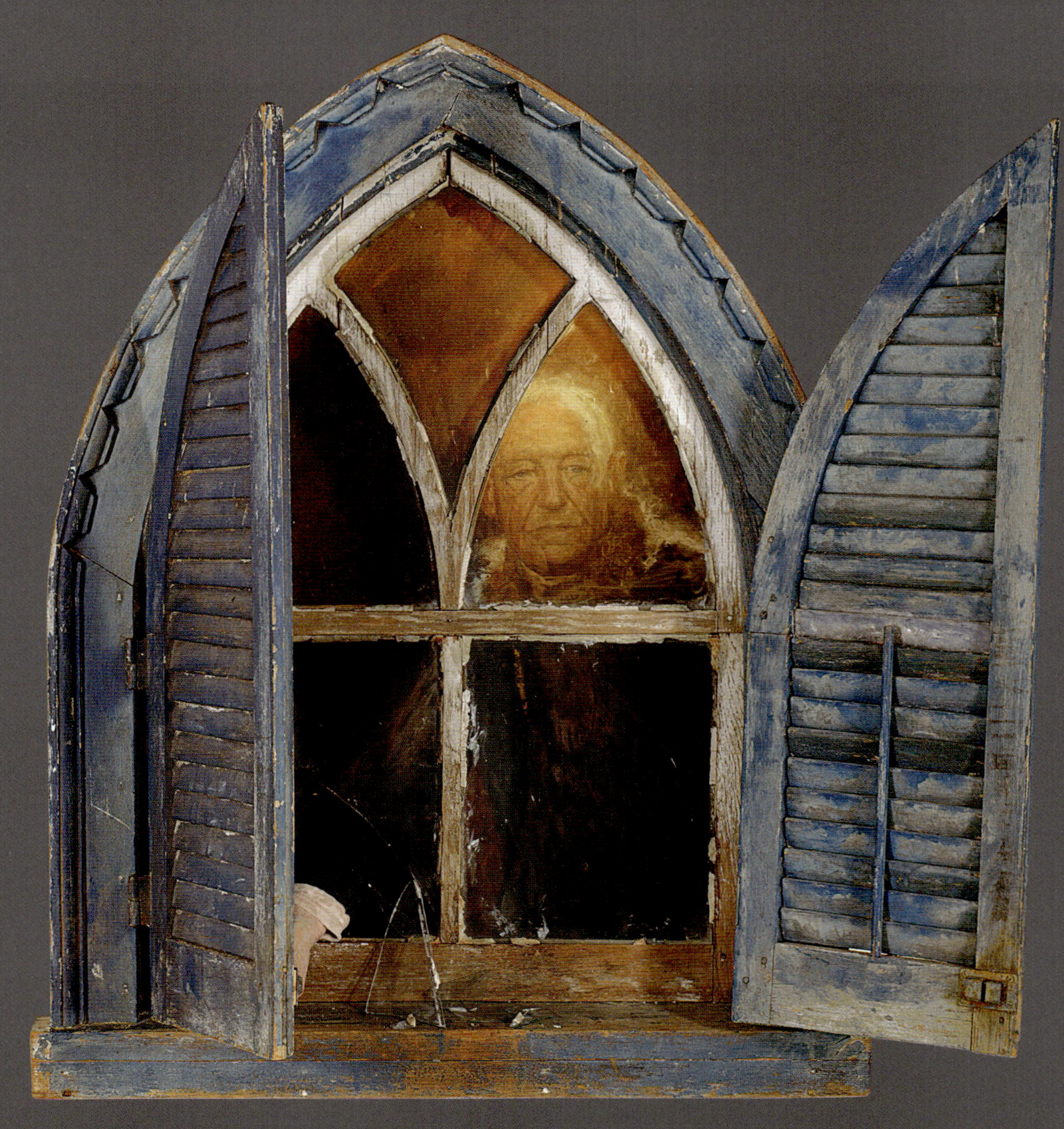

PLATE 14
Dormer: Third in the Screen Door Sequence, 2017

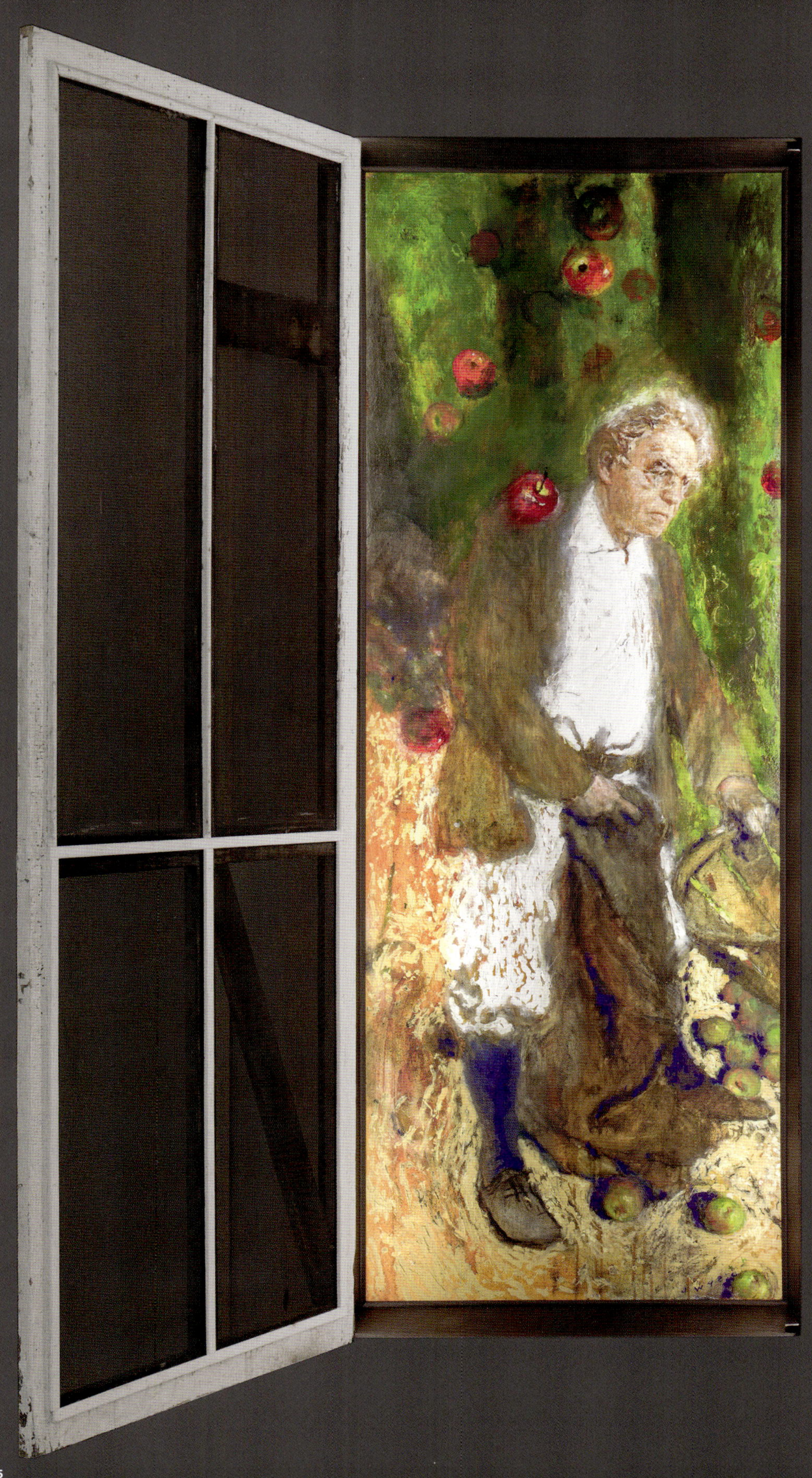

PLATE 15
Apples: Fifth in the Screen Door Sequence, 2021

PLATE 16
Spring, the Hanging of the Tree Rocks, 2017

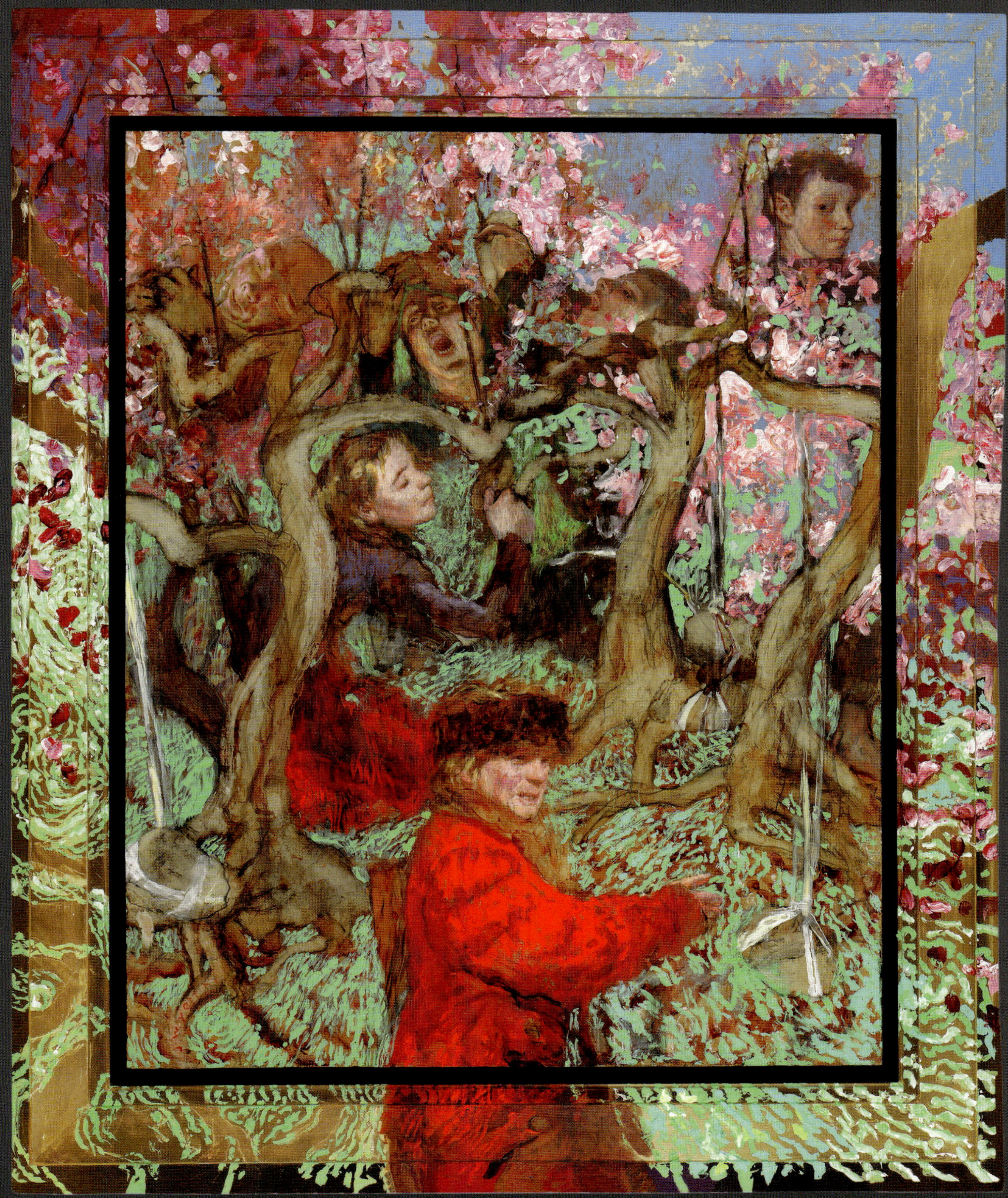

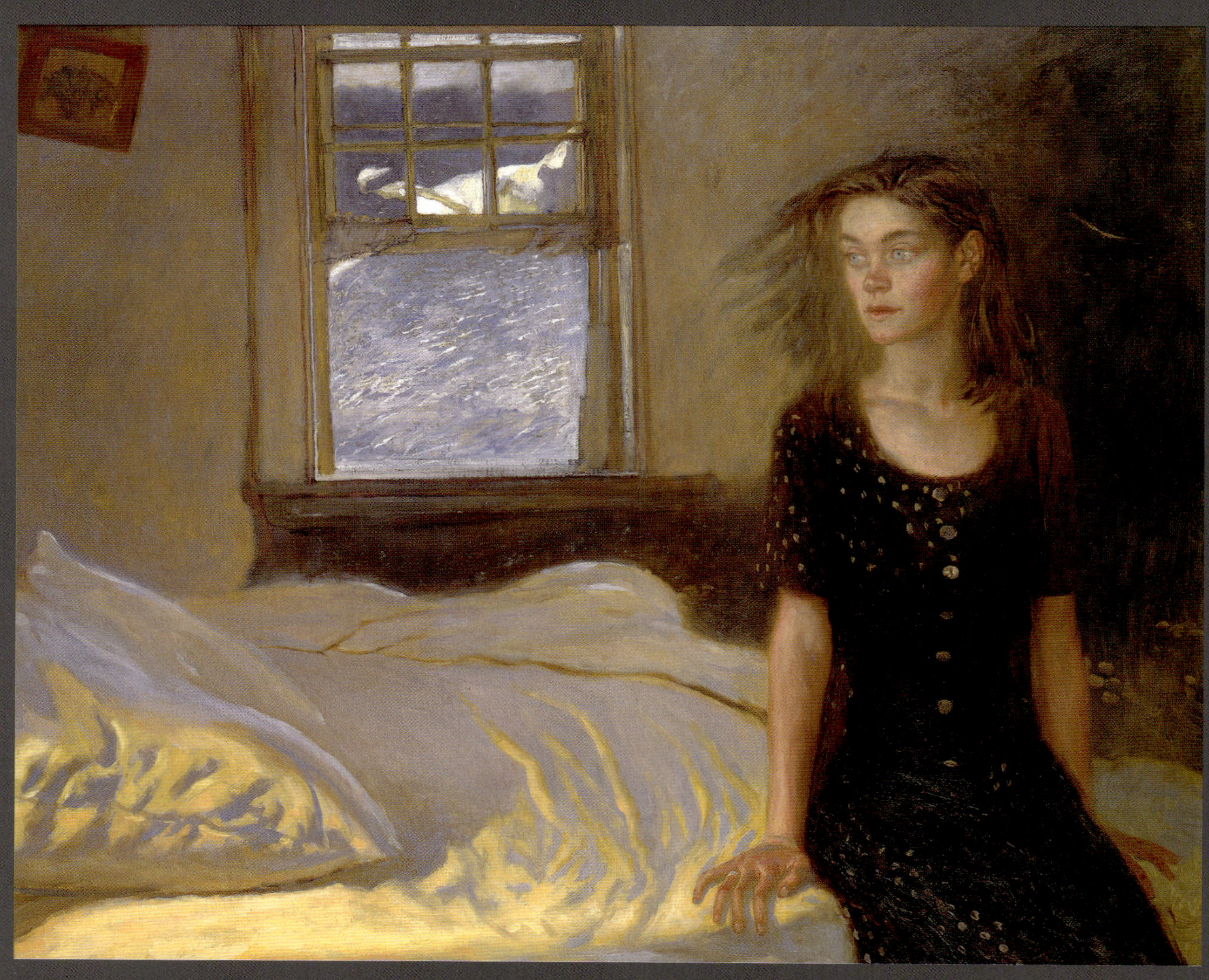

PLATE 17
If Once You Slept on an Island, 1996

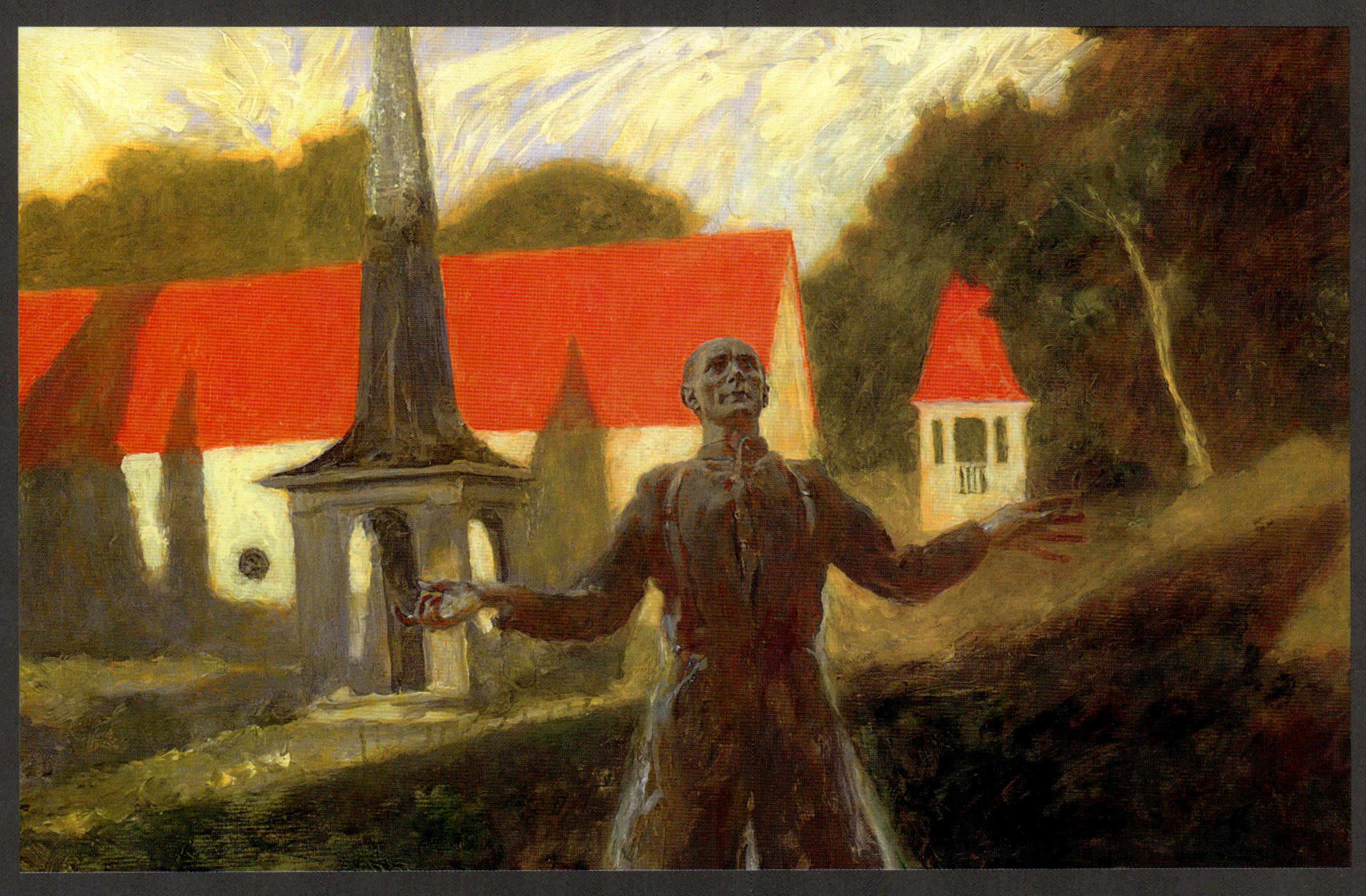

PLATE 18
The Steeple Salesman, 2012

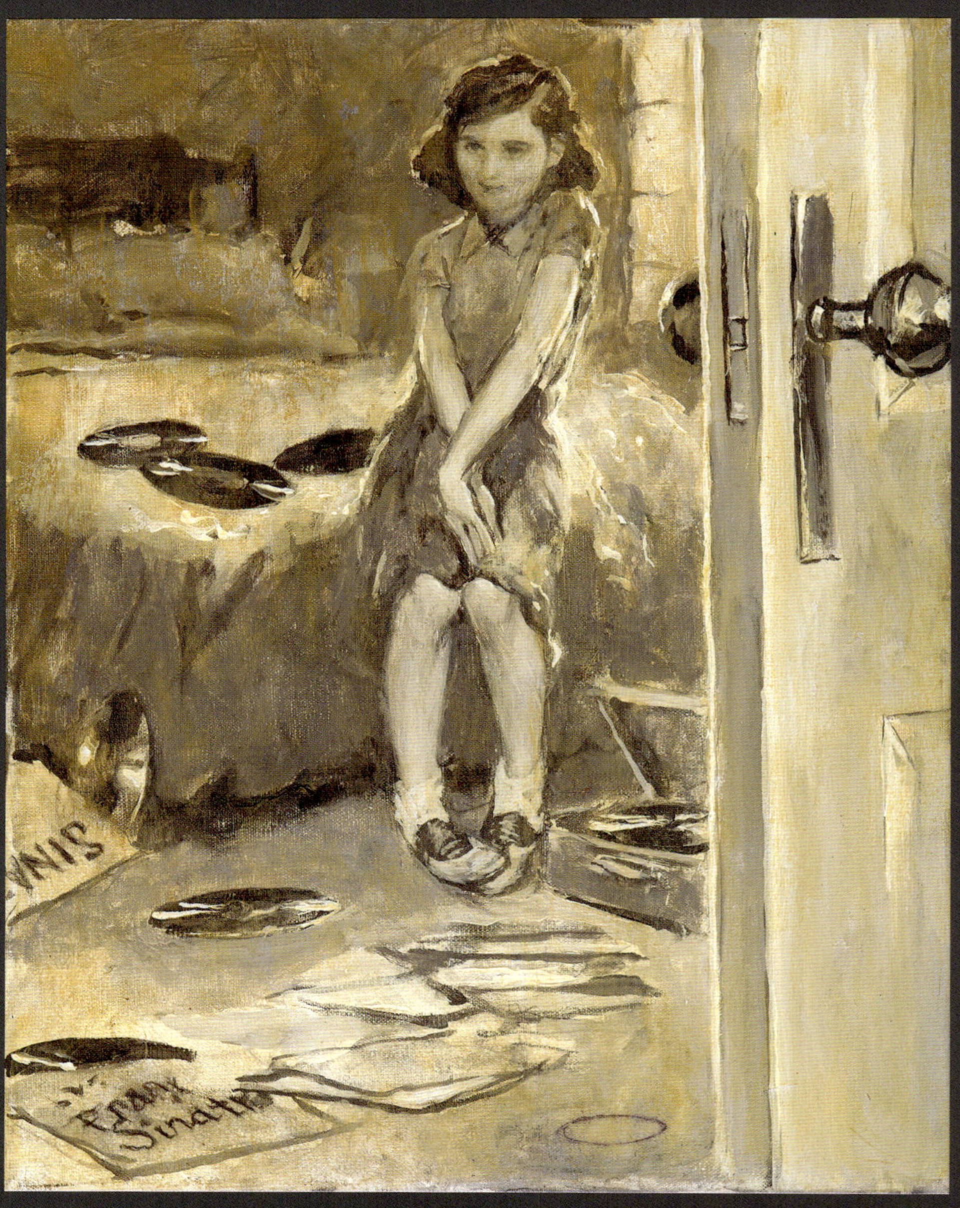

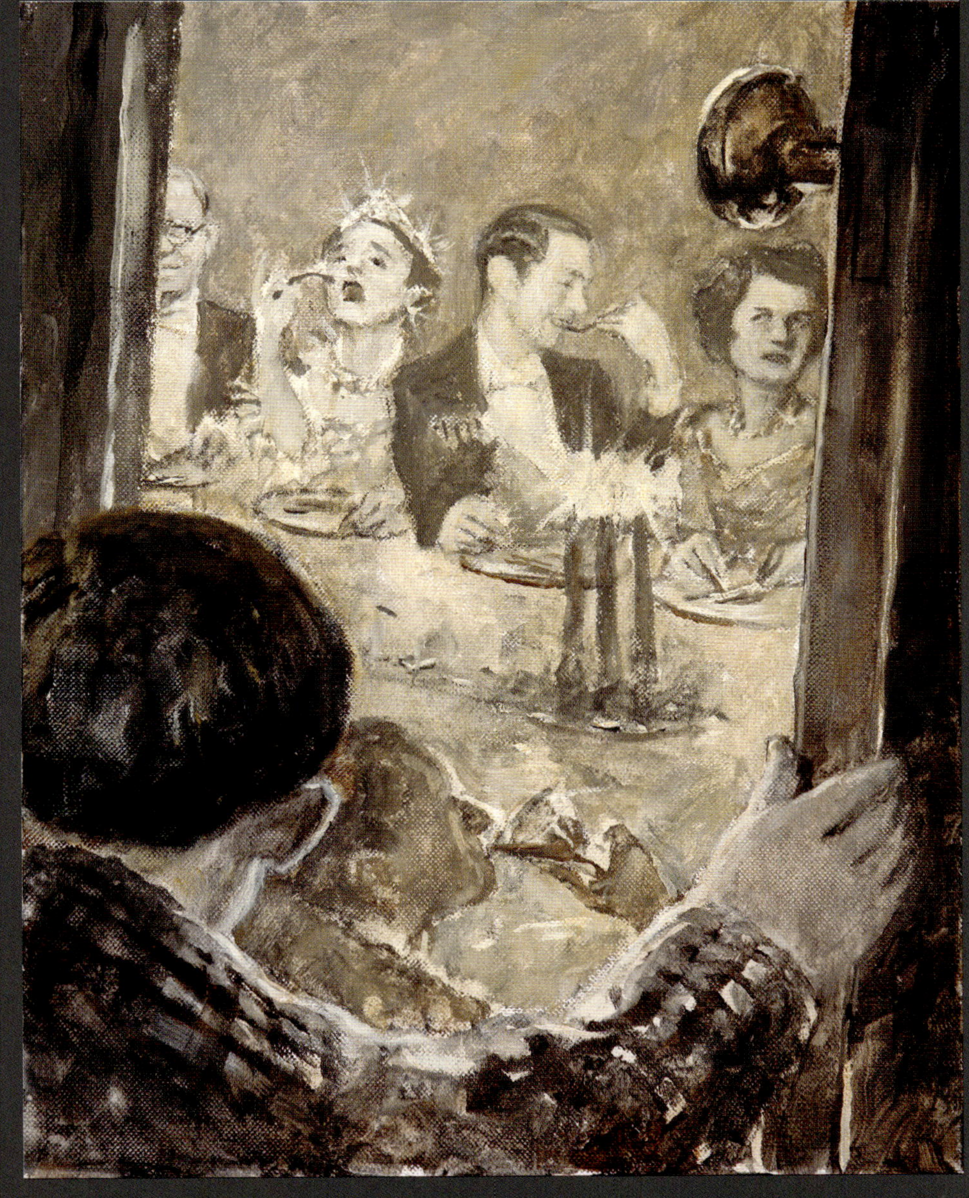

PLATE 20
Teddy Kennedy Observing the King and Queen of England, 2013

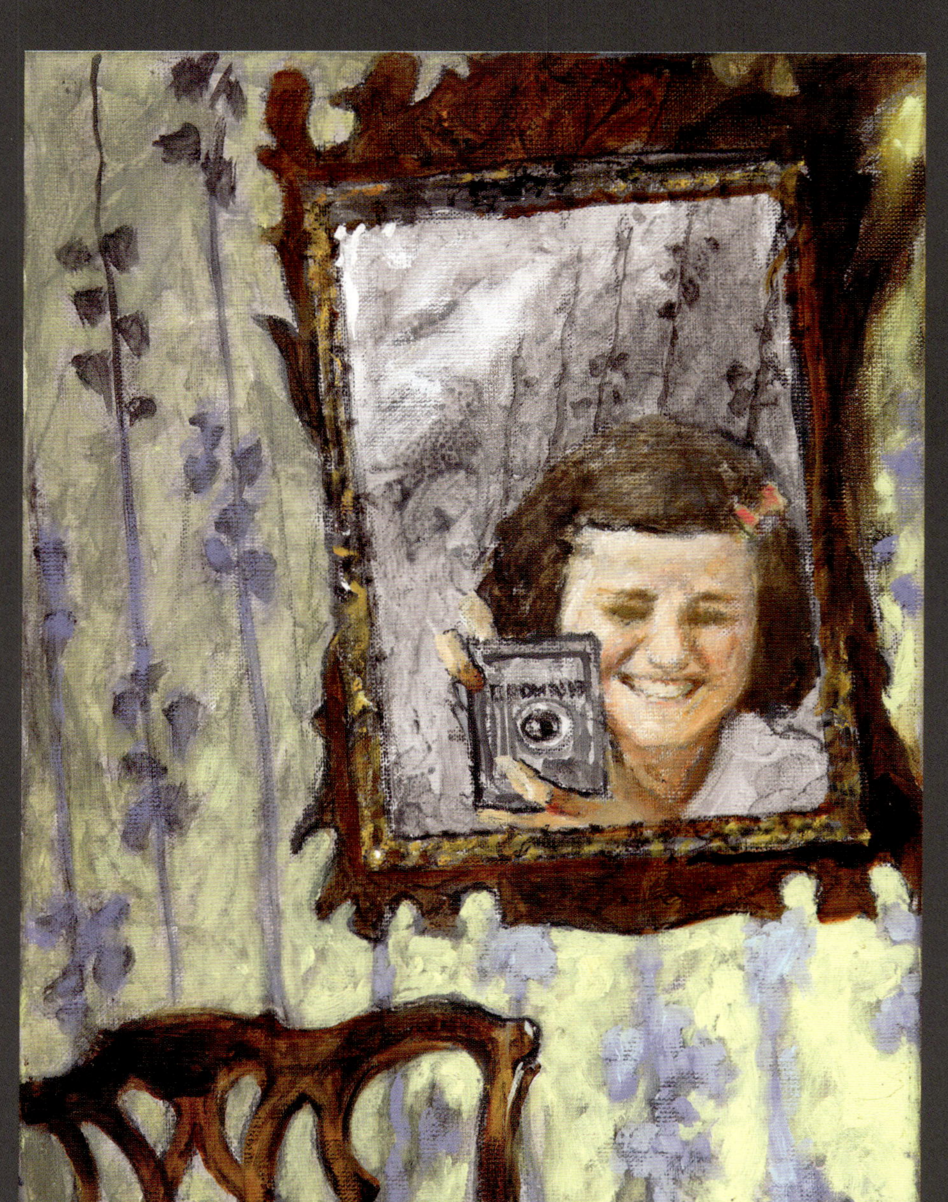

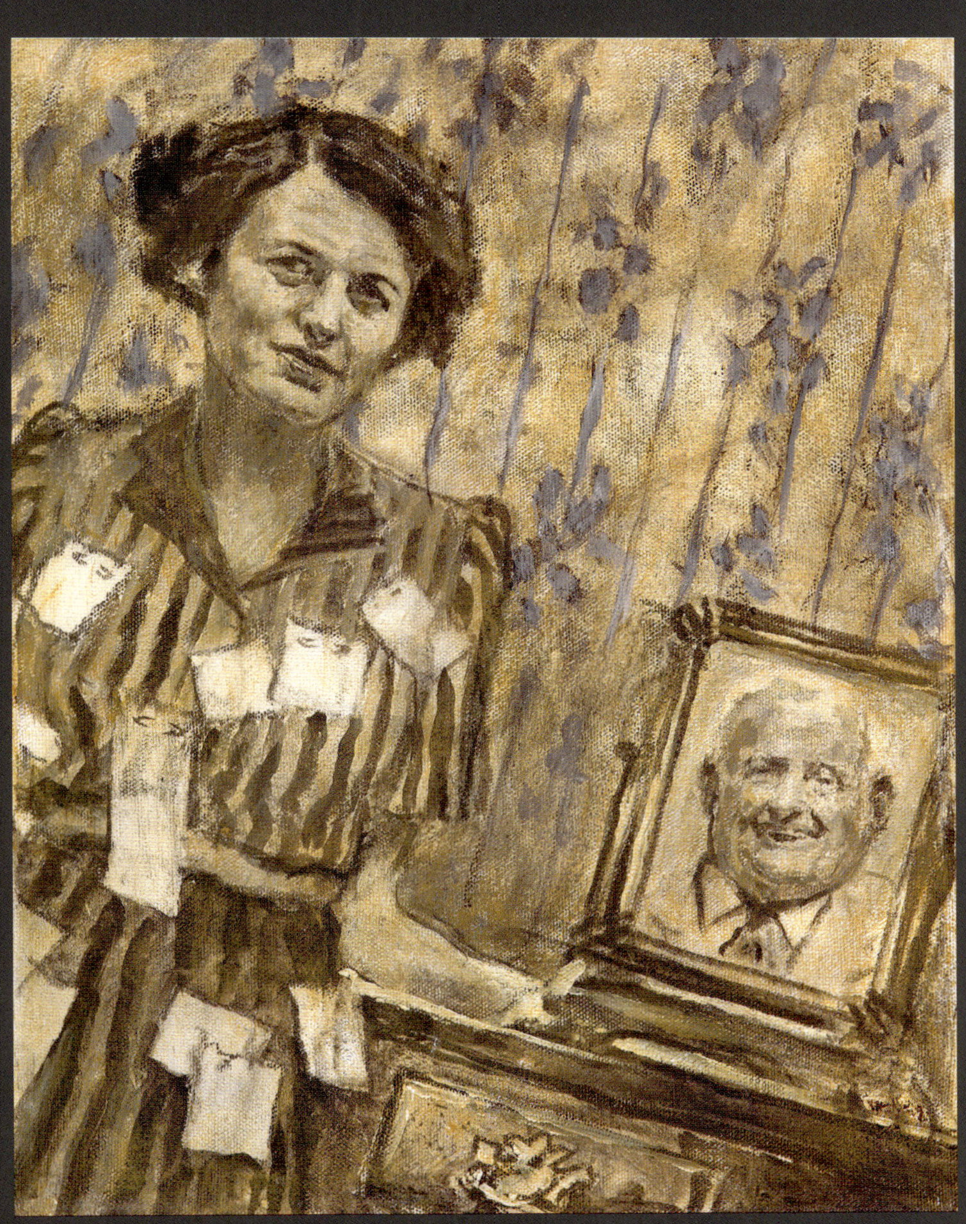

22
dy with Her Father's
ph, 2013

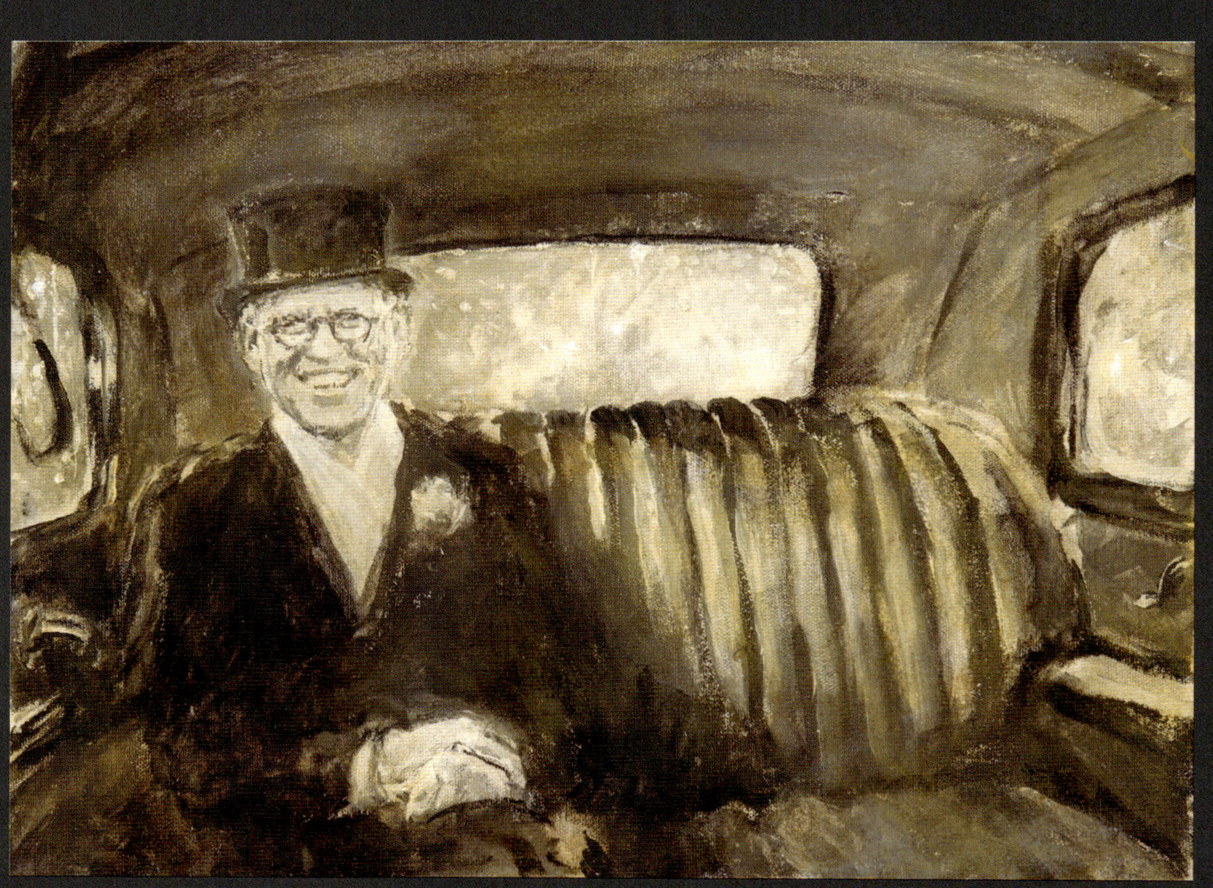

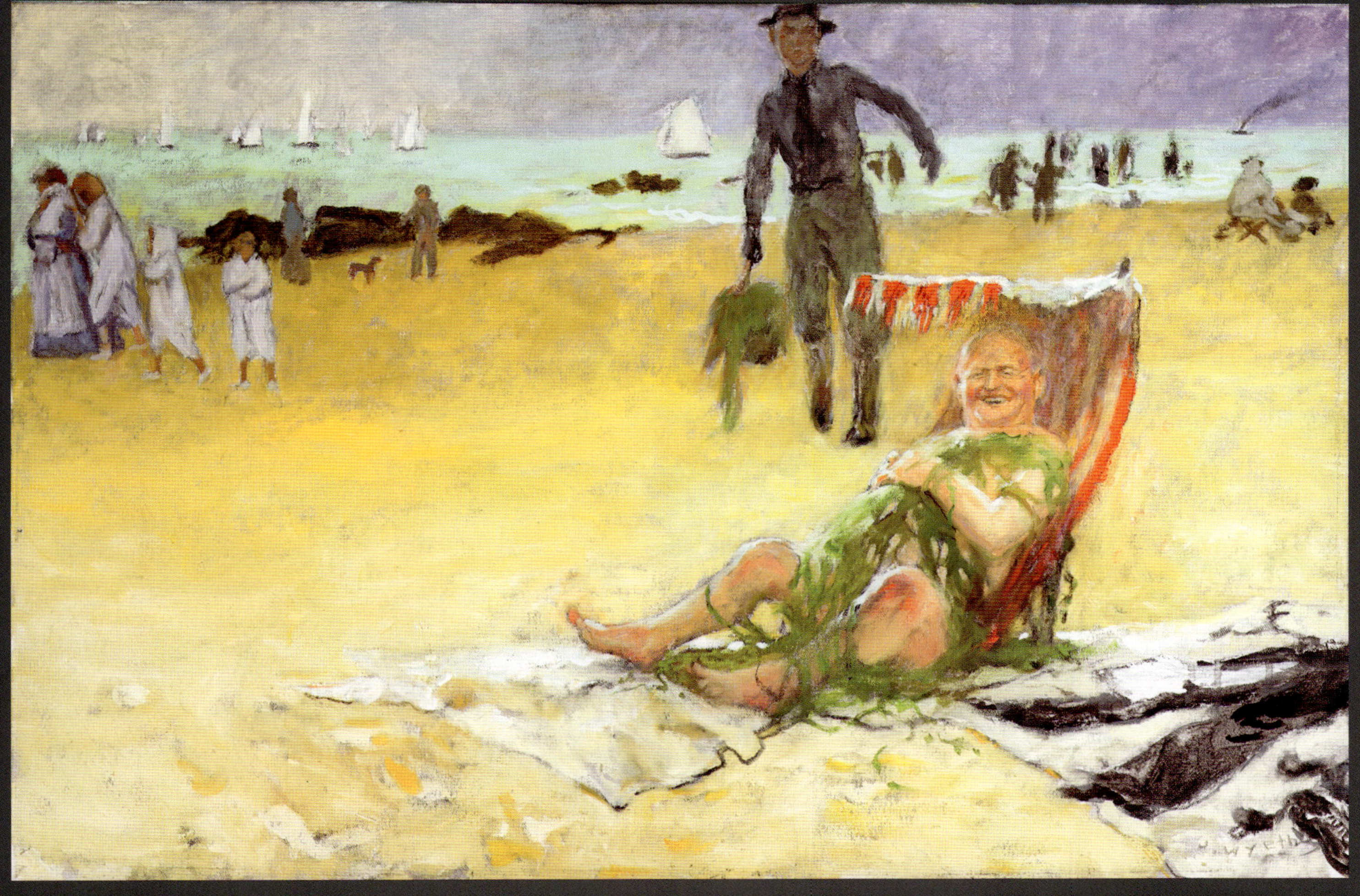

PLATE 24
The Seaweed and Honey Fitz, 2014

PLATE 25
Ramps, 2013

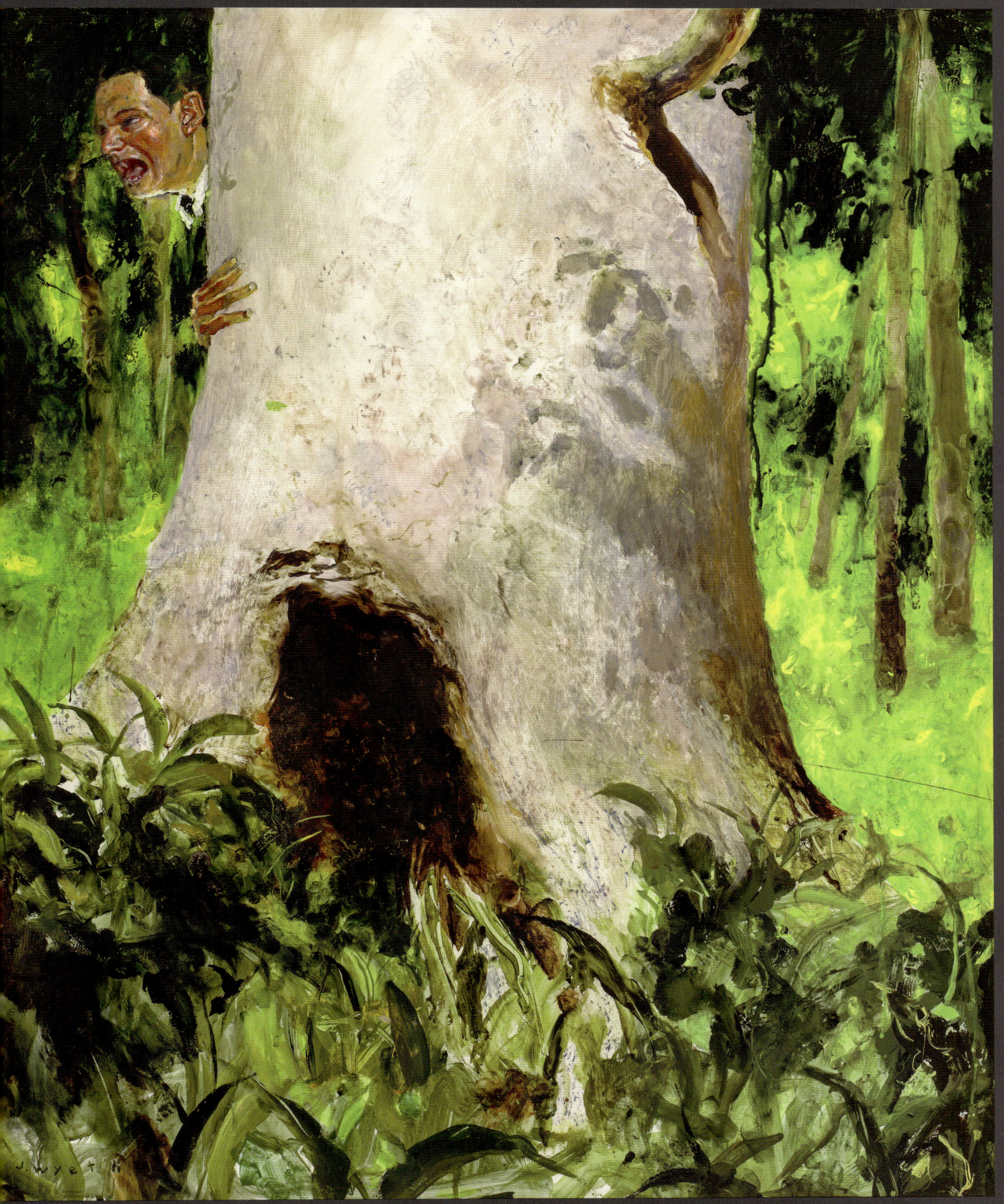

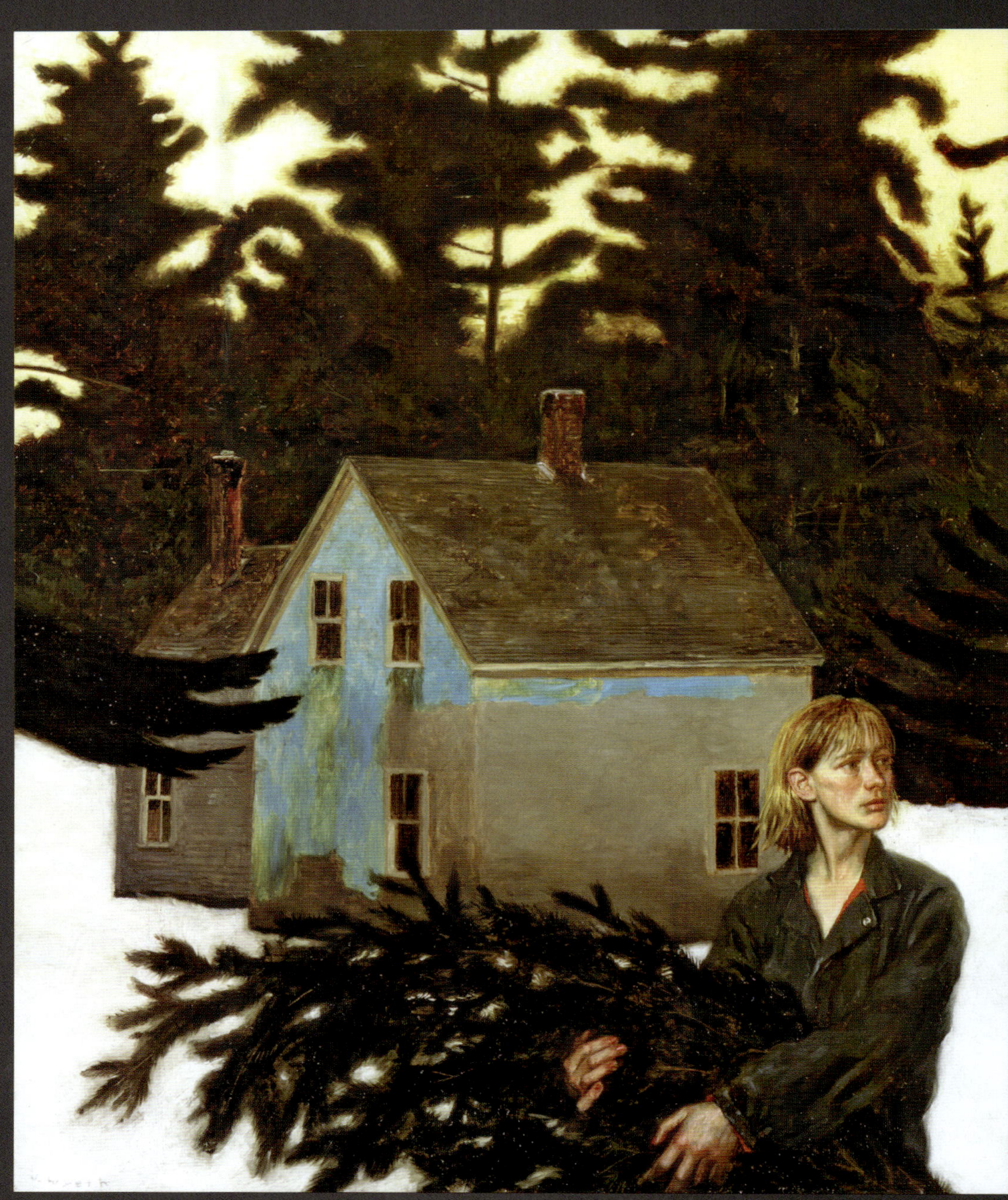

PLATE 26
Black Spruce, 1994

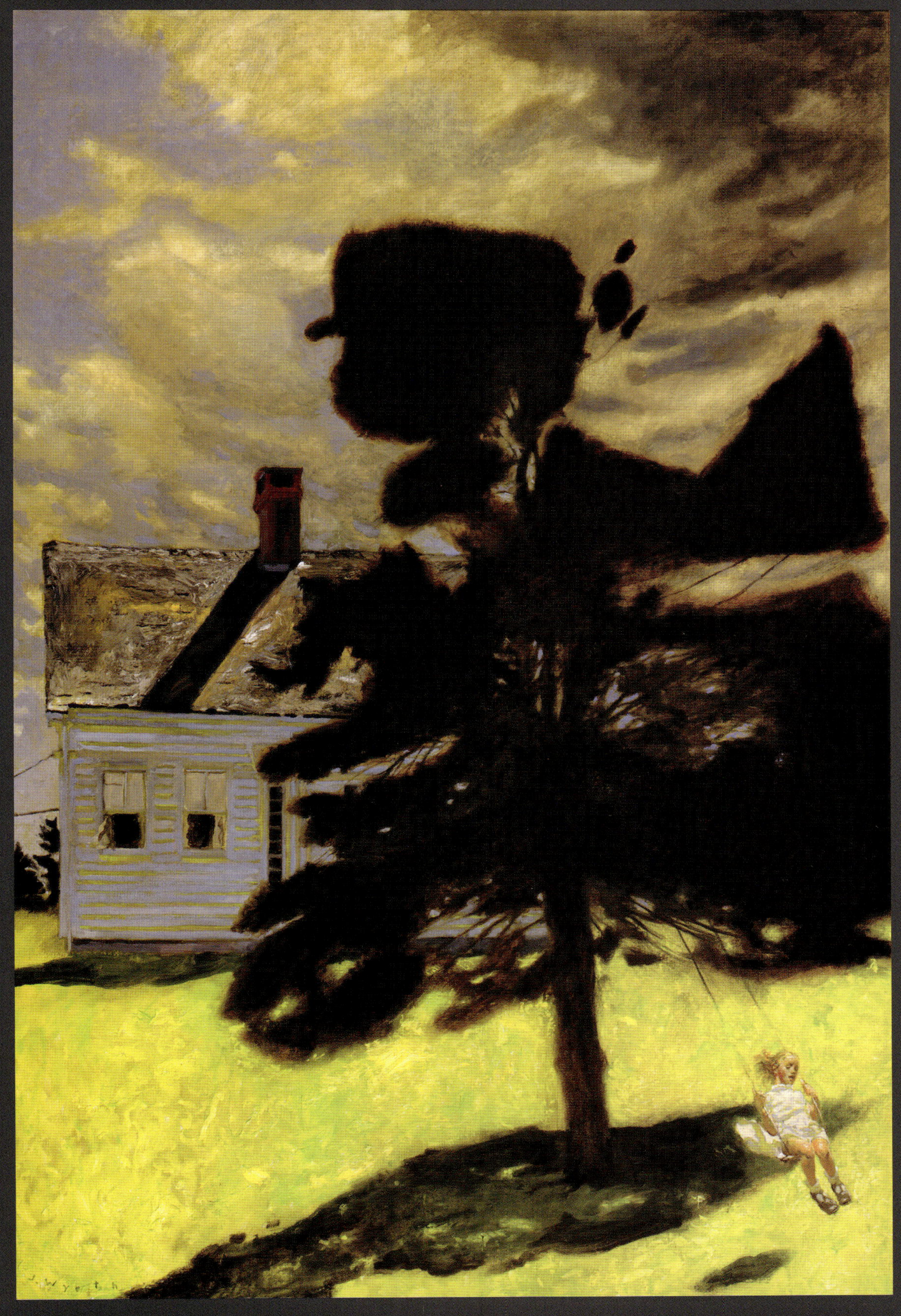

PLATE 27
Julia on the Swing, 1999

PLATE 28
Hill Girt Farm, 2000

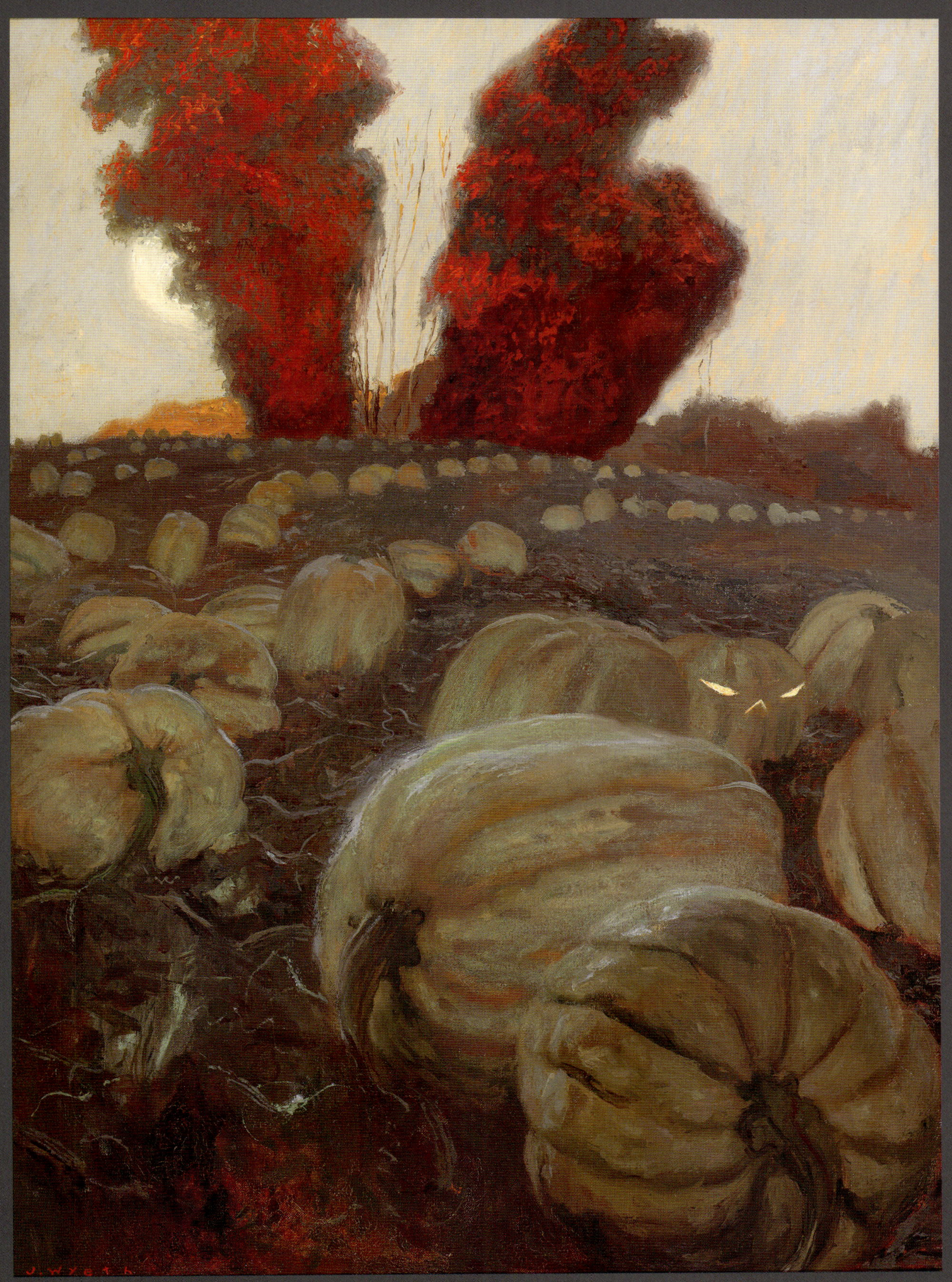
J. Wyeth

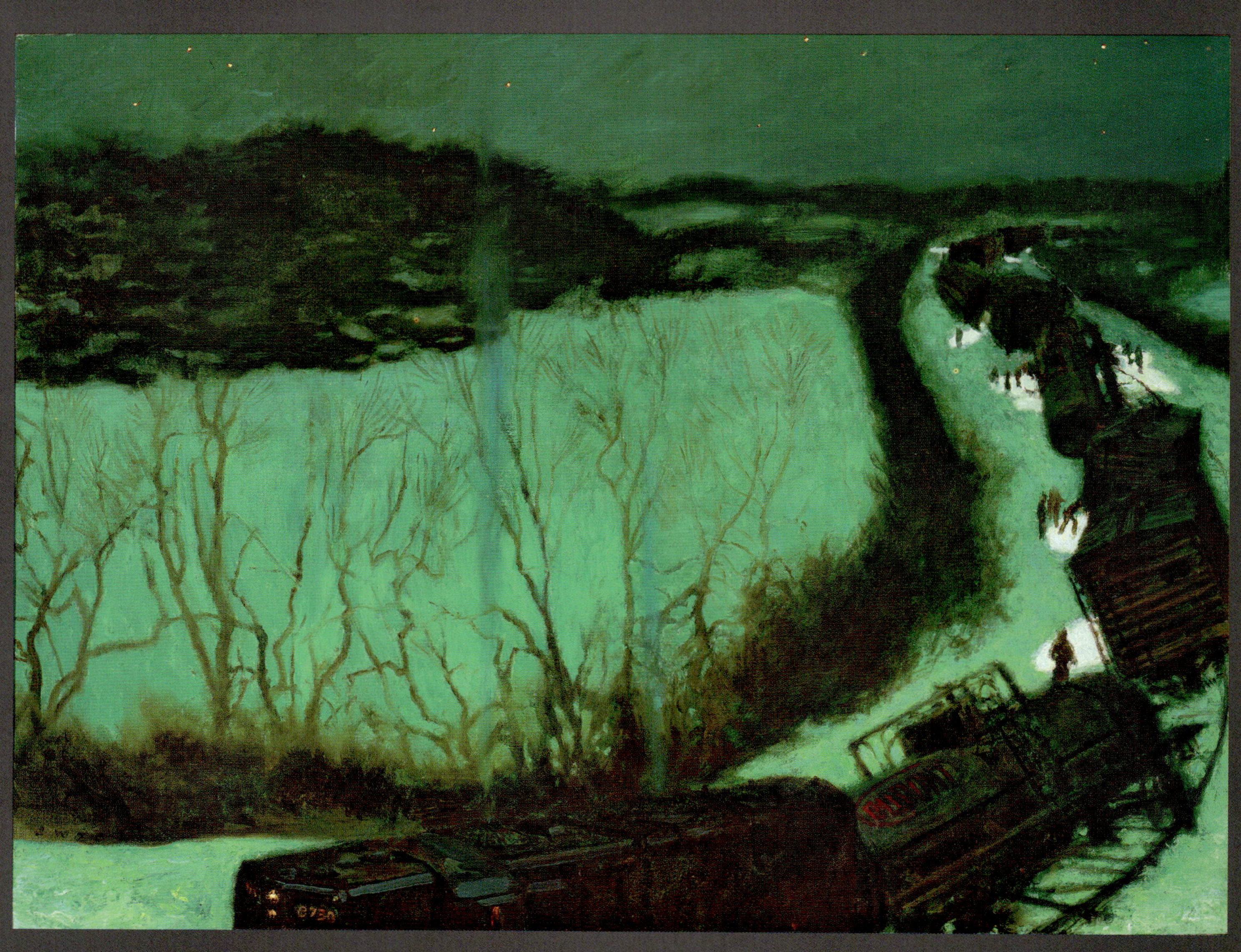

PLATE 29
The du Ponts of Delaware Study, 2010

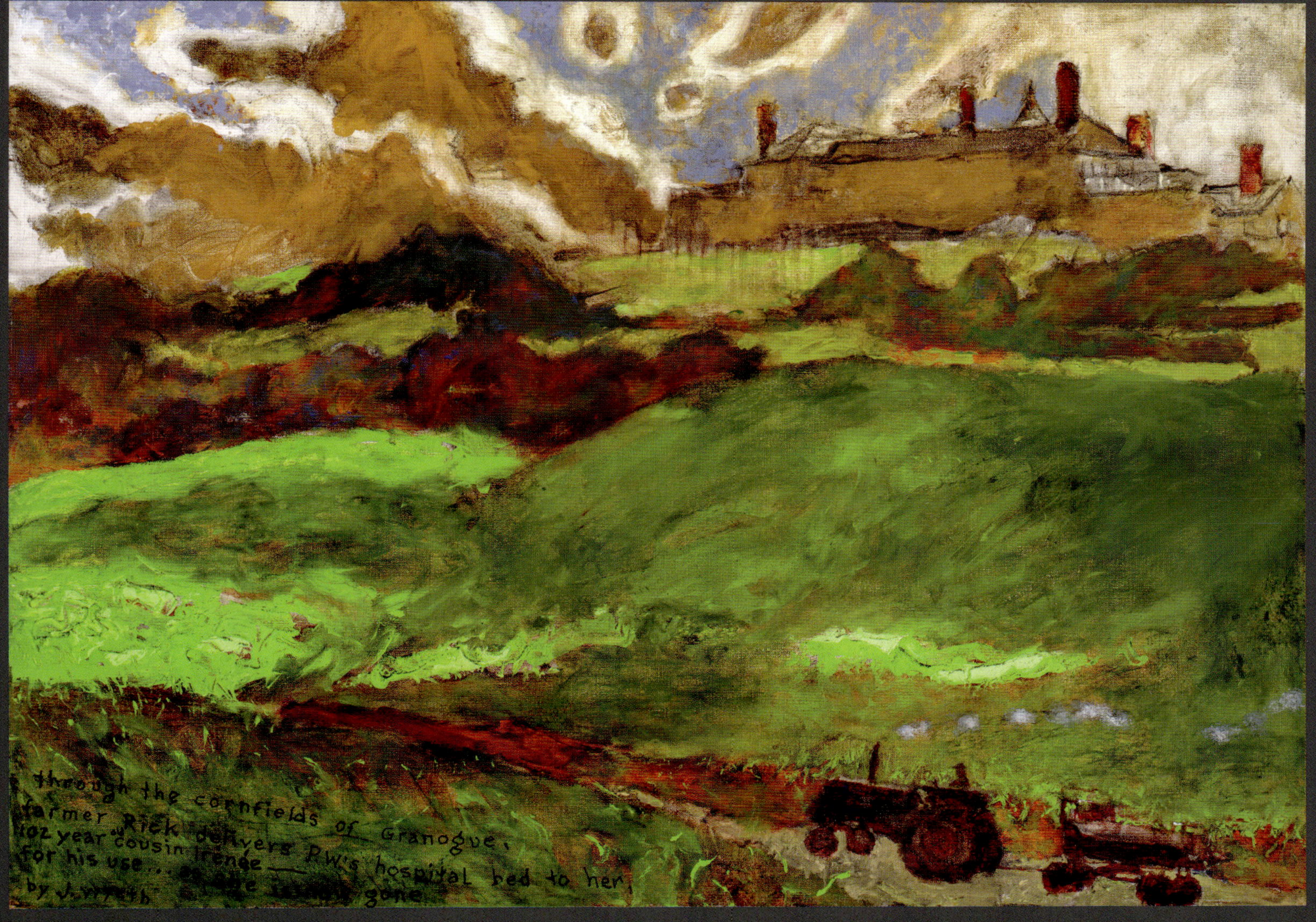

PLATE 30

Through the Cornfields of Granogue, 2022

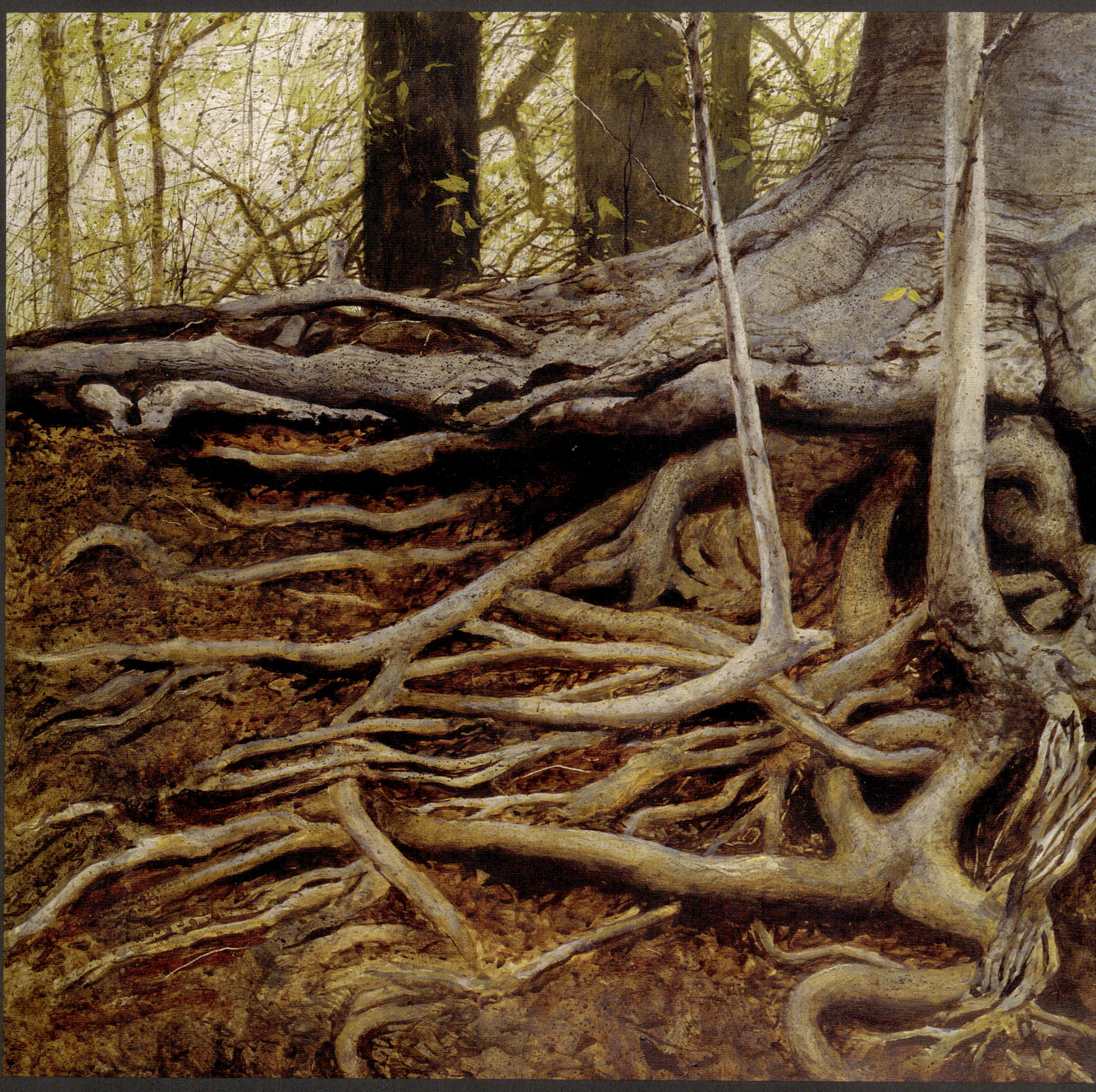

PLATE 31
Roots, 1971

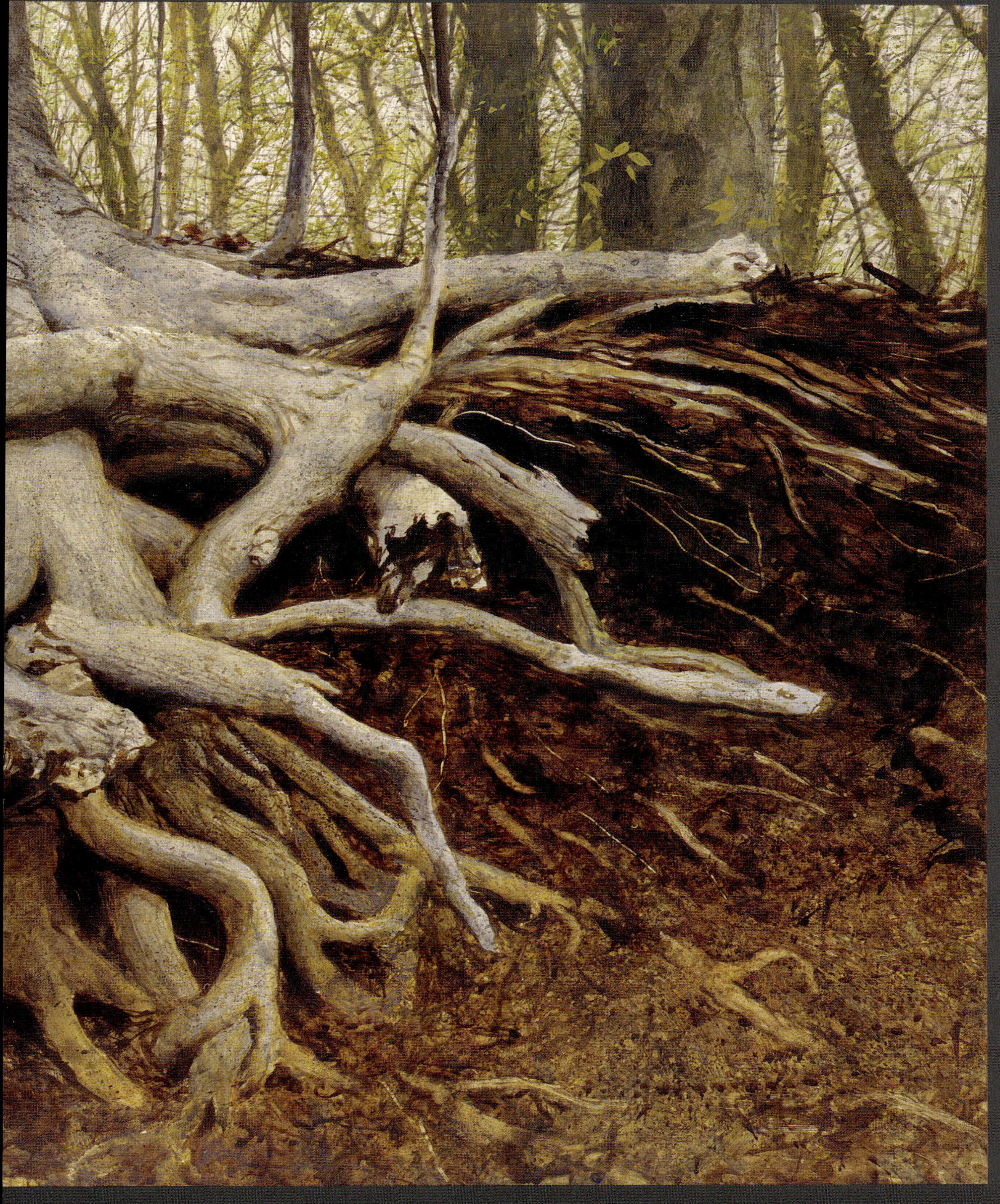

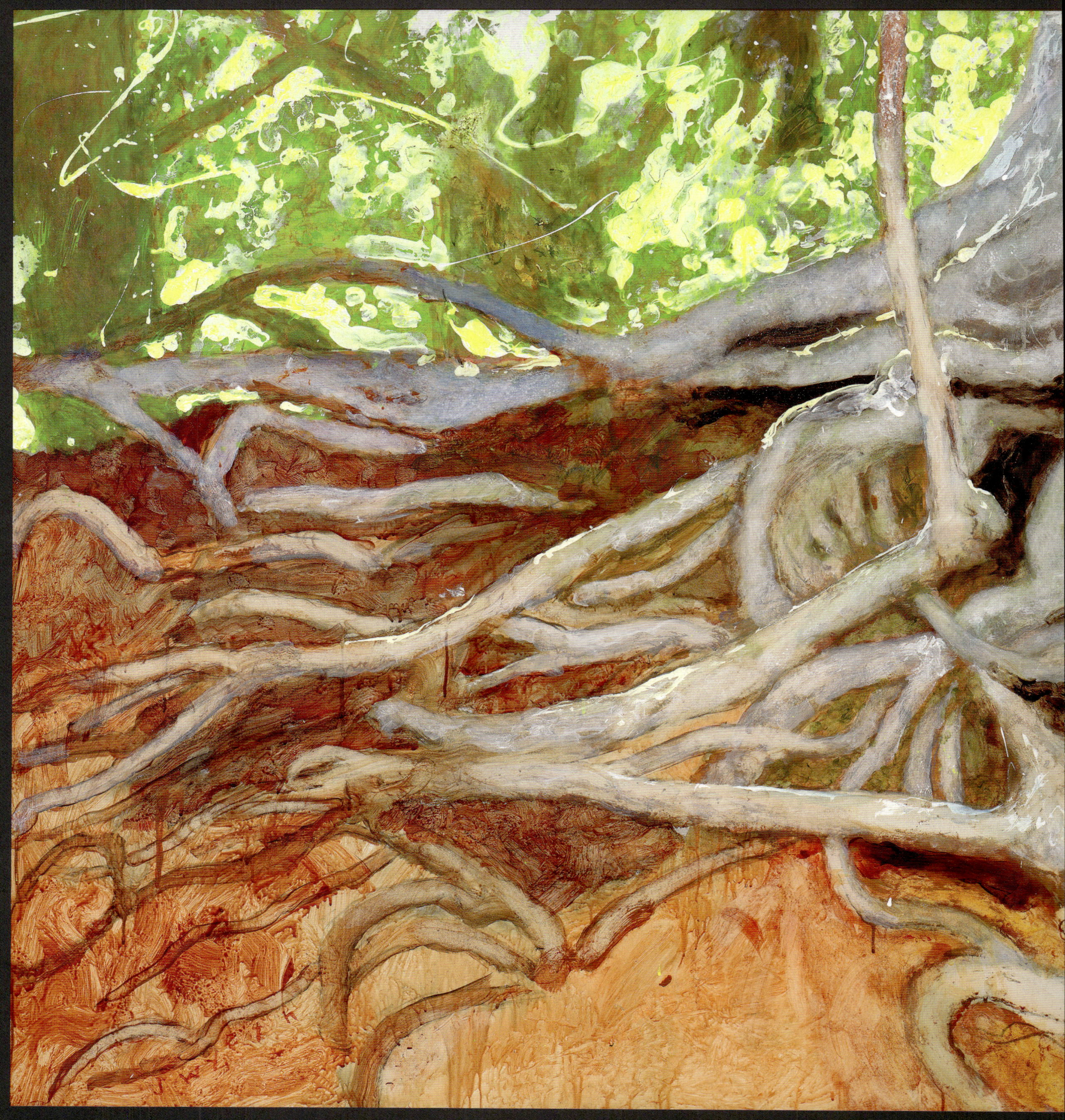

PLATE 32
Roots, Revisited, 2019

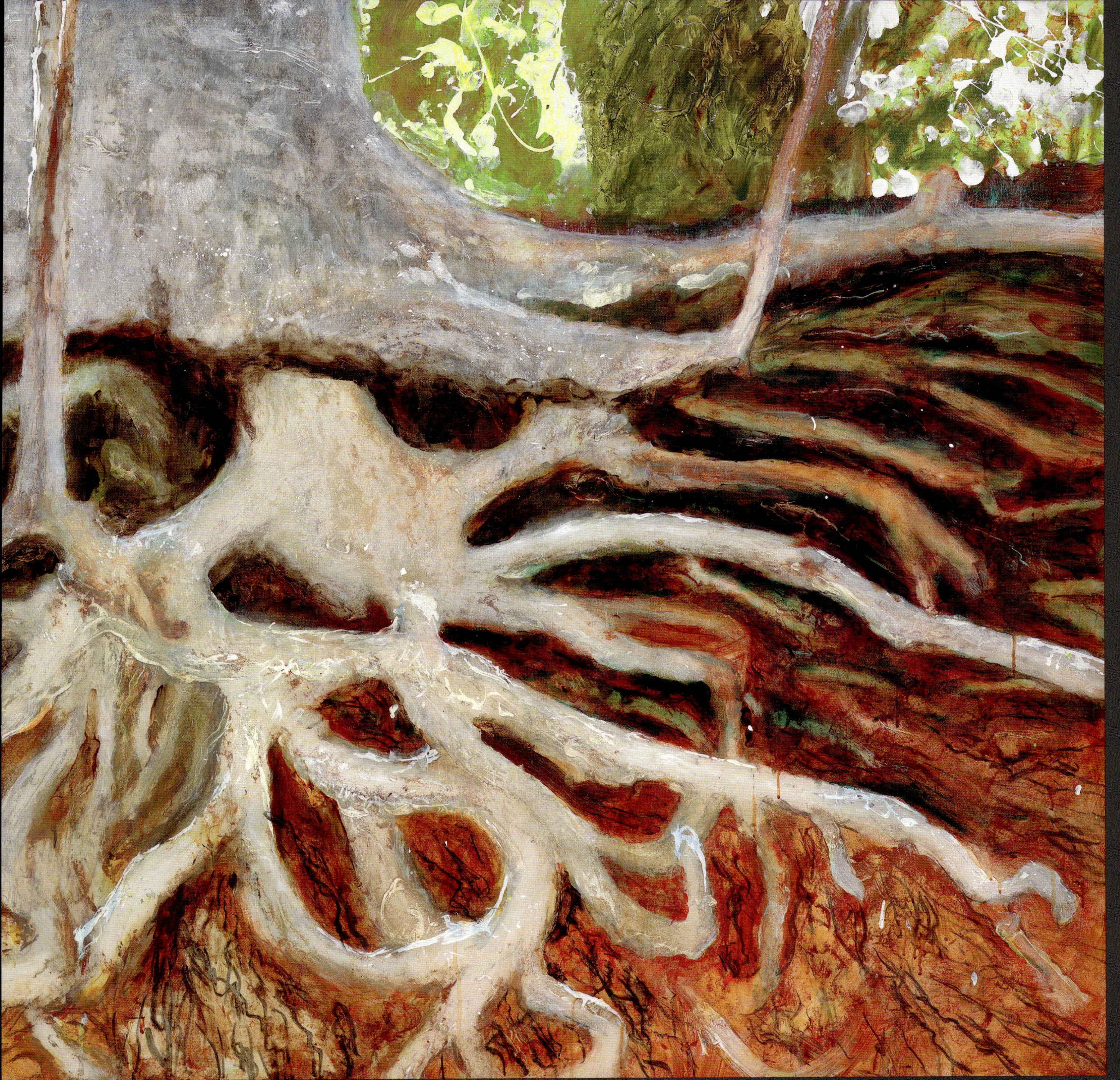

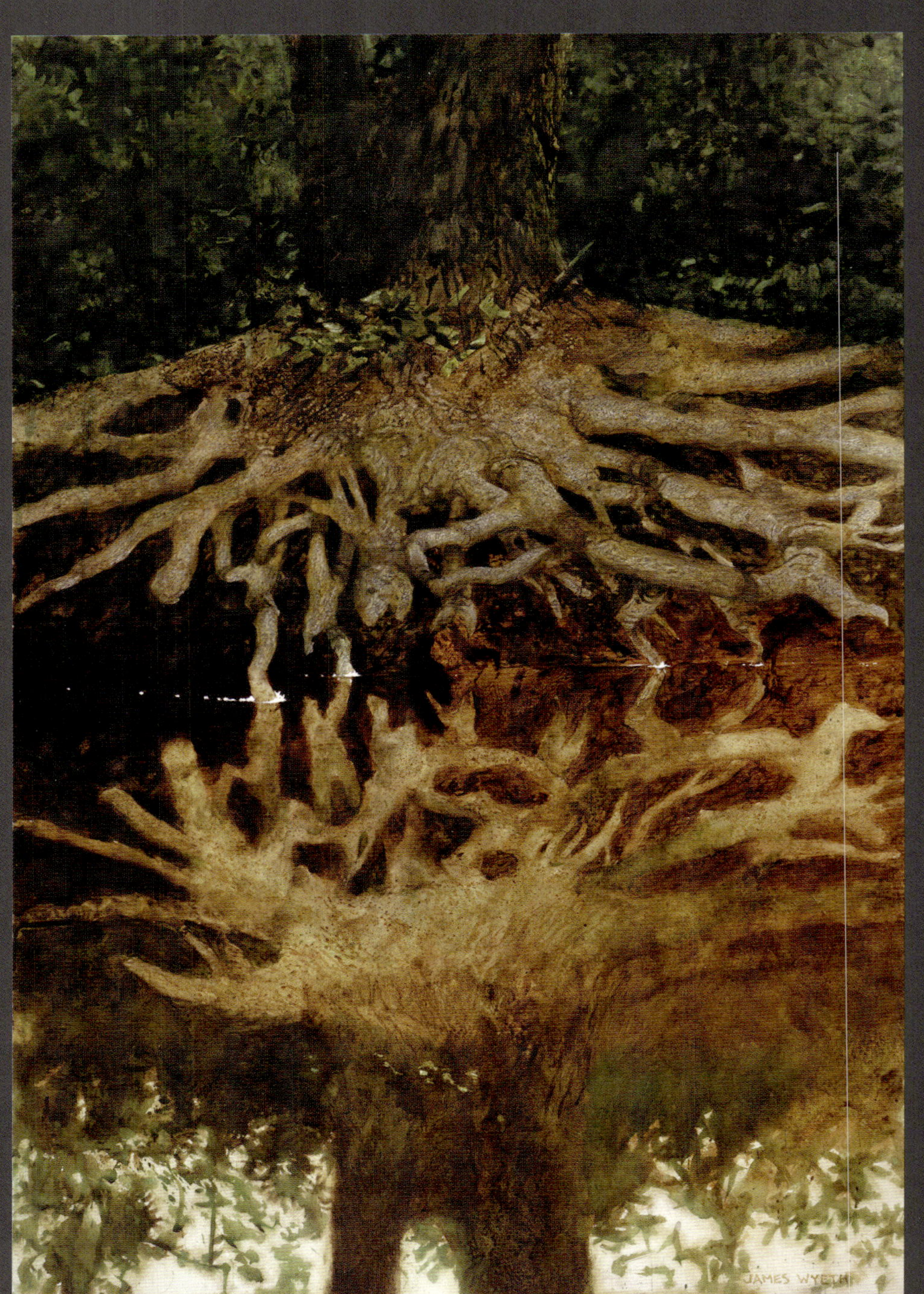
JAMES WYETH

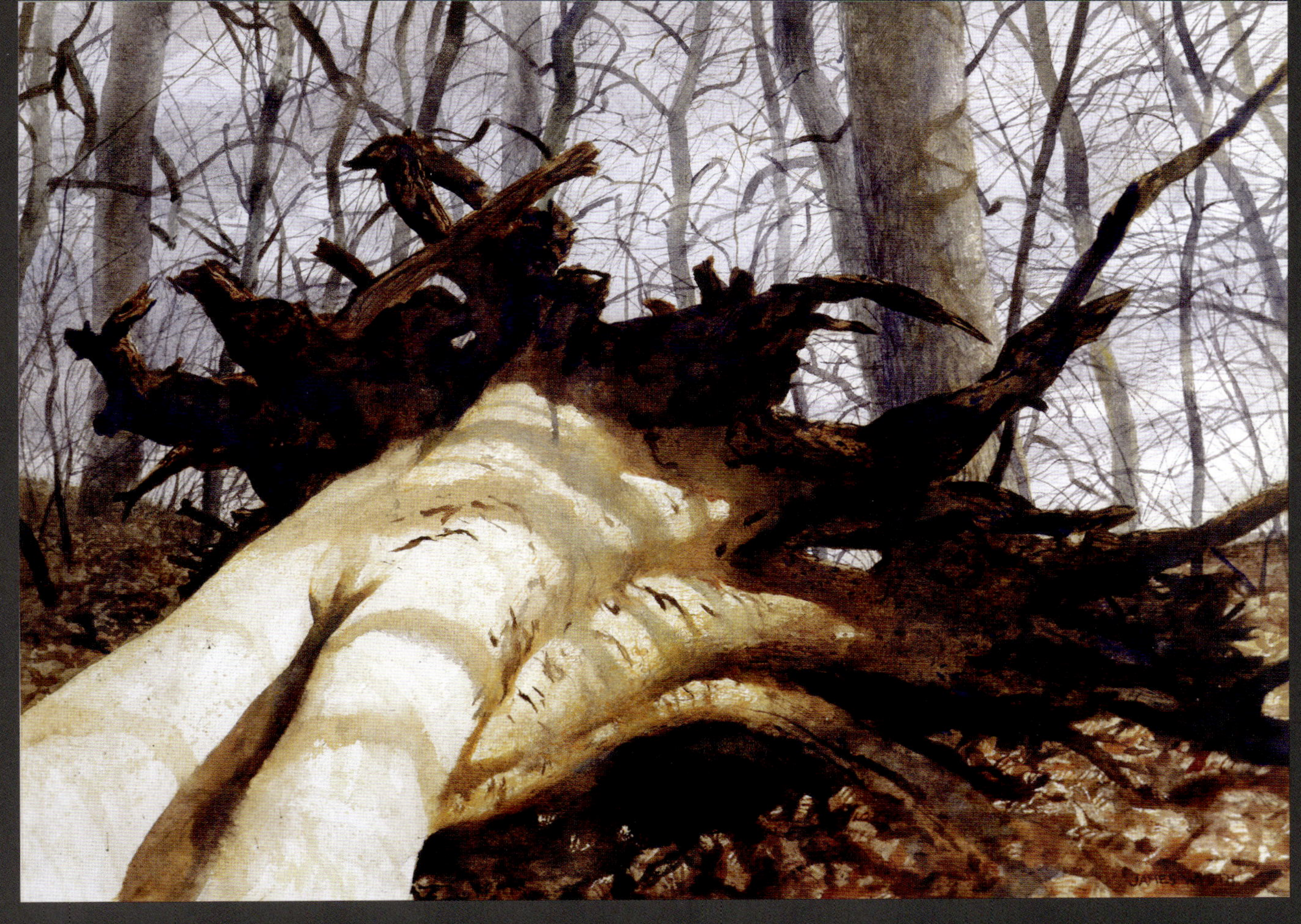

PLATE 34
Fallen, 1975

PLATE 35
River Trunk, 1968

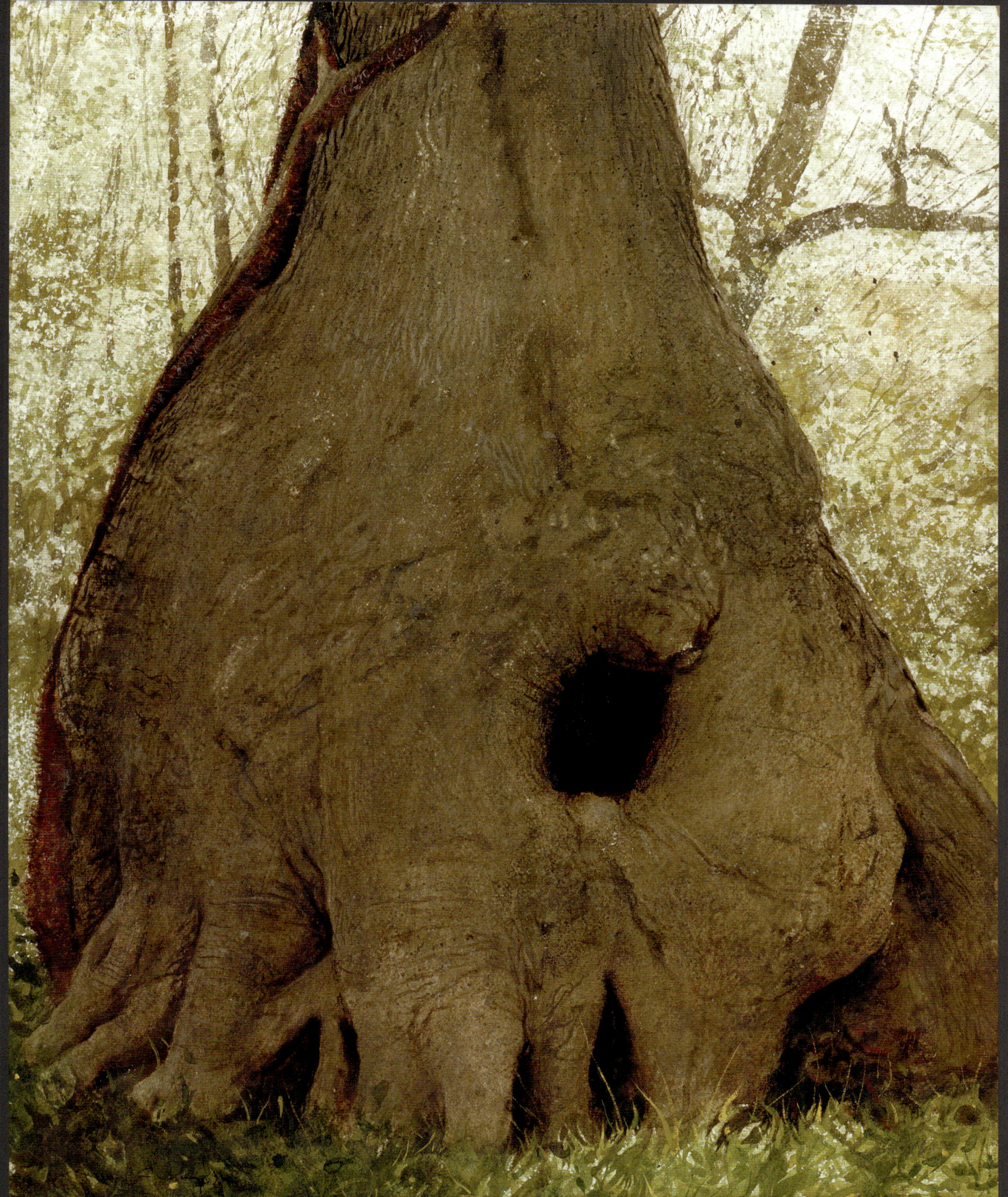

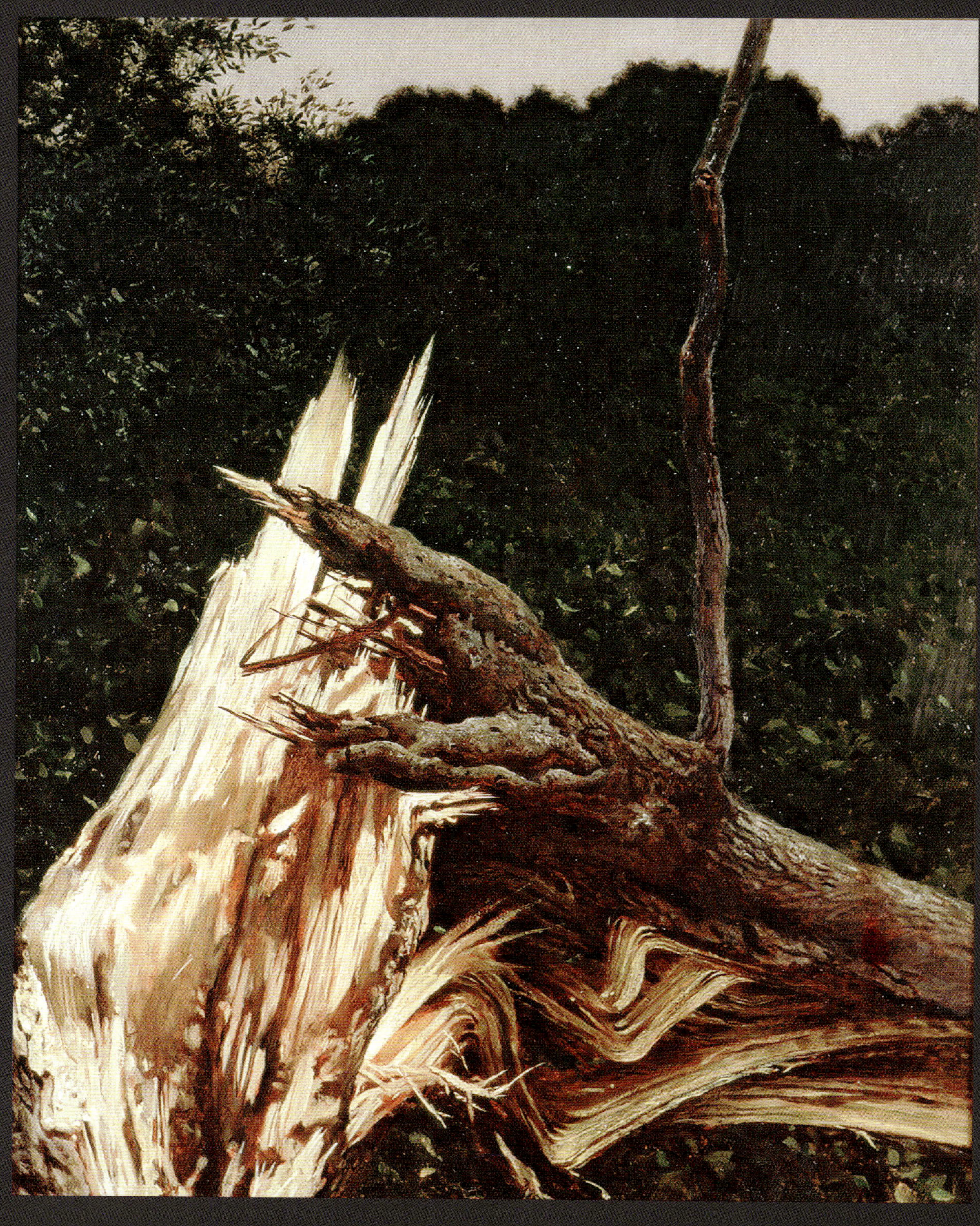

PLATE 36
Lightning Struck, 1975

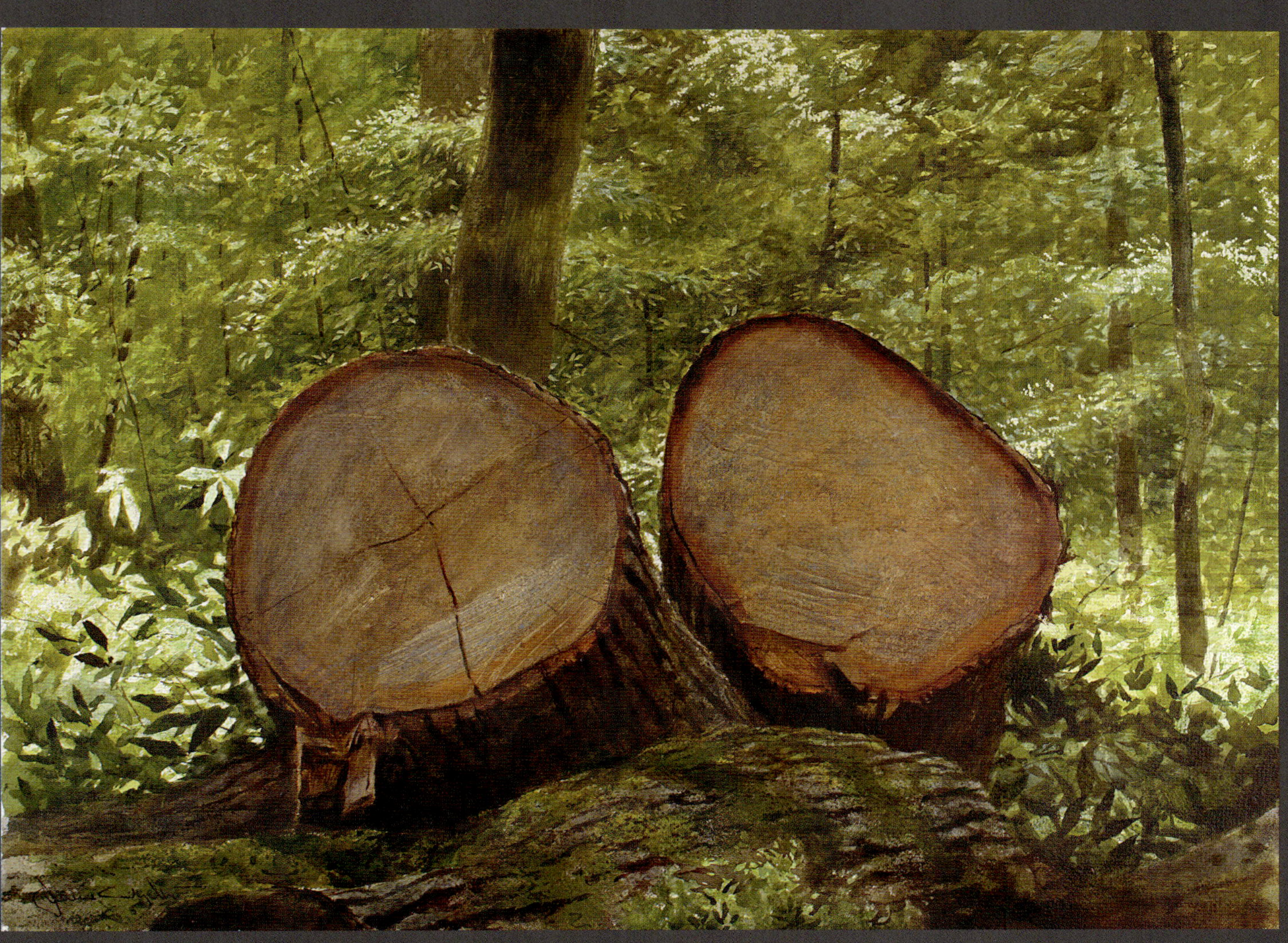

PLATE 37
Butts, 1973

PLATE 38
Portrait of a Moon Curser, Fifteenth in a Suite of Untoward Occurrences on Monhegan Island, 2020

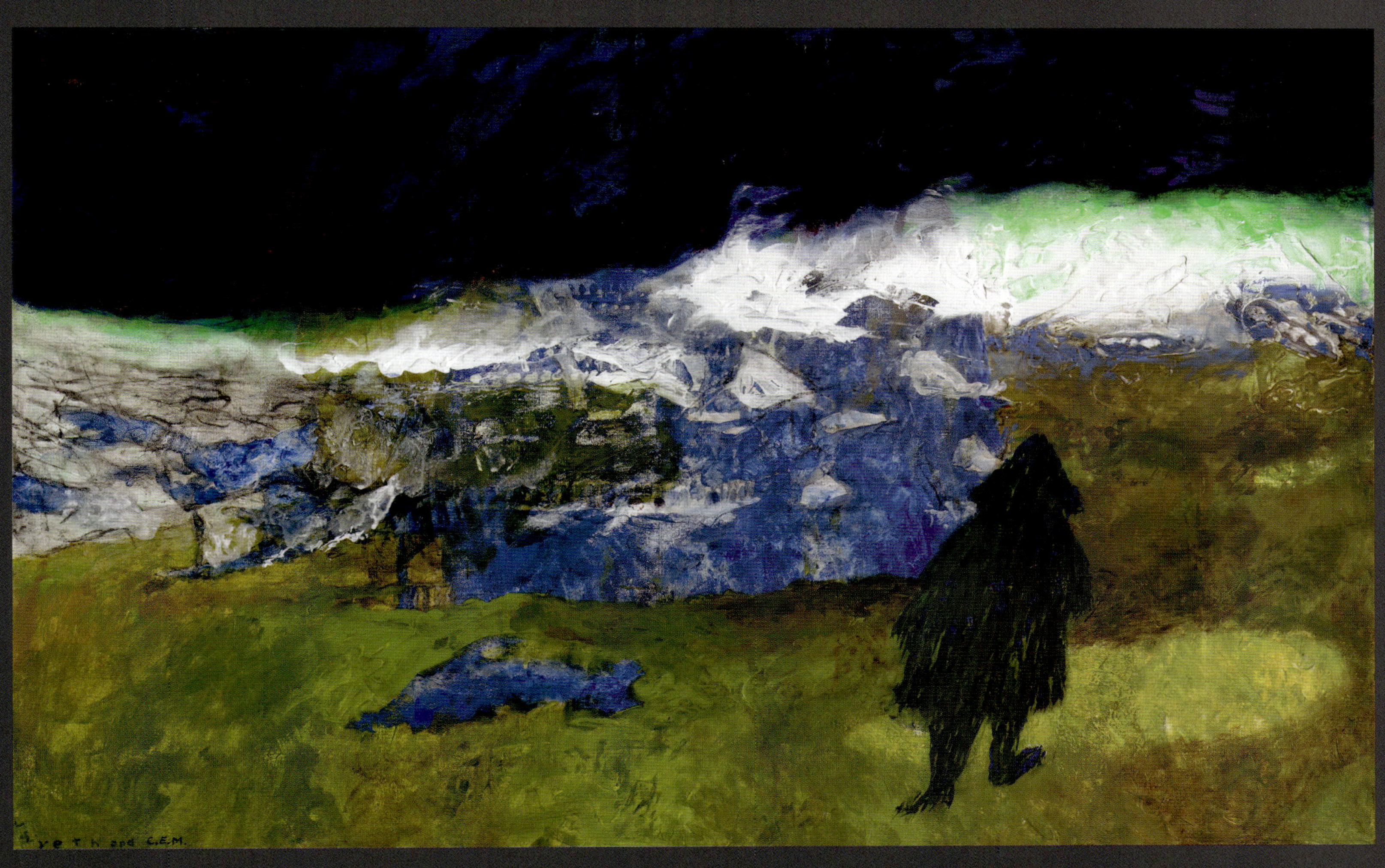
Wyeth and C.E.M.

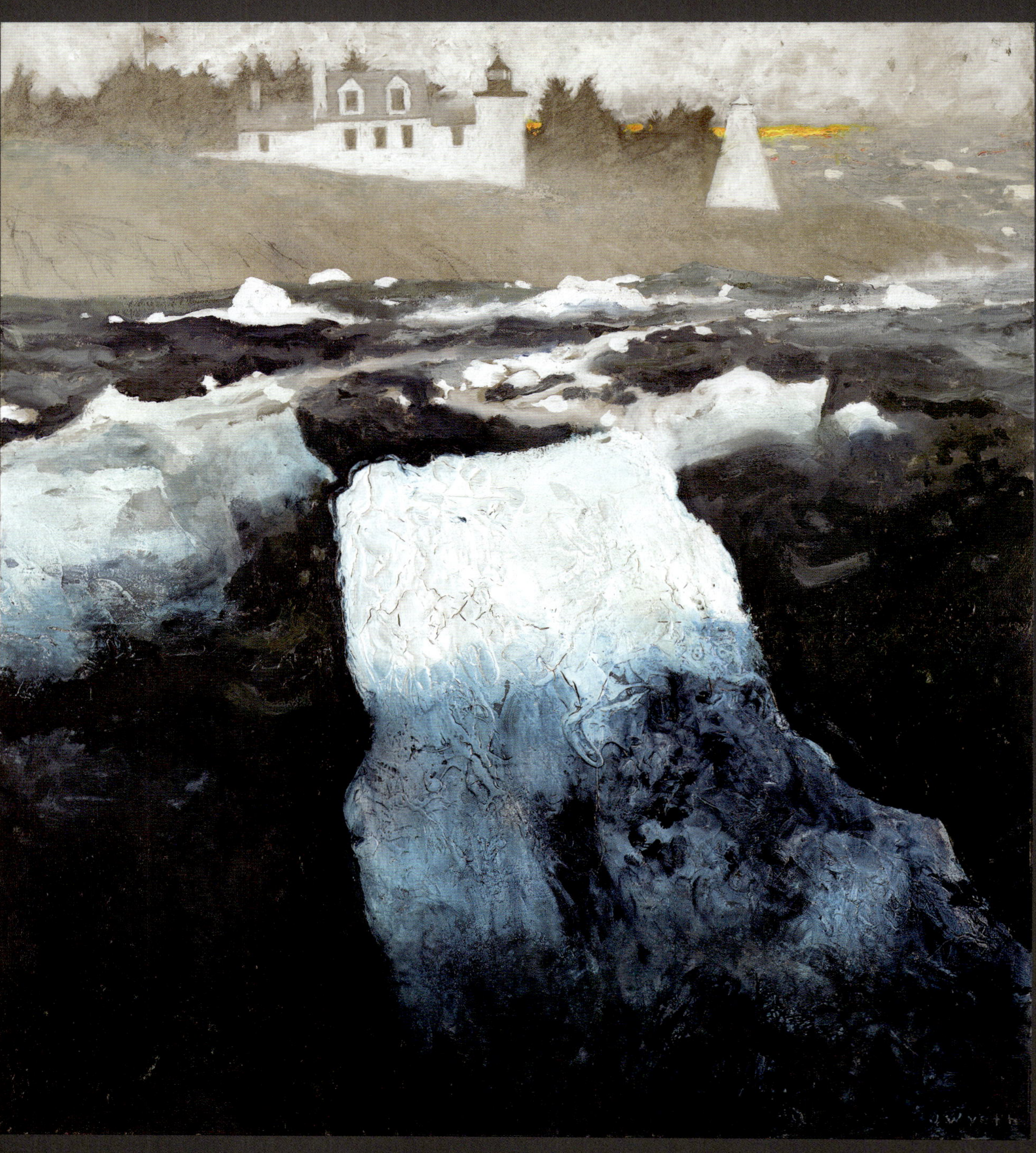

PLATE 39
Berg, 2011

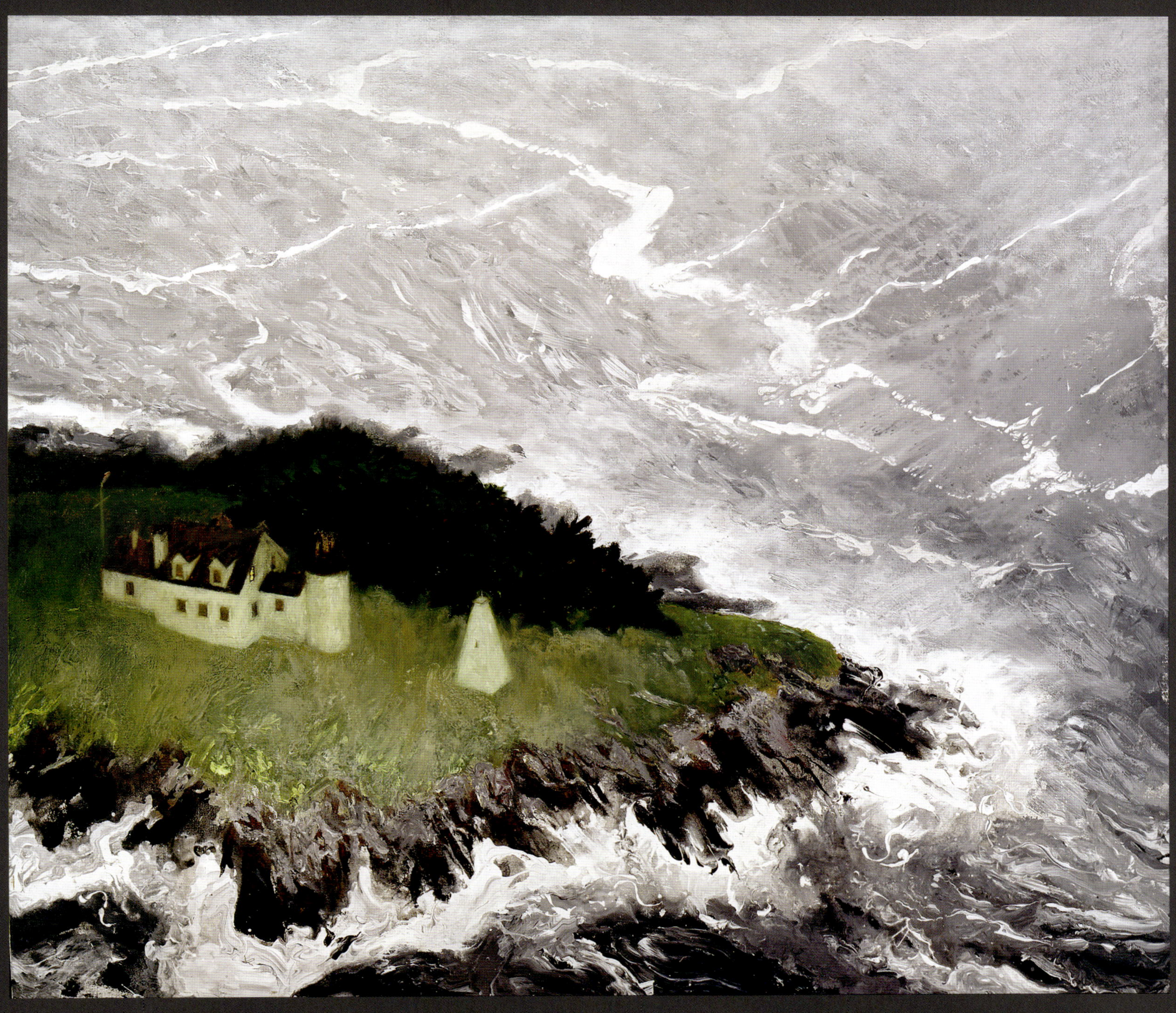

PLATE 40
Spindrift, 2010

PLATE 41
My Mother and the Squall, 2016

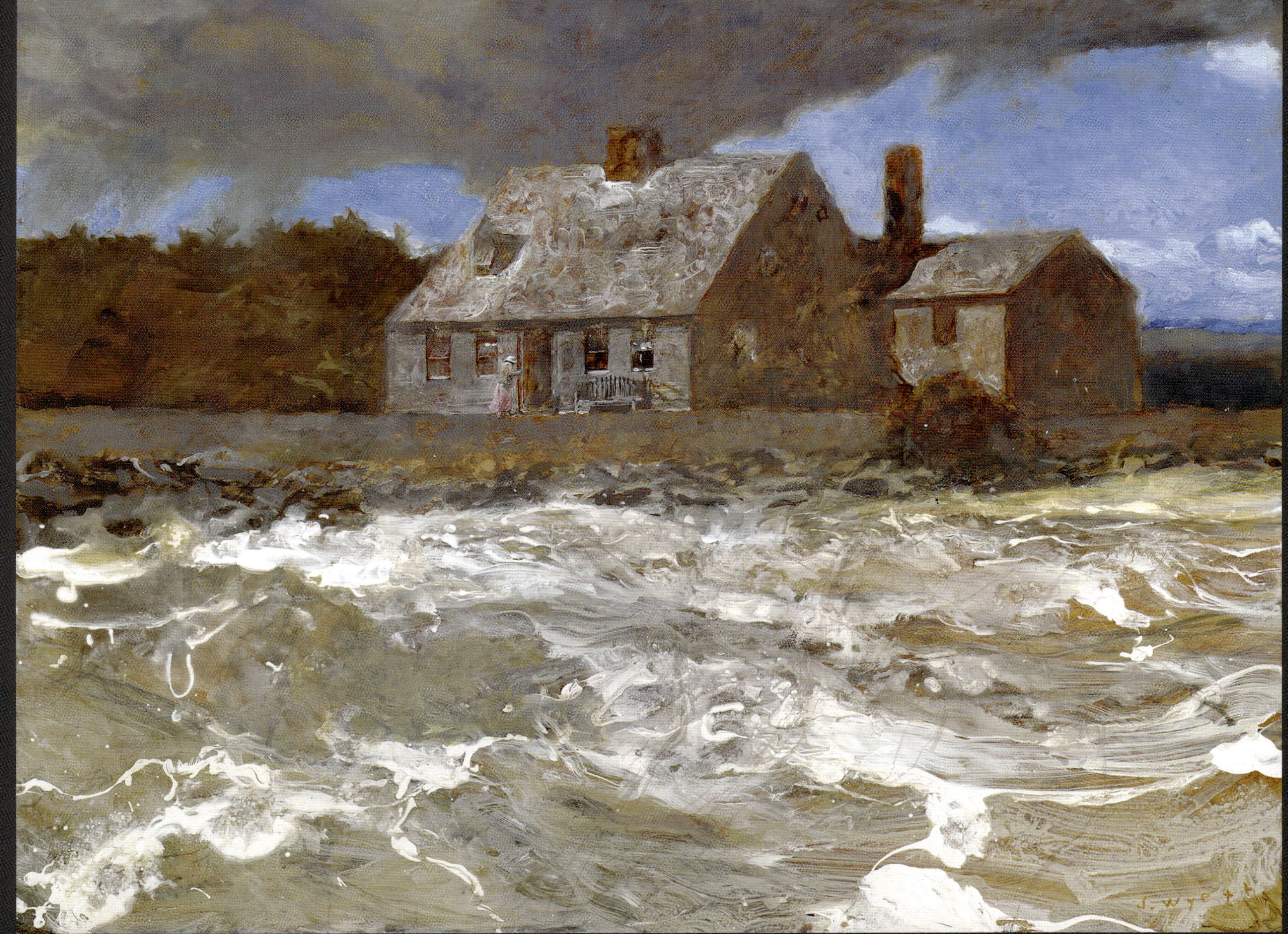

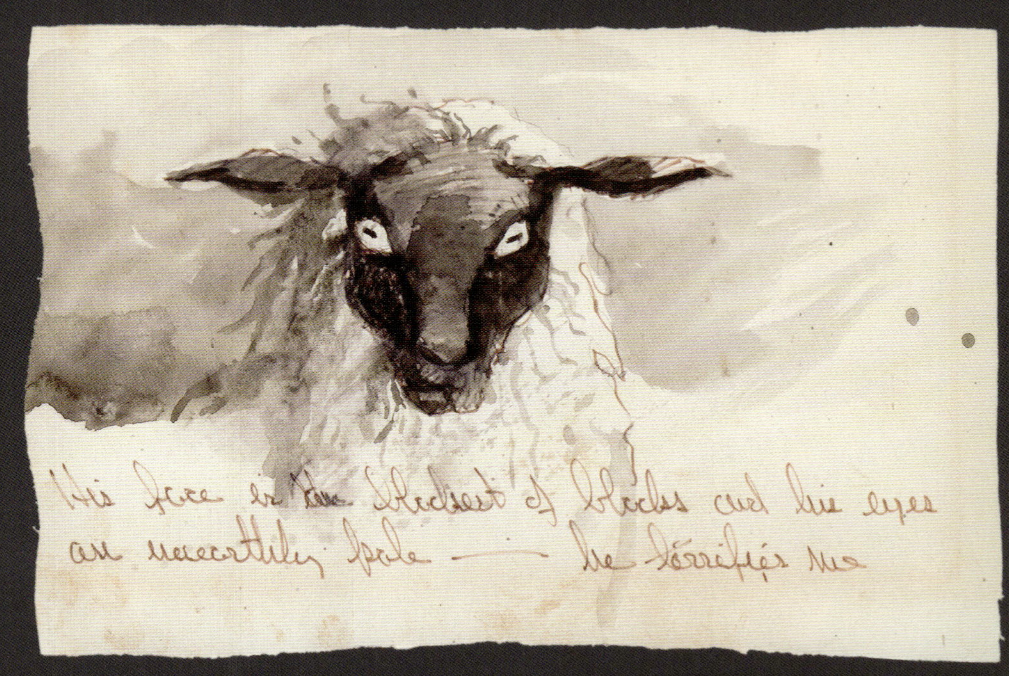

PLATE 42
Sheep Drawing with Letter, 1968

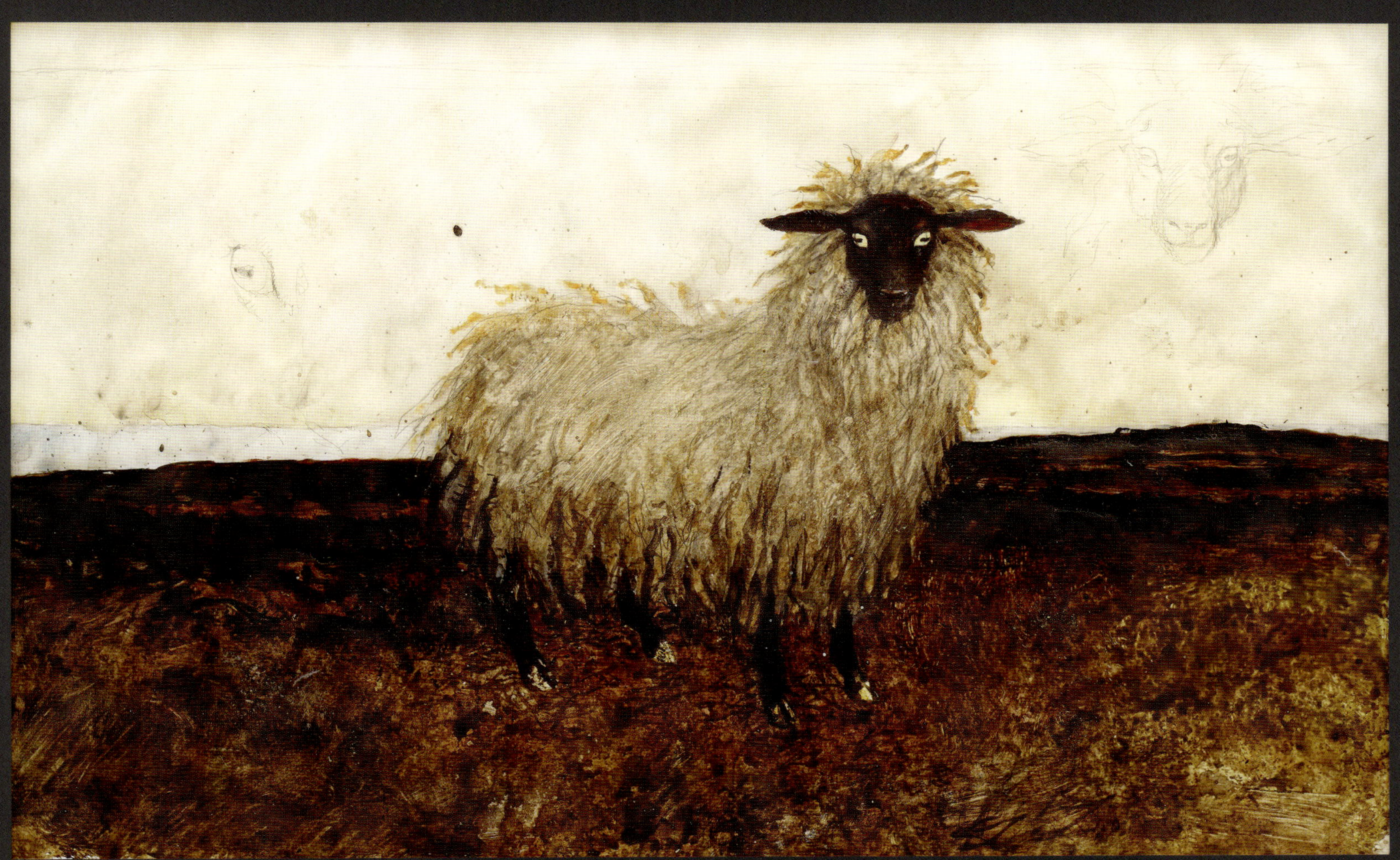

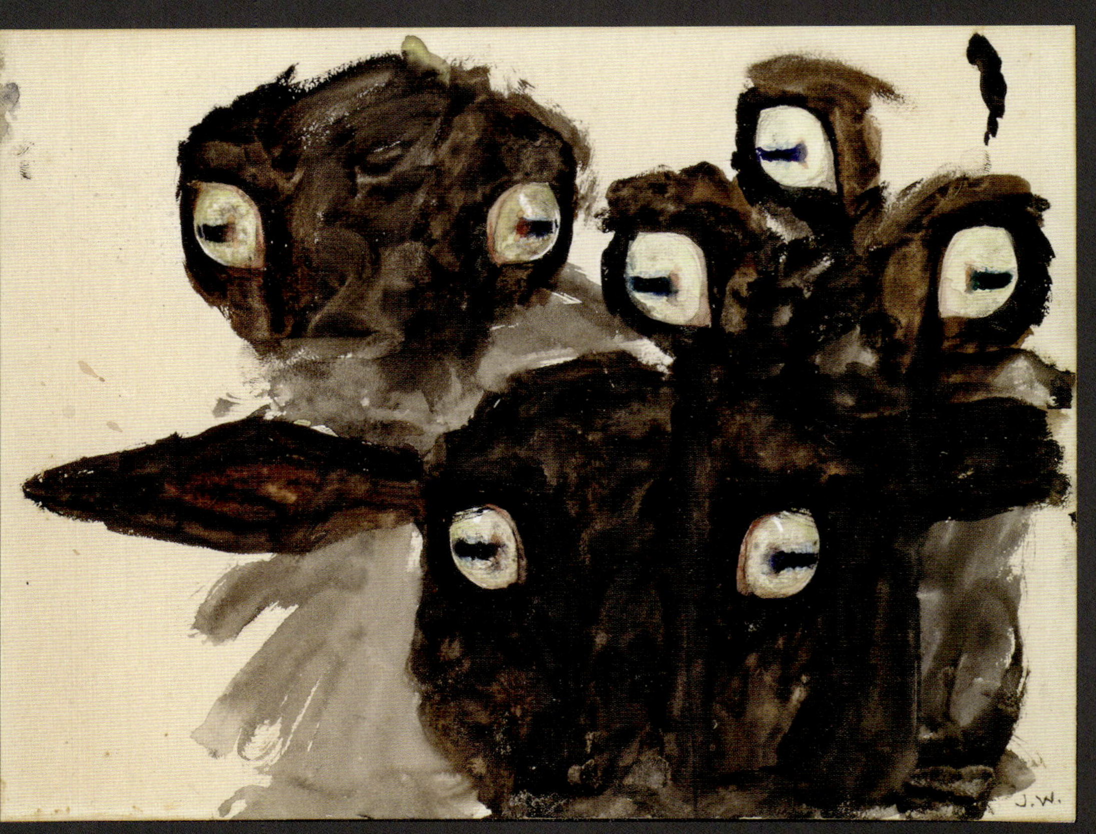

TE 44
yes, 1968

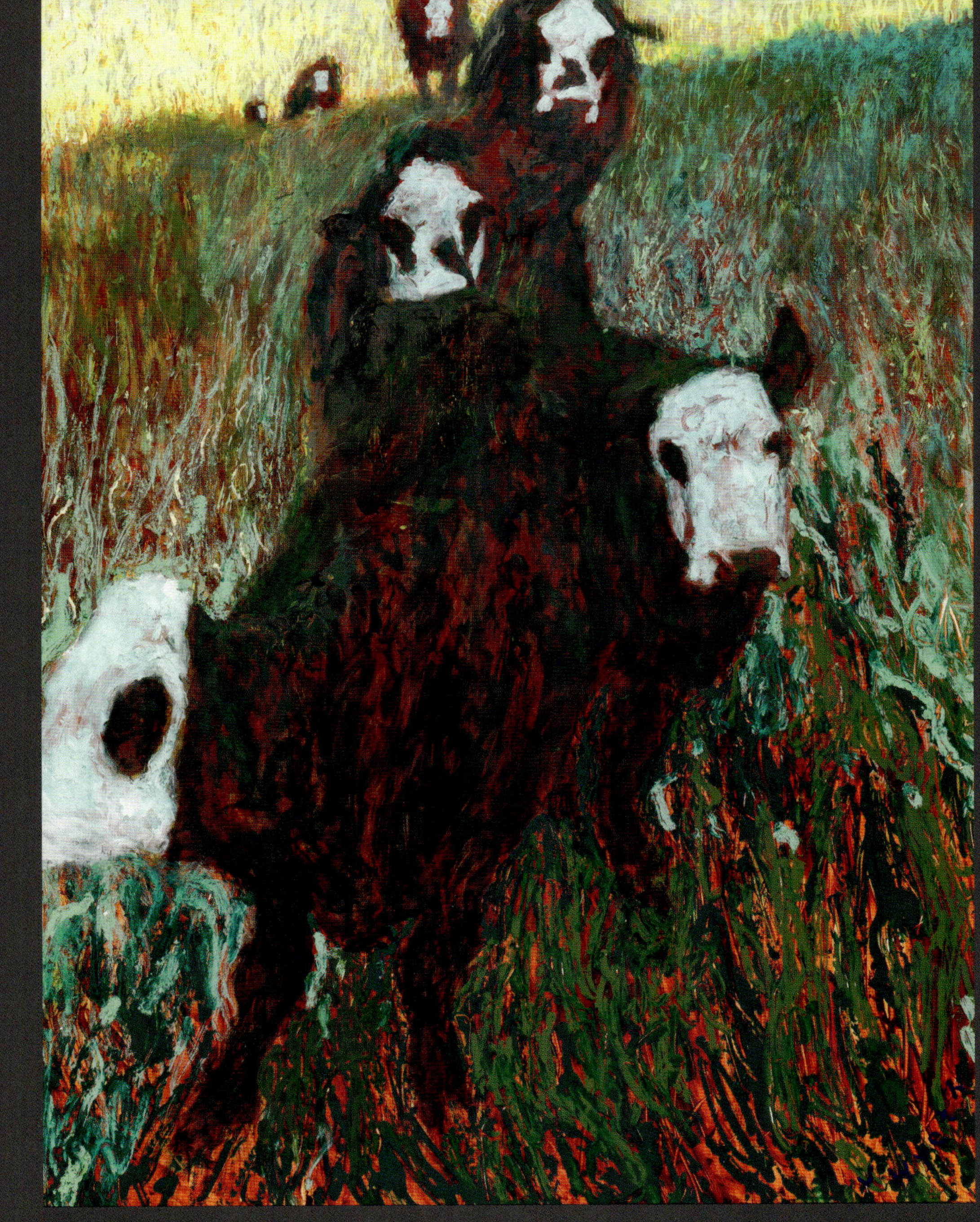

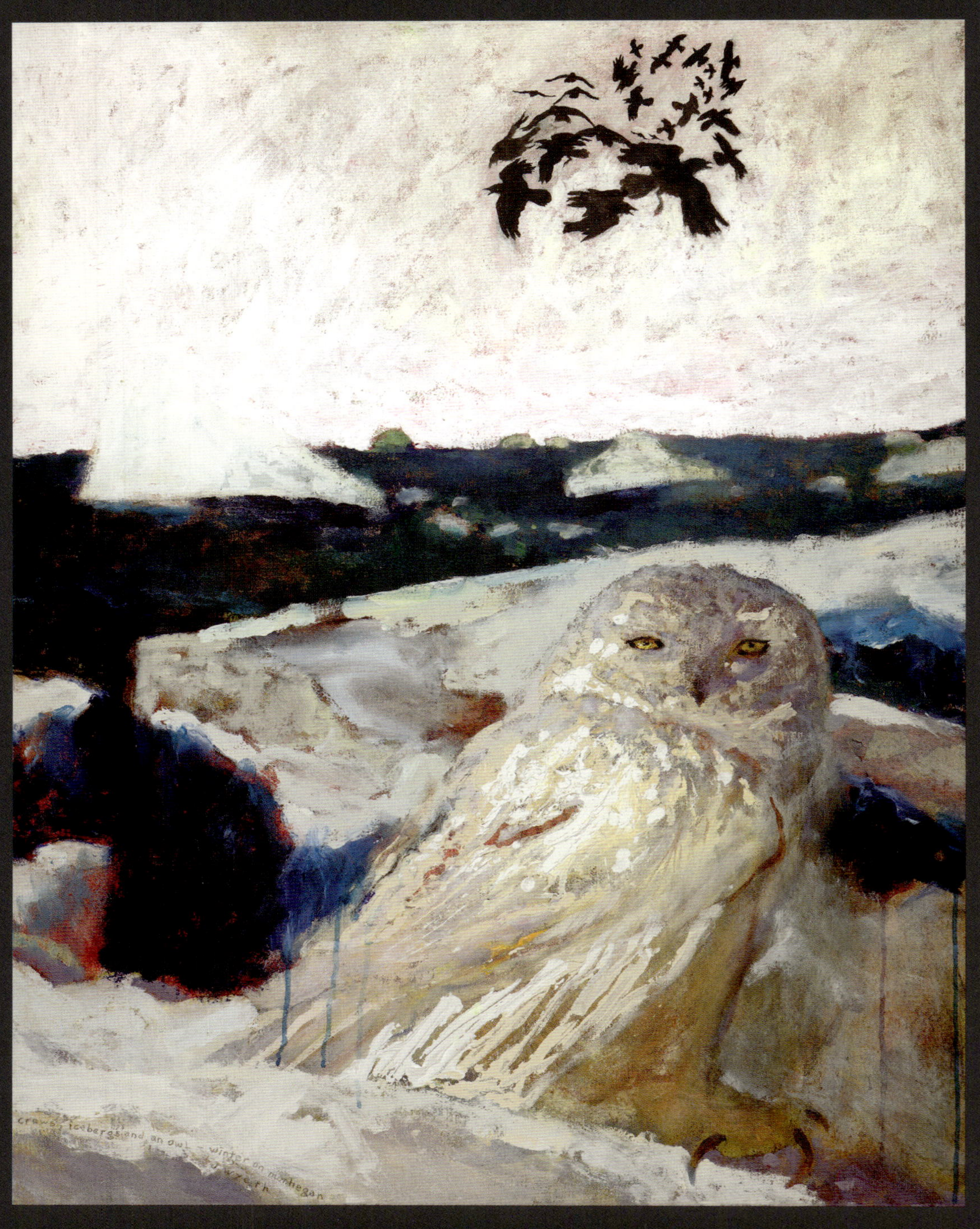

PLATE 46
Snow Owl, Fourteenth in a Suite of Untoward Occurrences on Monhegan Island, 2020

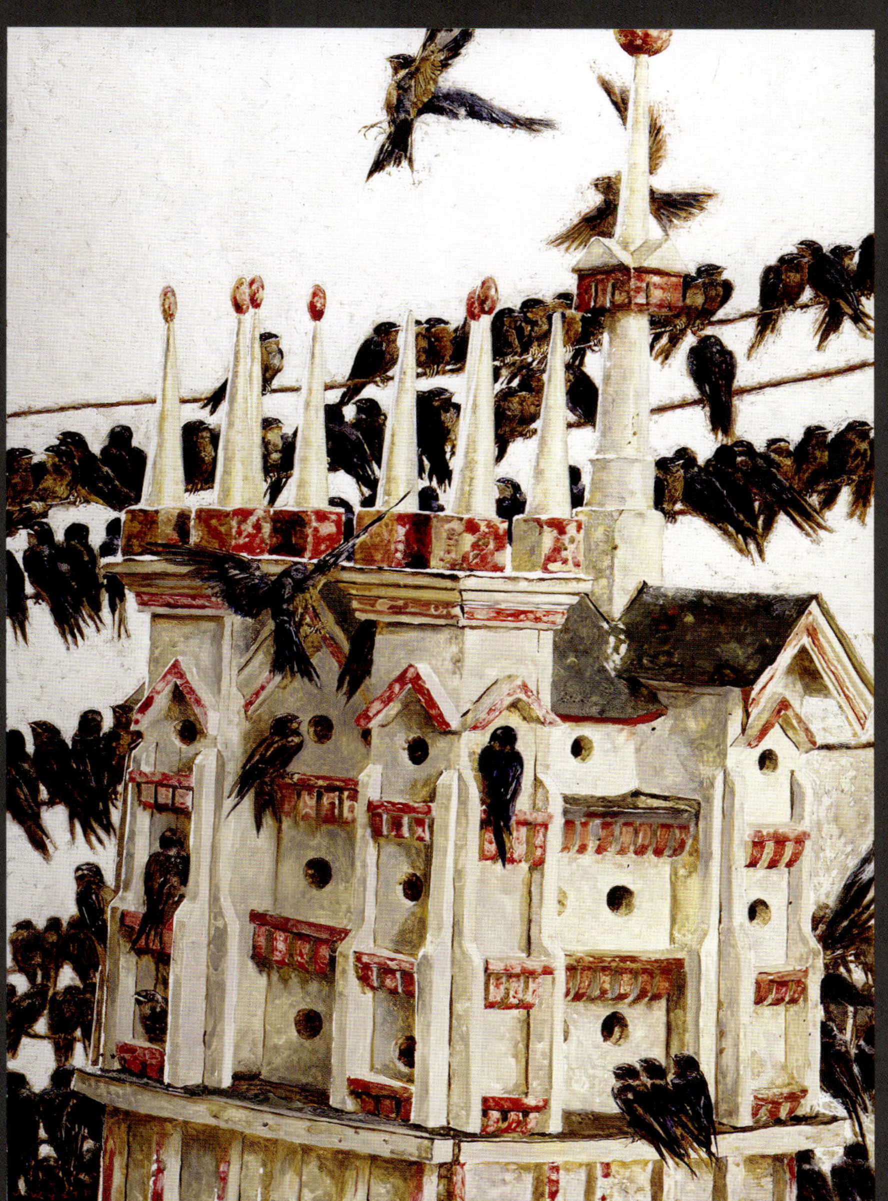

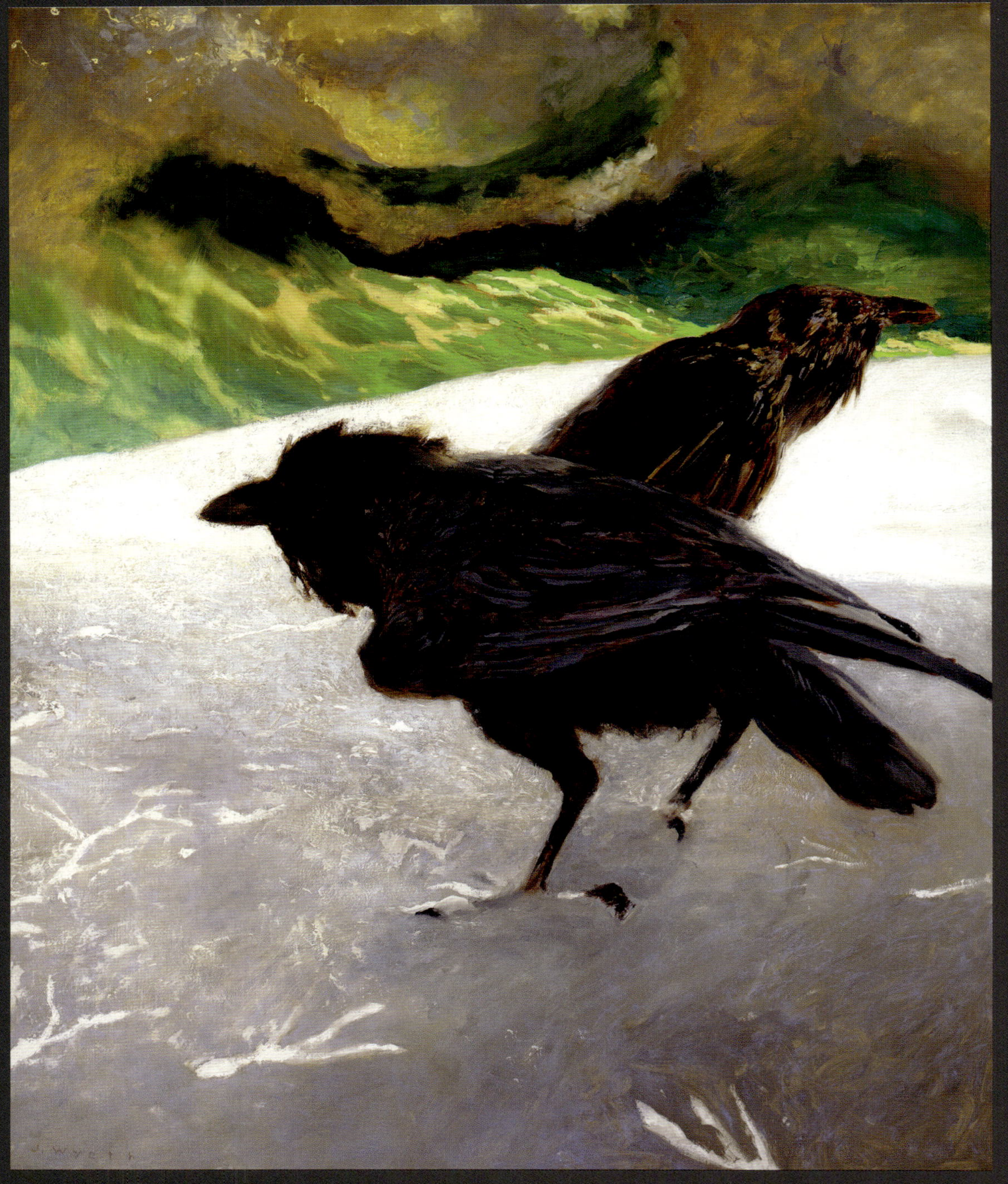

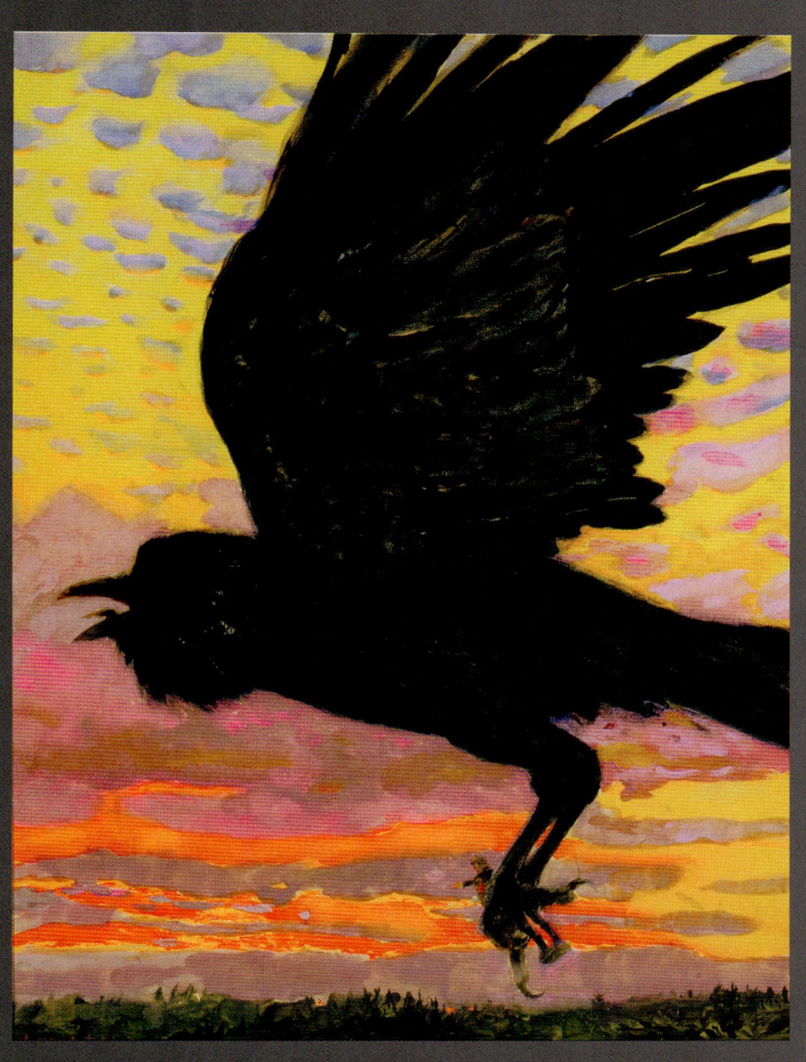

PLATE 49

Rudolf Hess and the Raven, 1997

PLATE 50
Wake, 2008

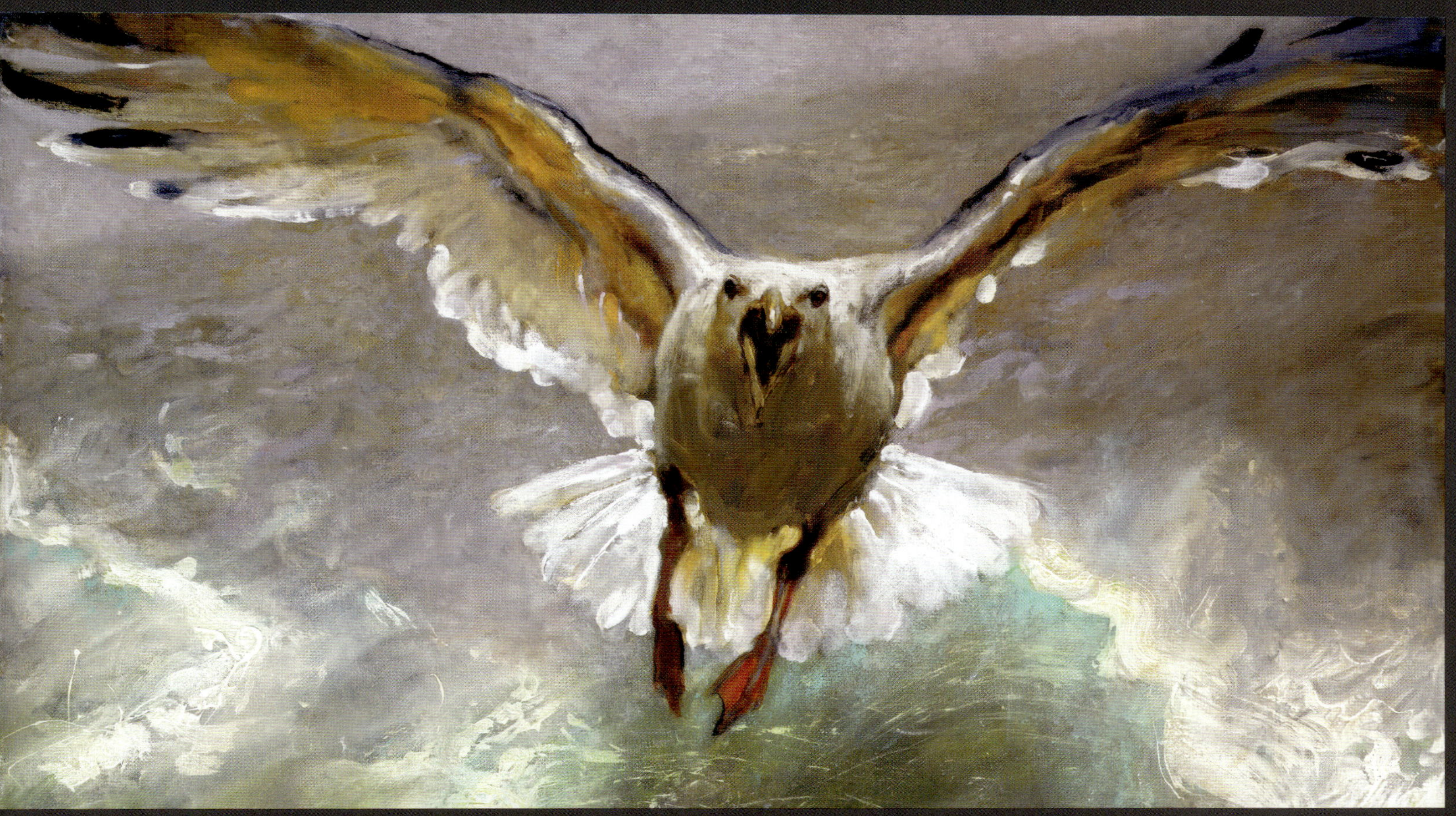

PLATE 51
Poisoned: Seventh in the Screen Door Sequence, 2022

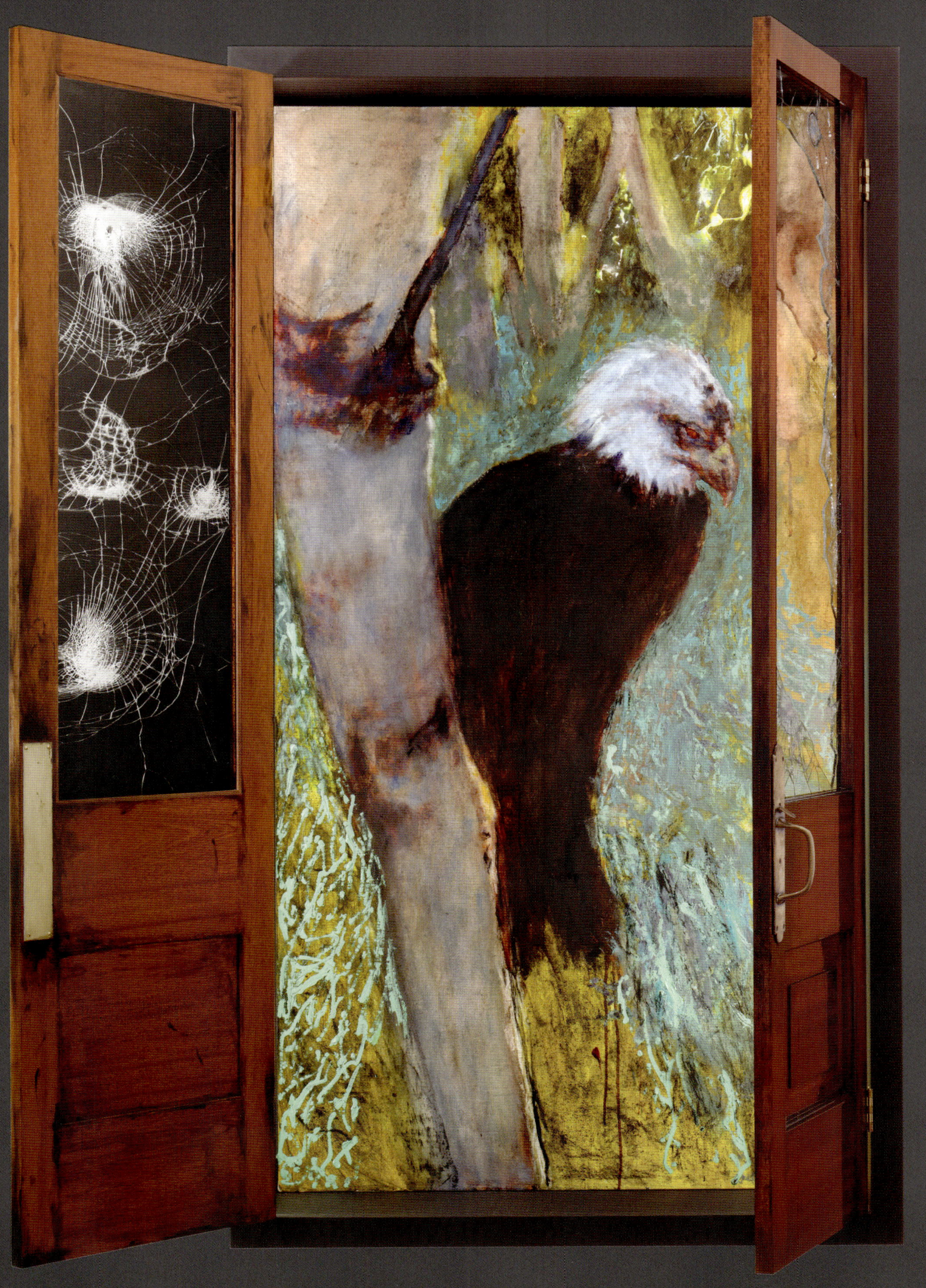

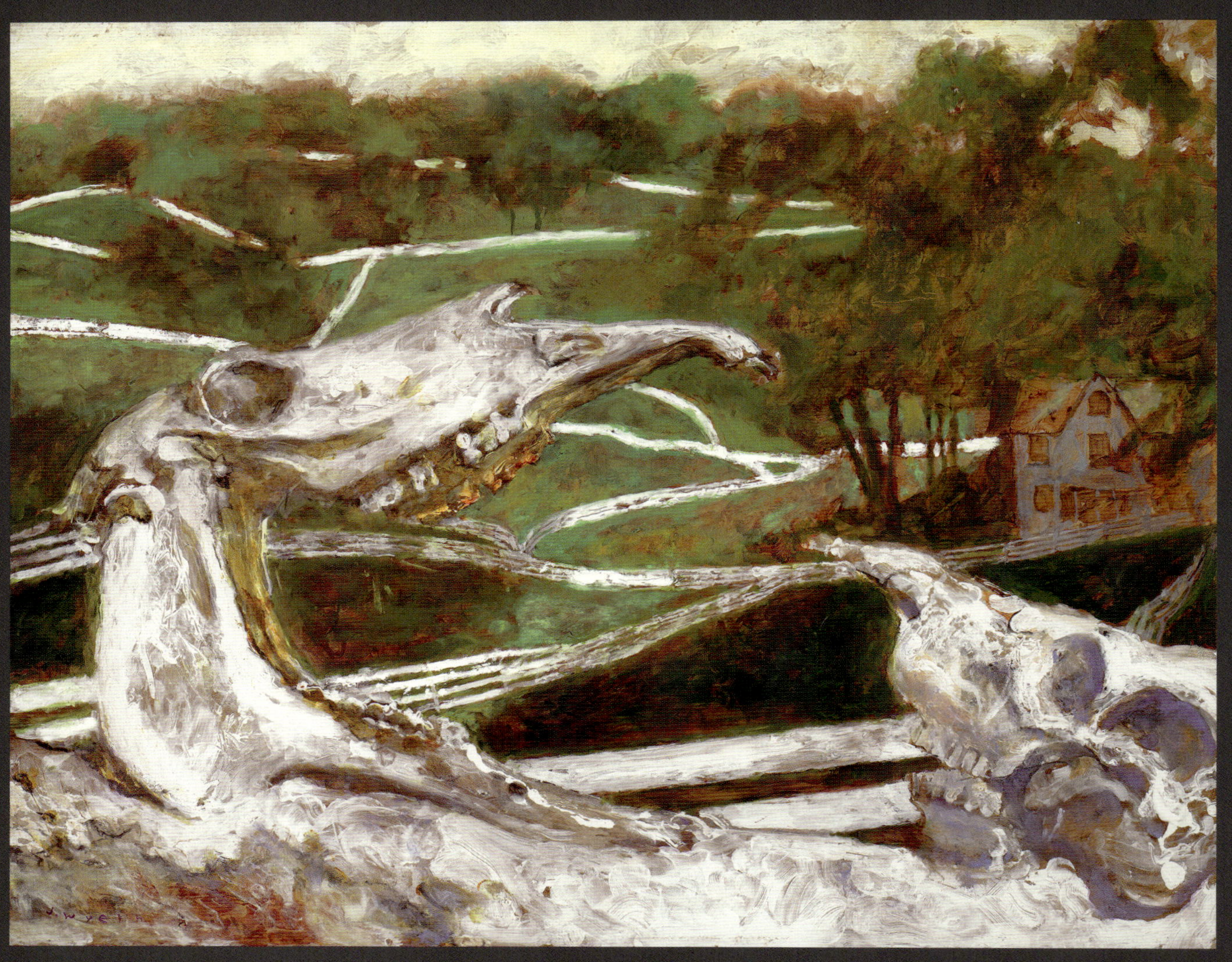

PLATE 52
Farm Talk, 2016

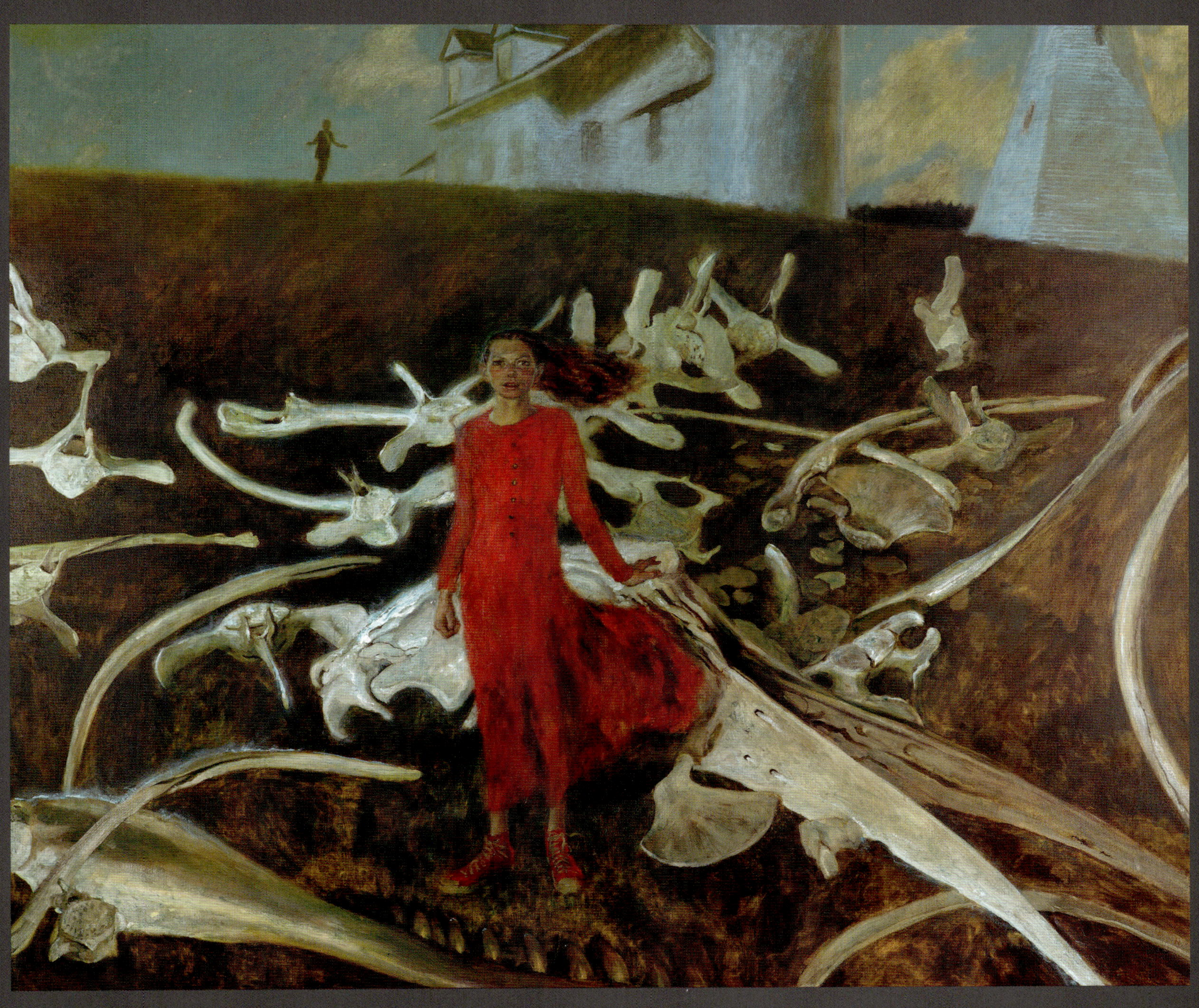

PLATE 53
Bones of a Whale, 2006

PLATE 54
Great White Shark, 2011

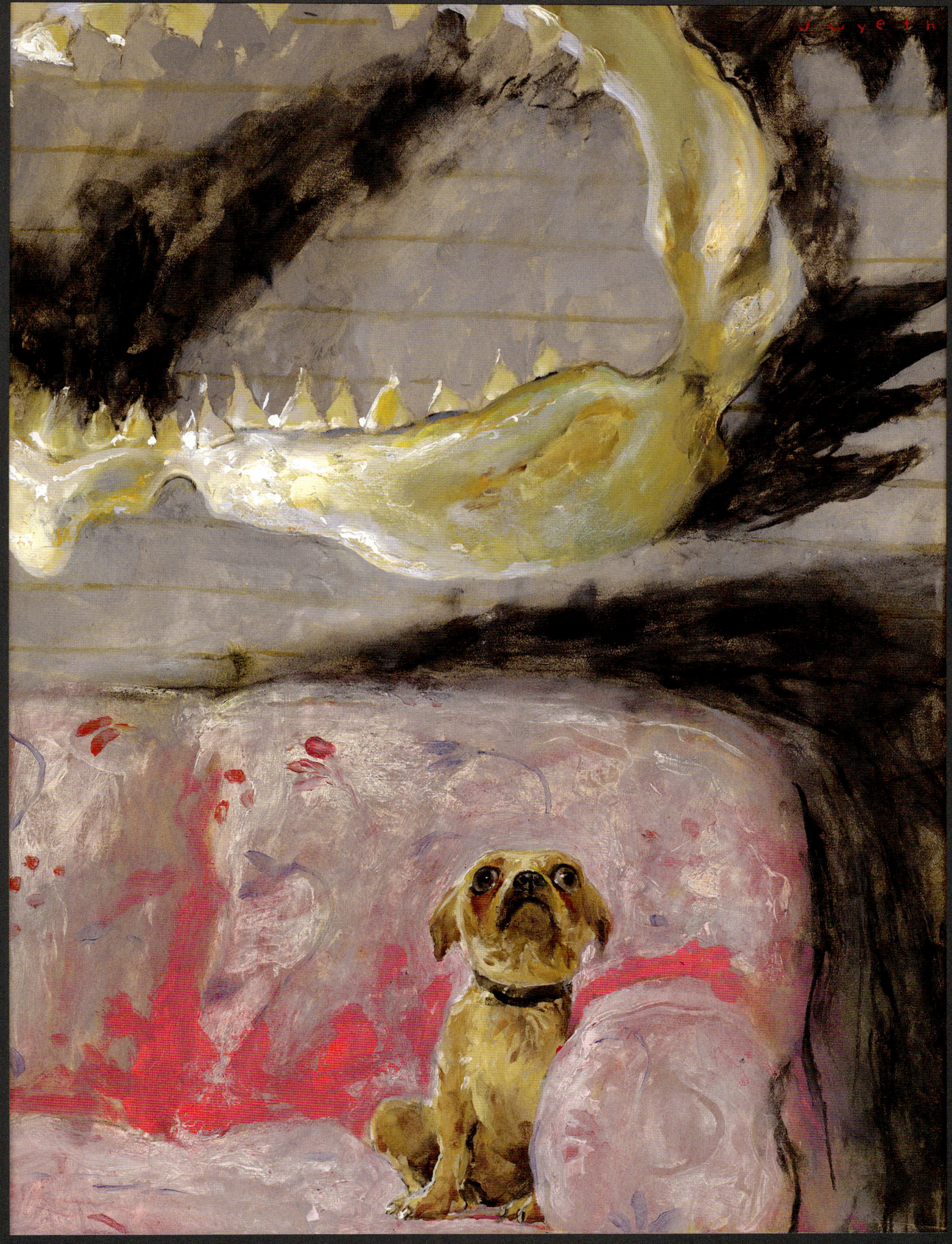

PLATE 55
Below the Barn, 1965

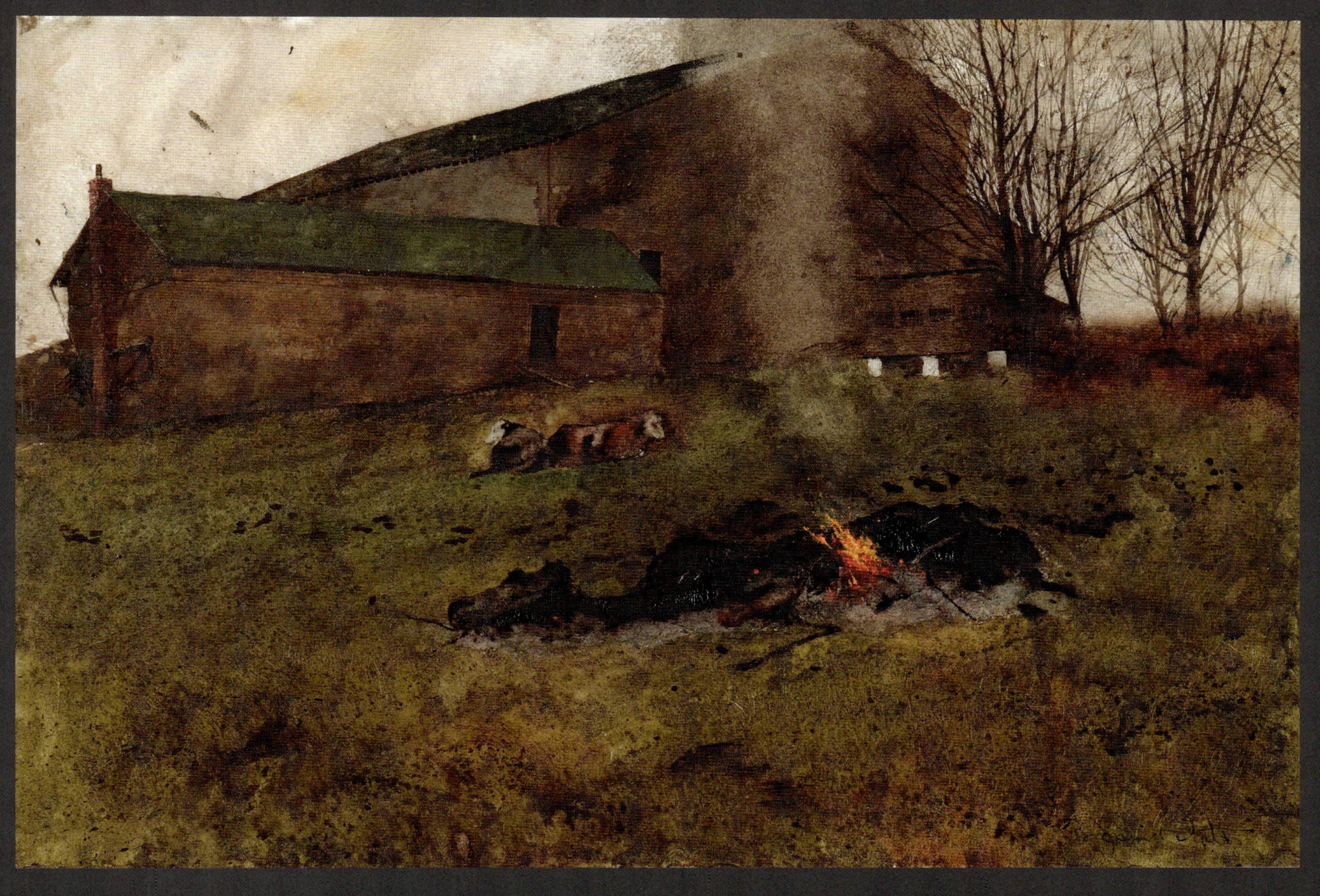

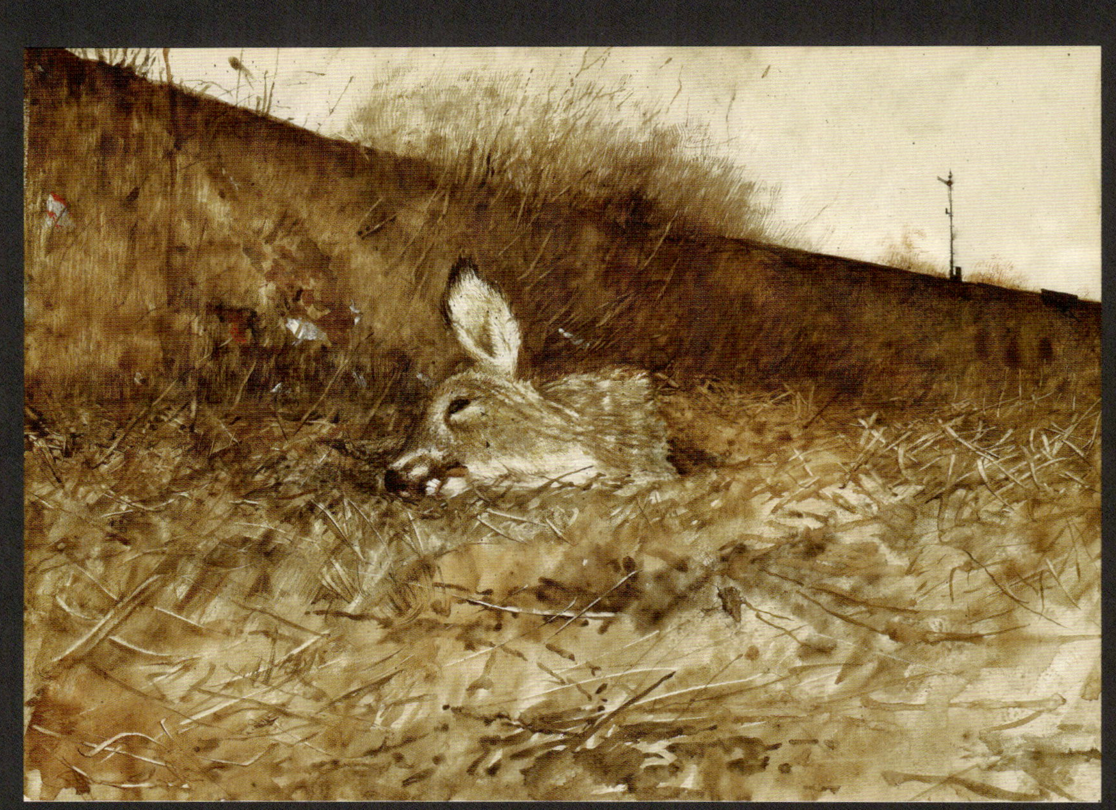

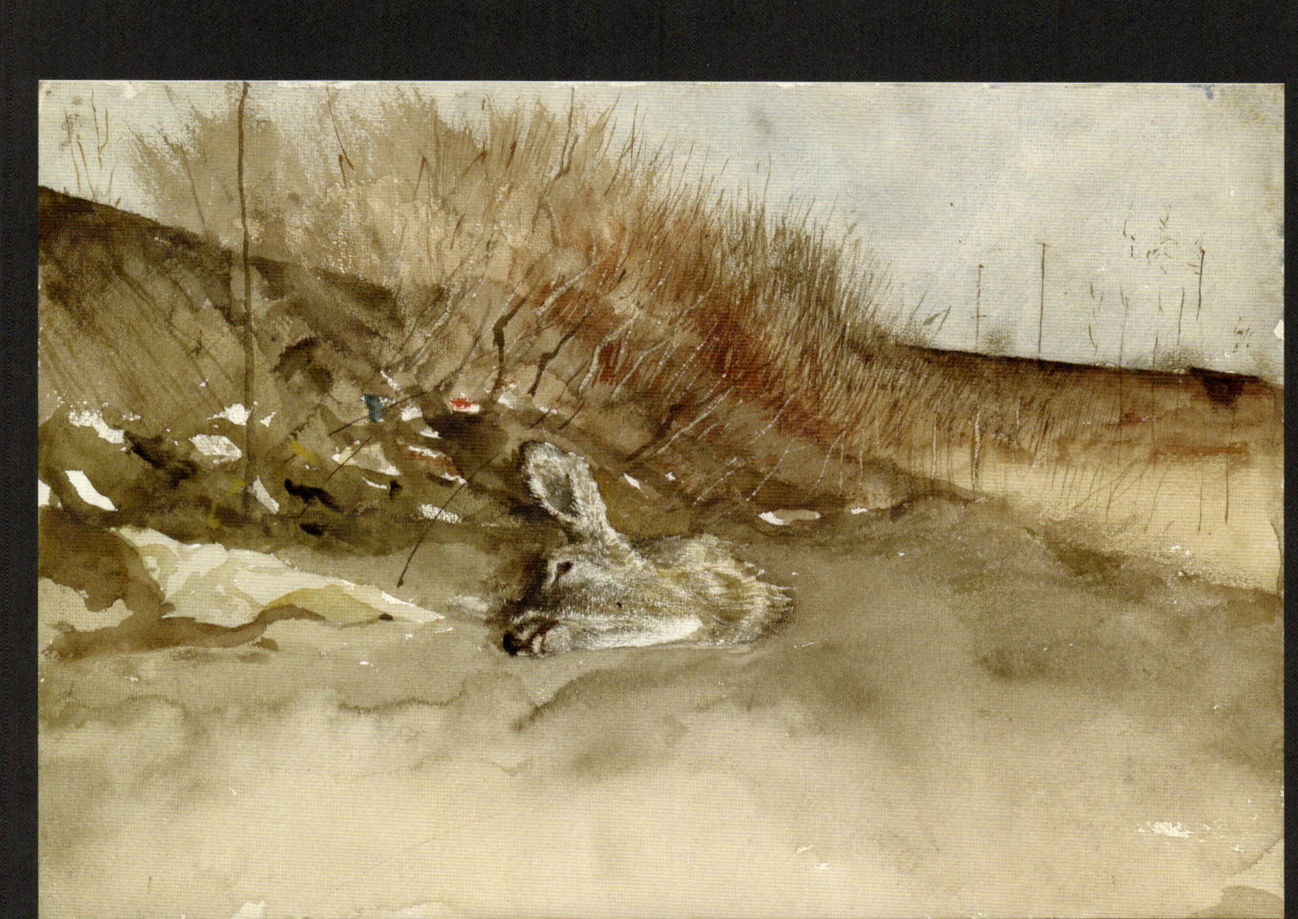

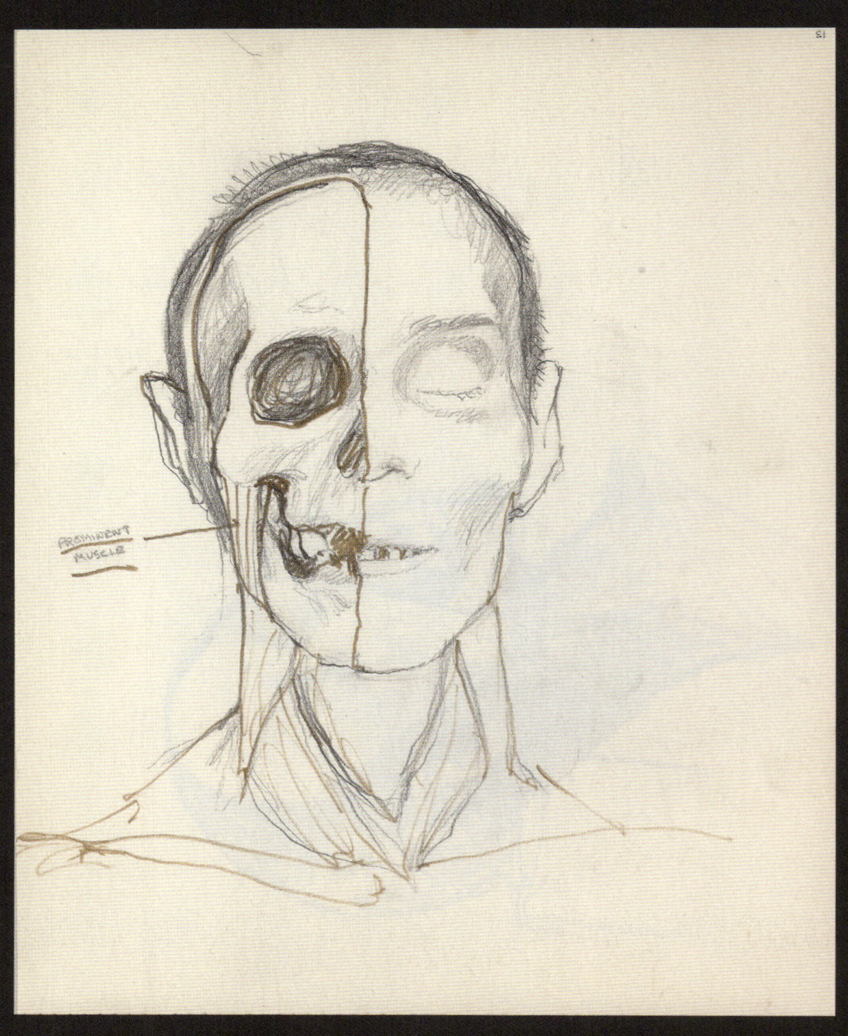
PROMINENT
MUSCLE

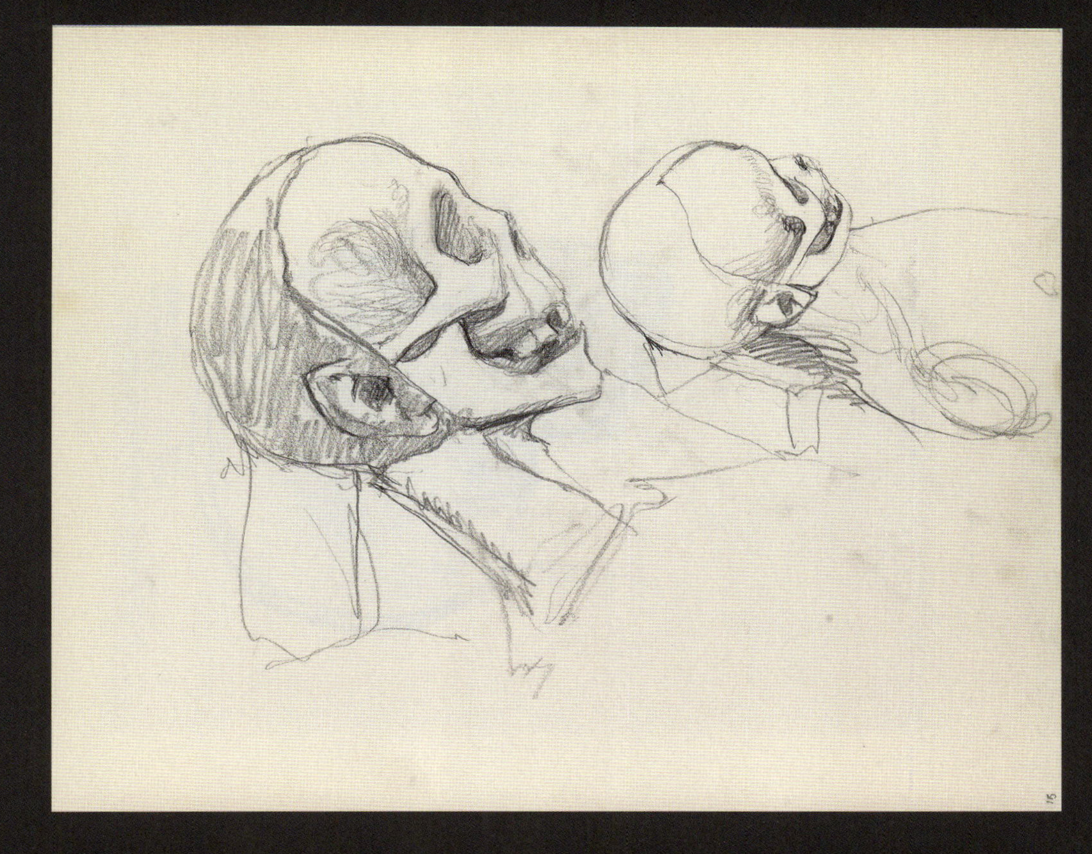

PLATE 60
Butcher Shop, 2015

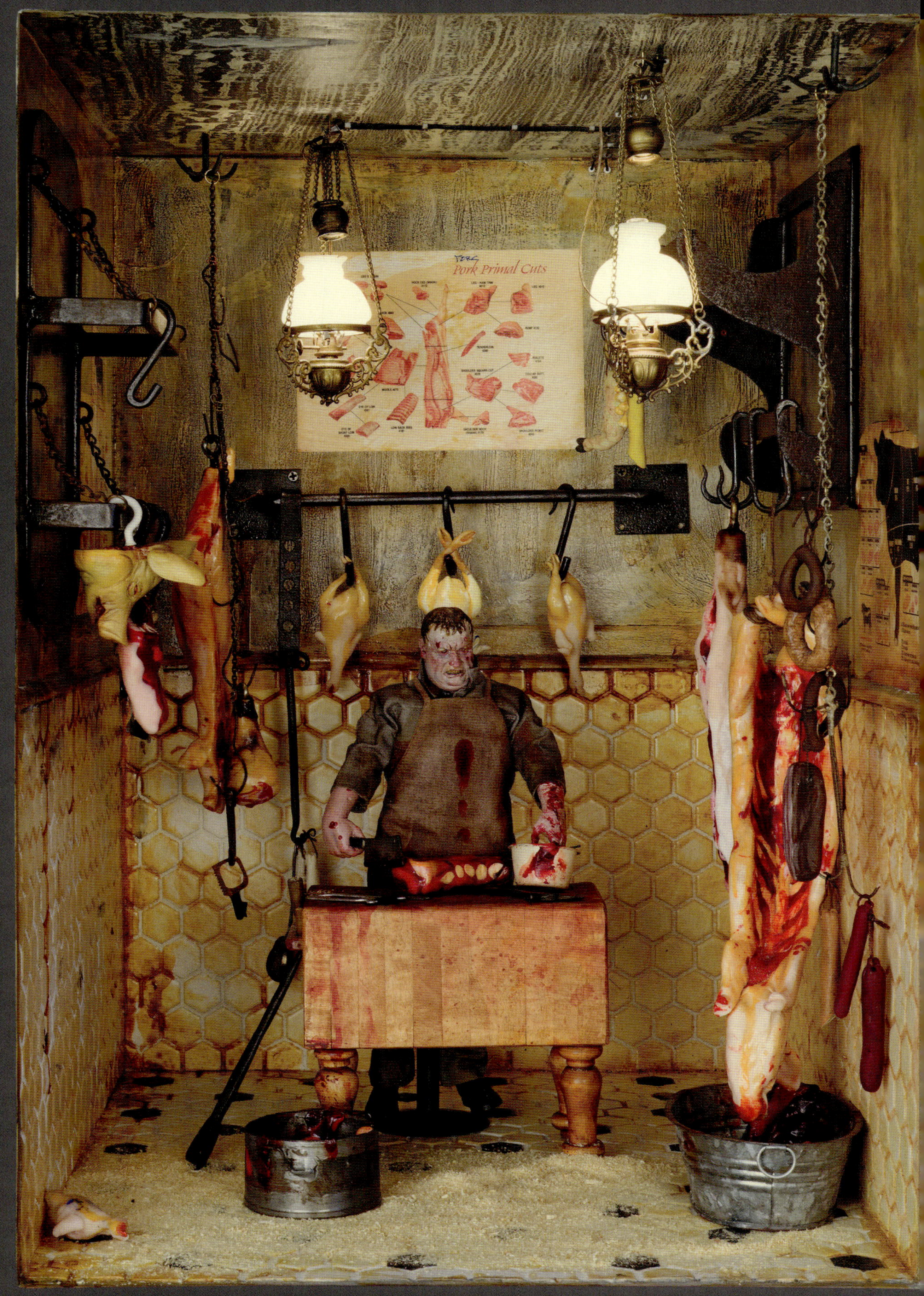
Pork Primal Cuts

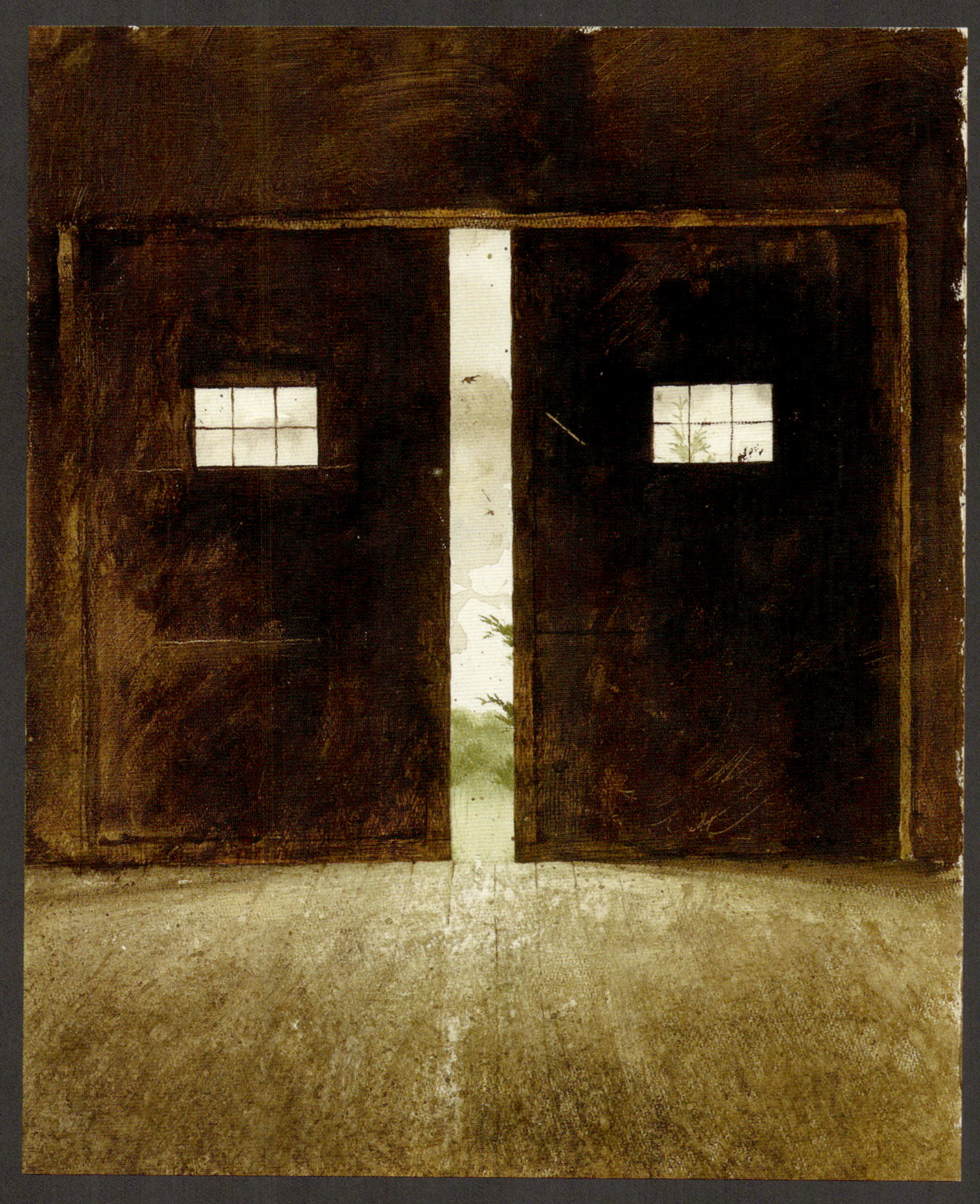

PLATE 61
Cove Farmhay, ca. 1965

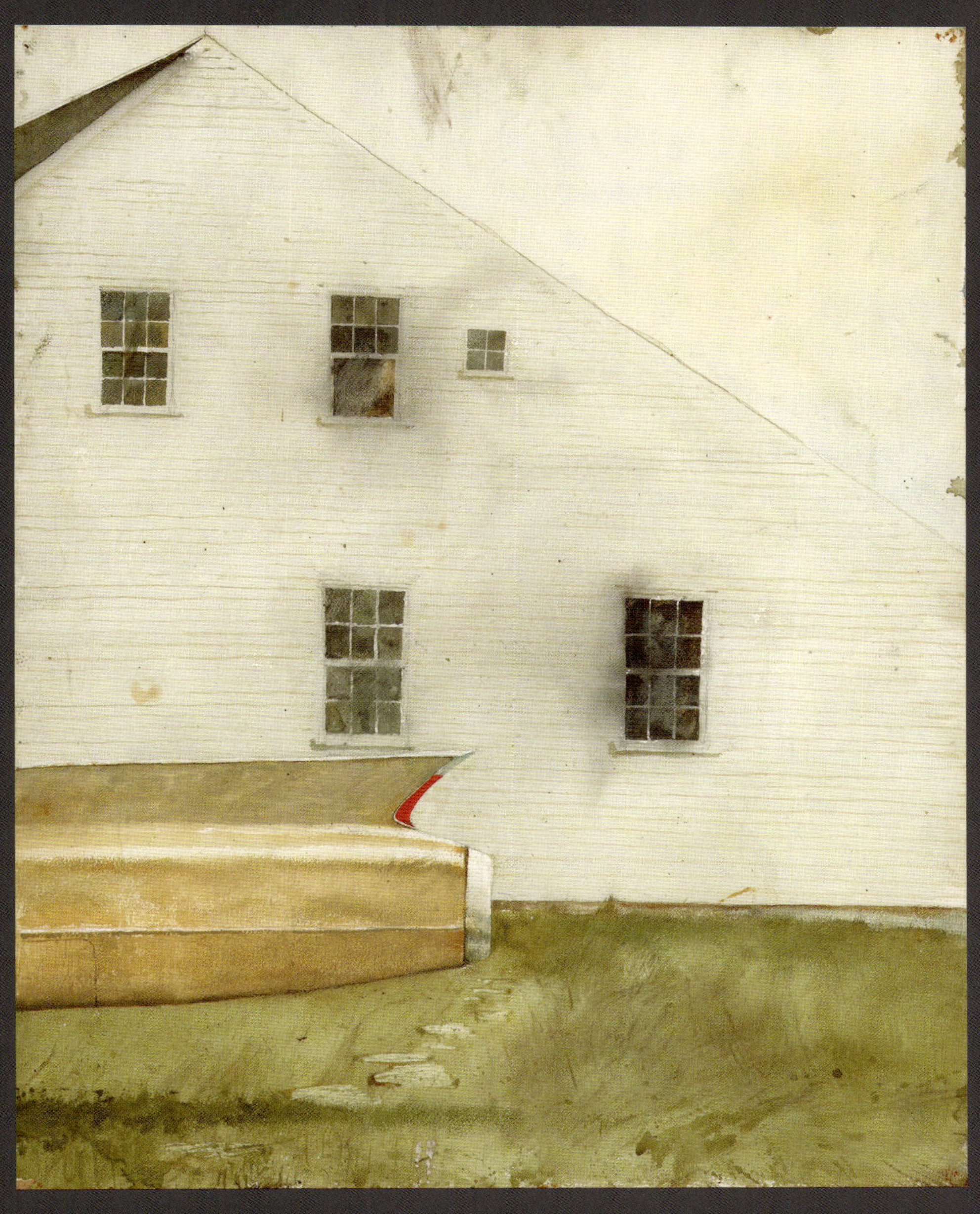

PLATE 62
Pom Pom's Cadillac, Broad Cove Farm, ca. 1965

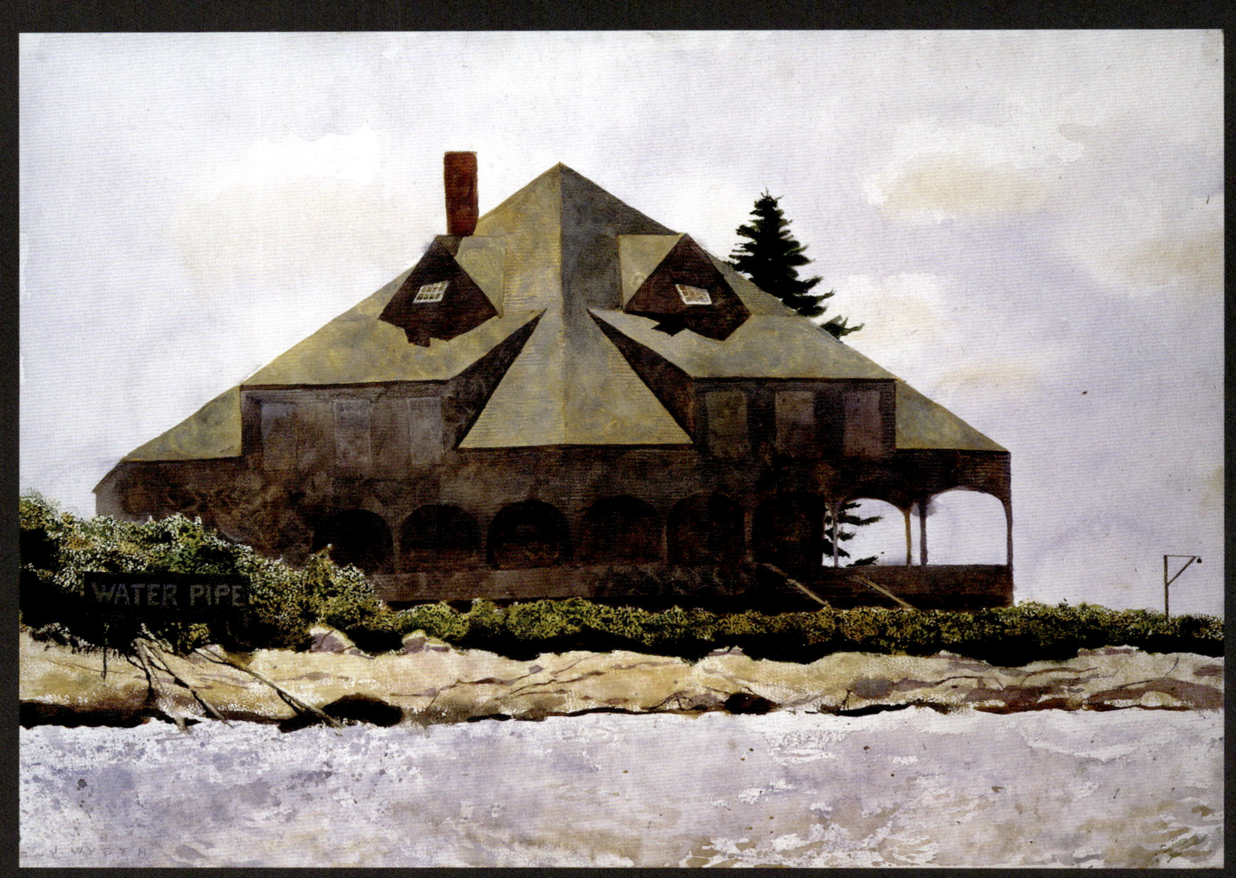

PLATE 63
Squirrel Island, 1986

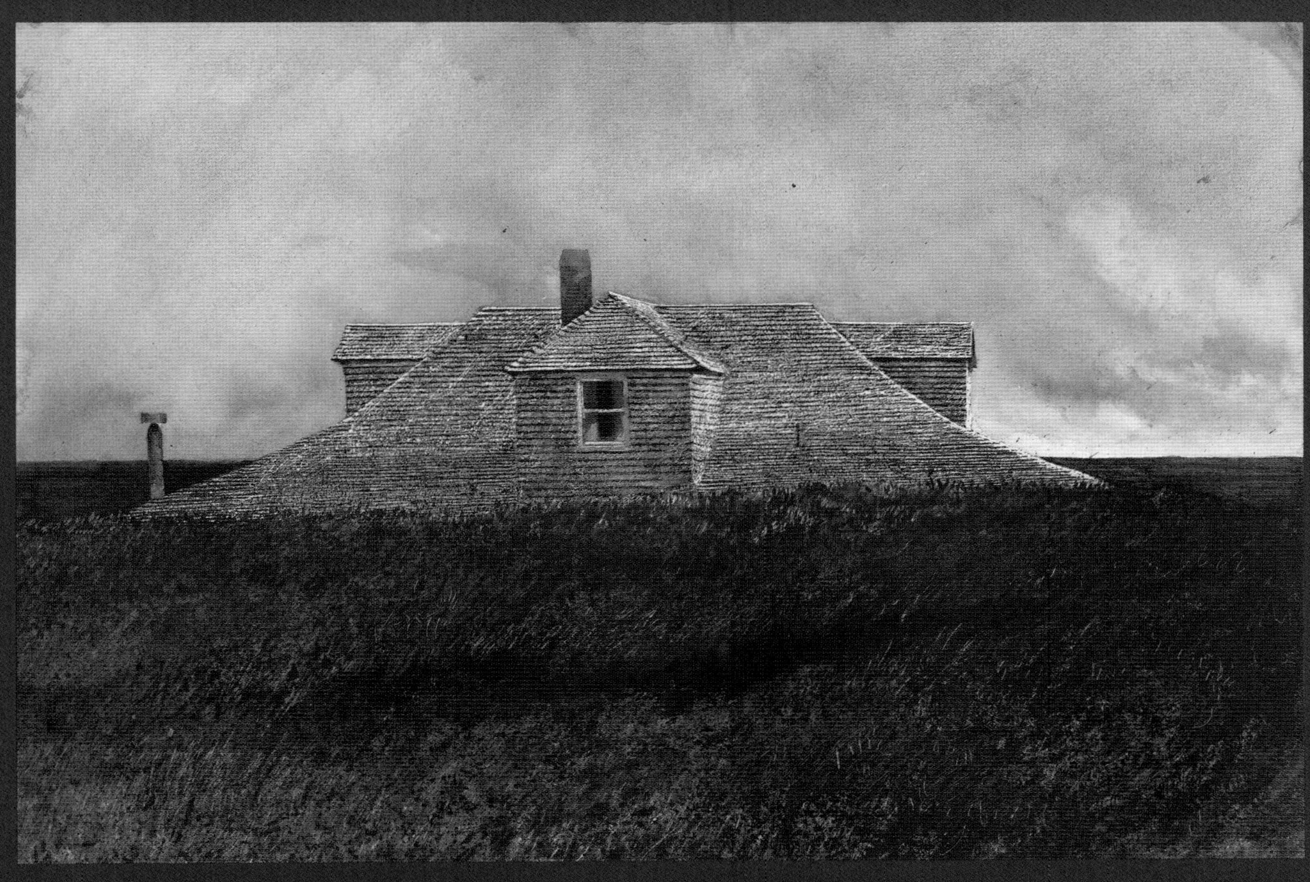

PLATE 64
Hekking House, 1968

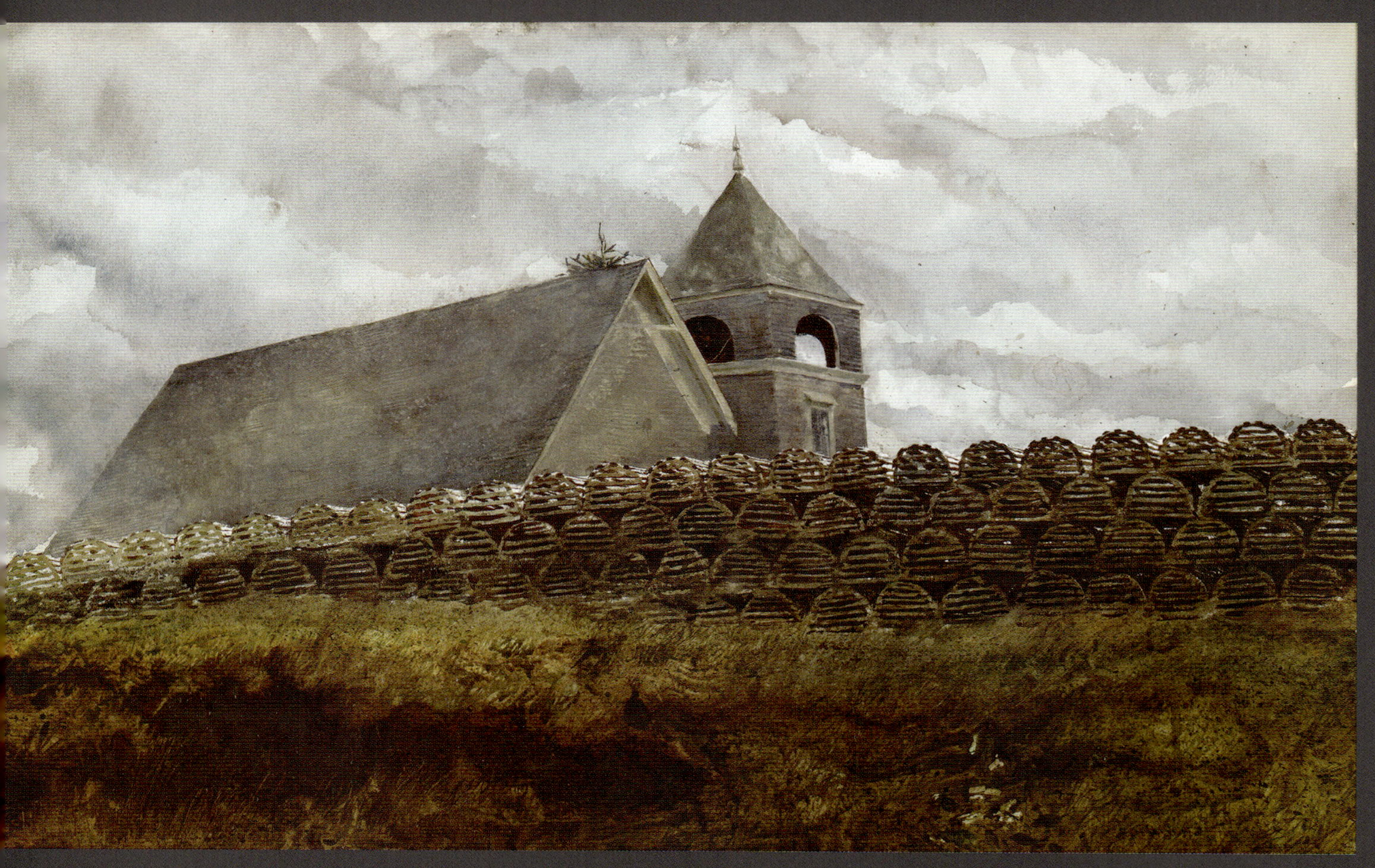

PLATE 65
Island Church, 1968

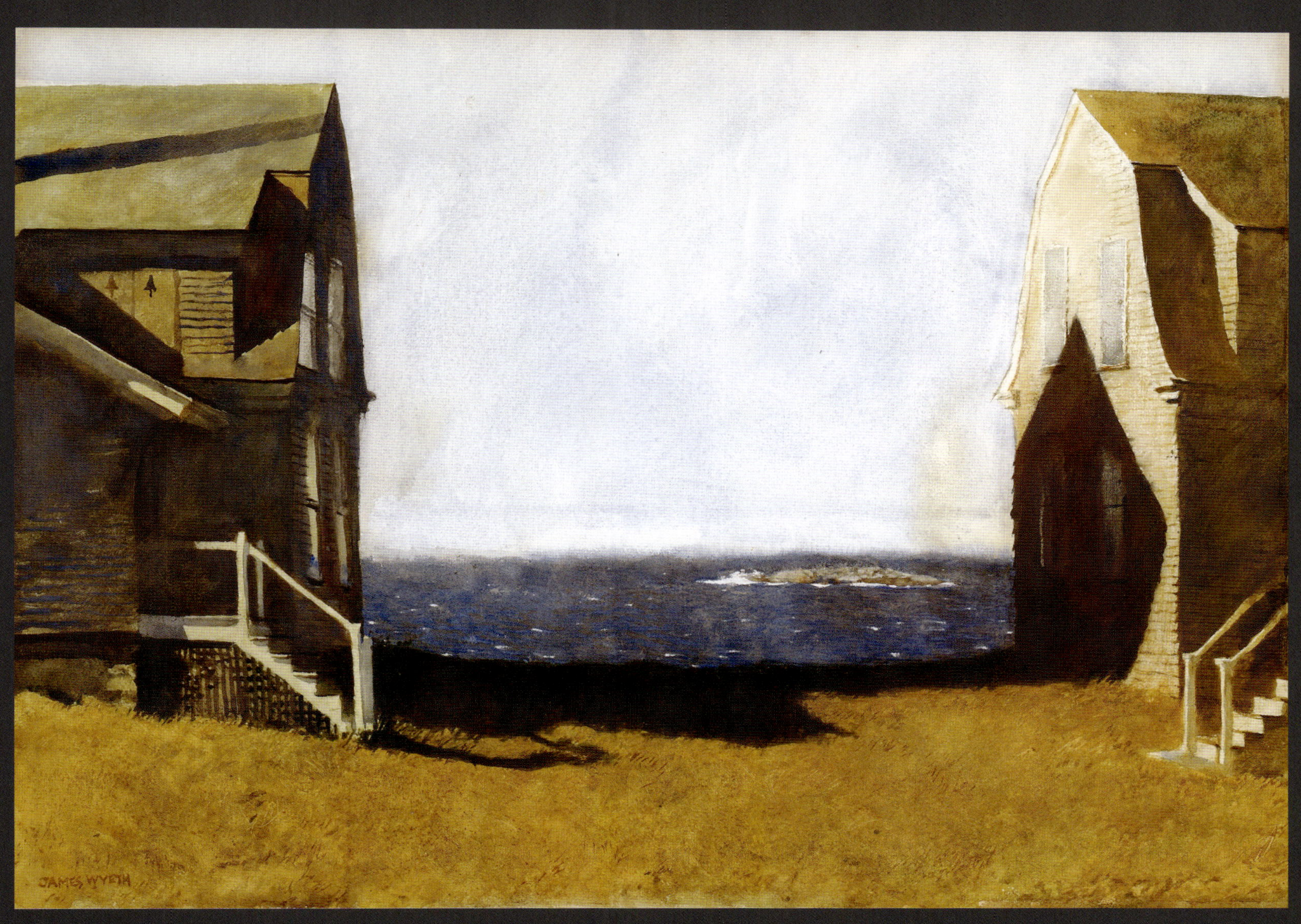

PLATE 66
Summer House, Winter House, 1975

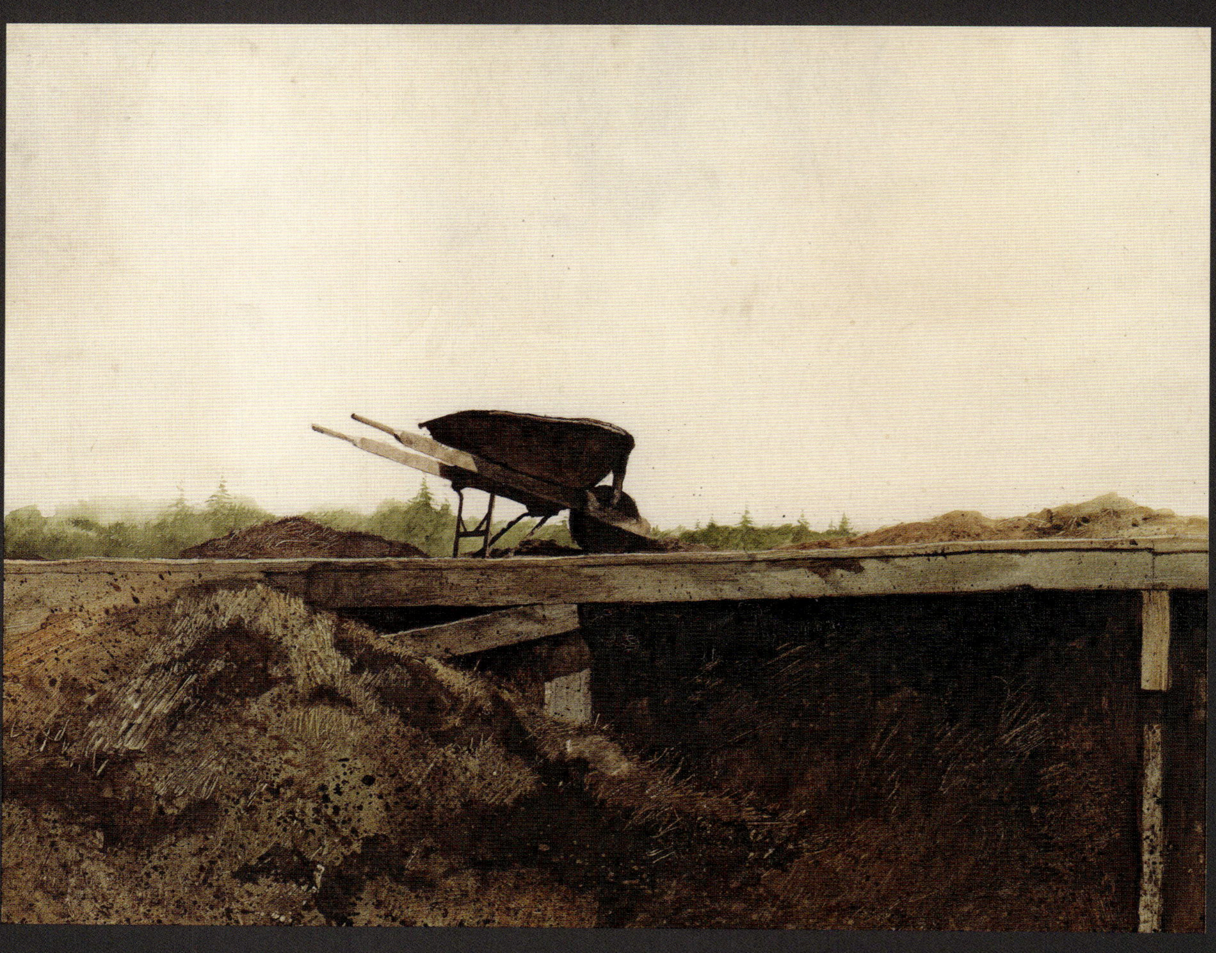

PLATE 67
Wheelbarrow, 1963

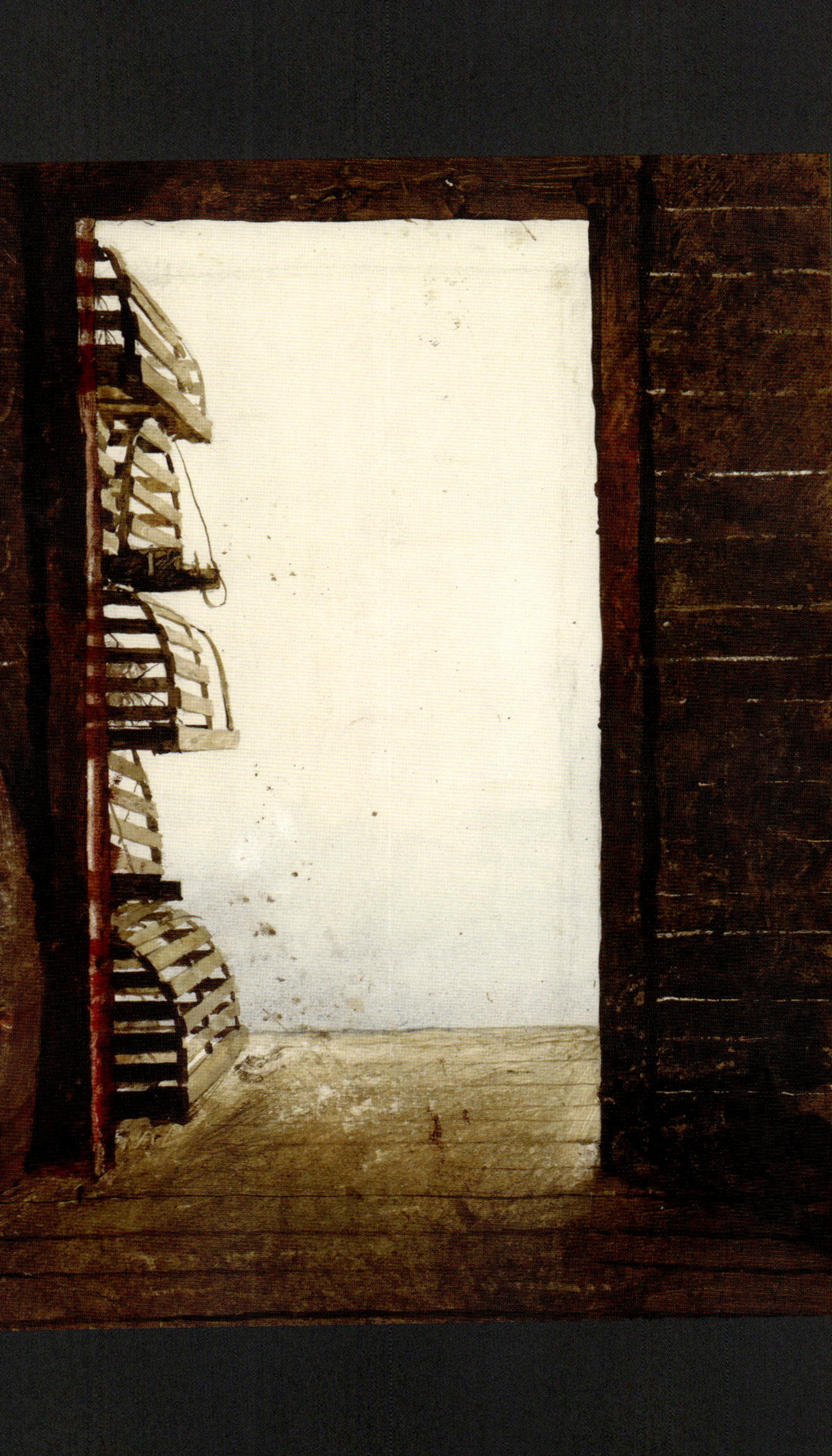

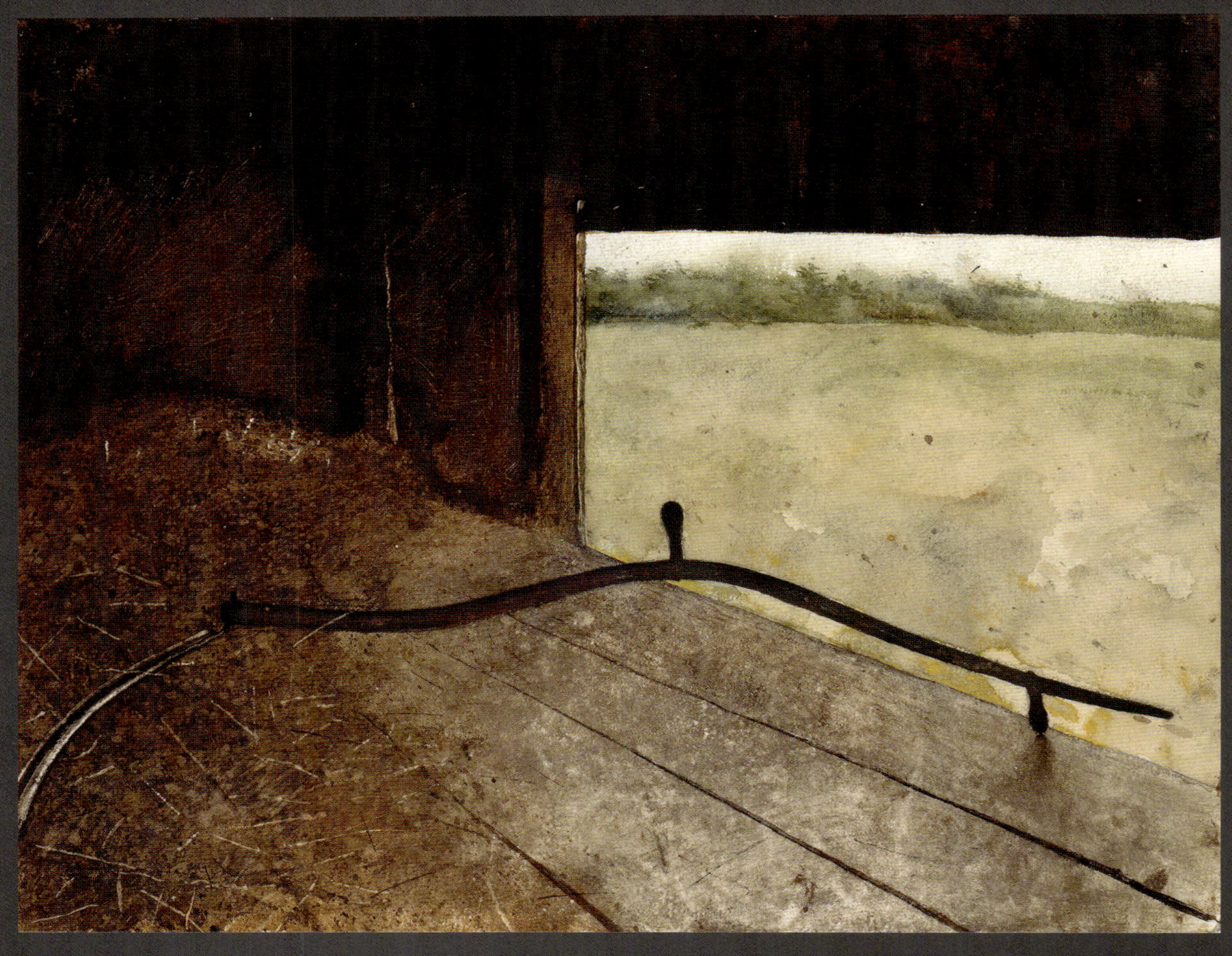

PLATE 69
The Scythe, 1966

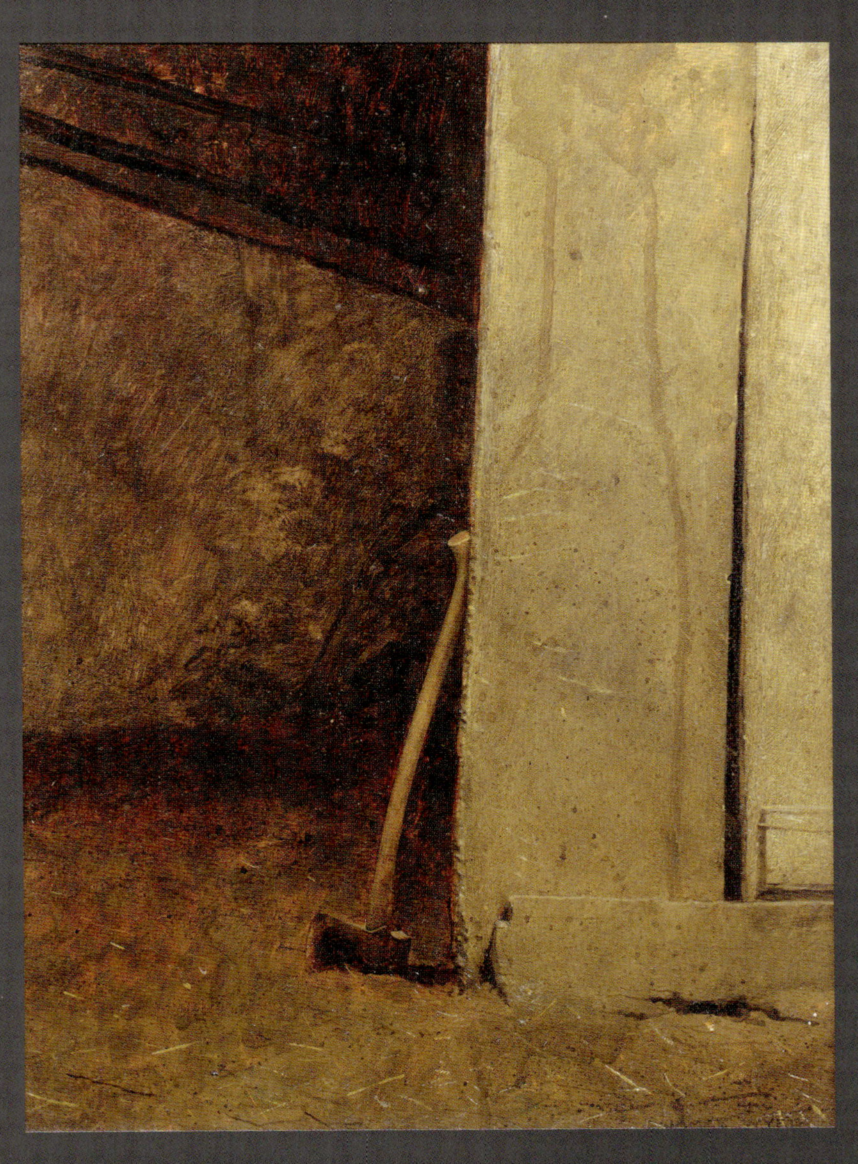

PLATE 70
The Axe, 1964

PLATE 71
Buzz Saw, 1969

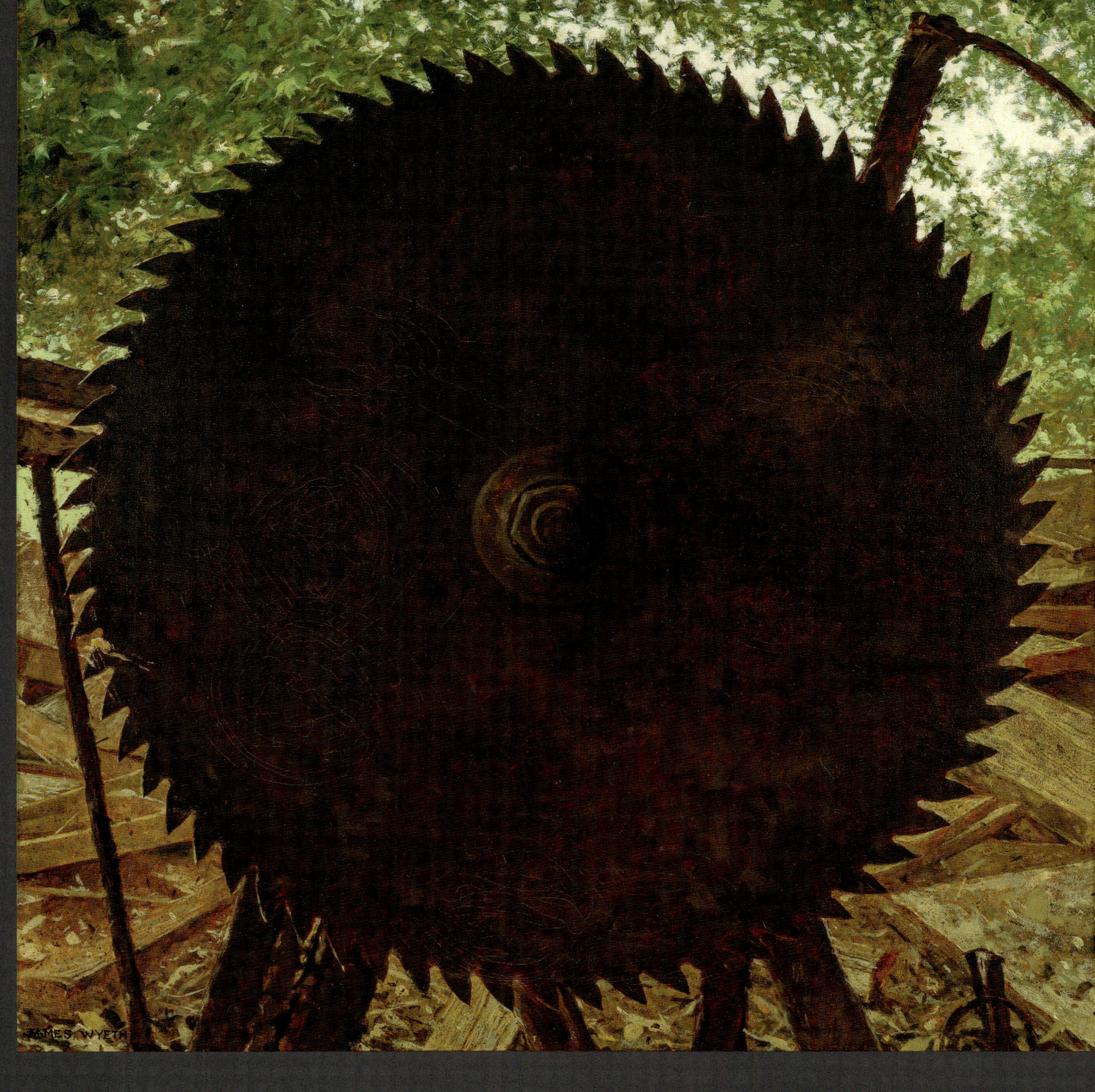
JAMES WYETH

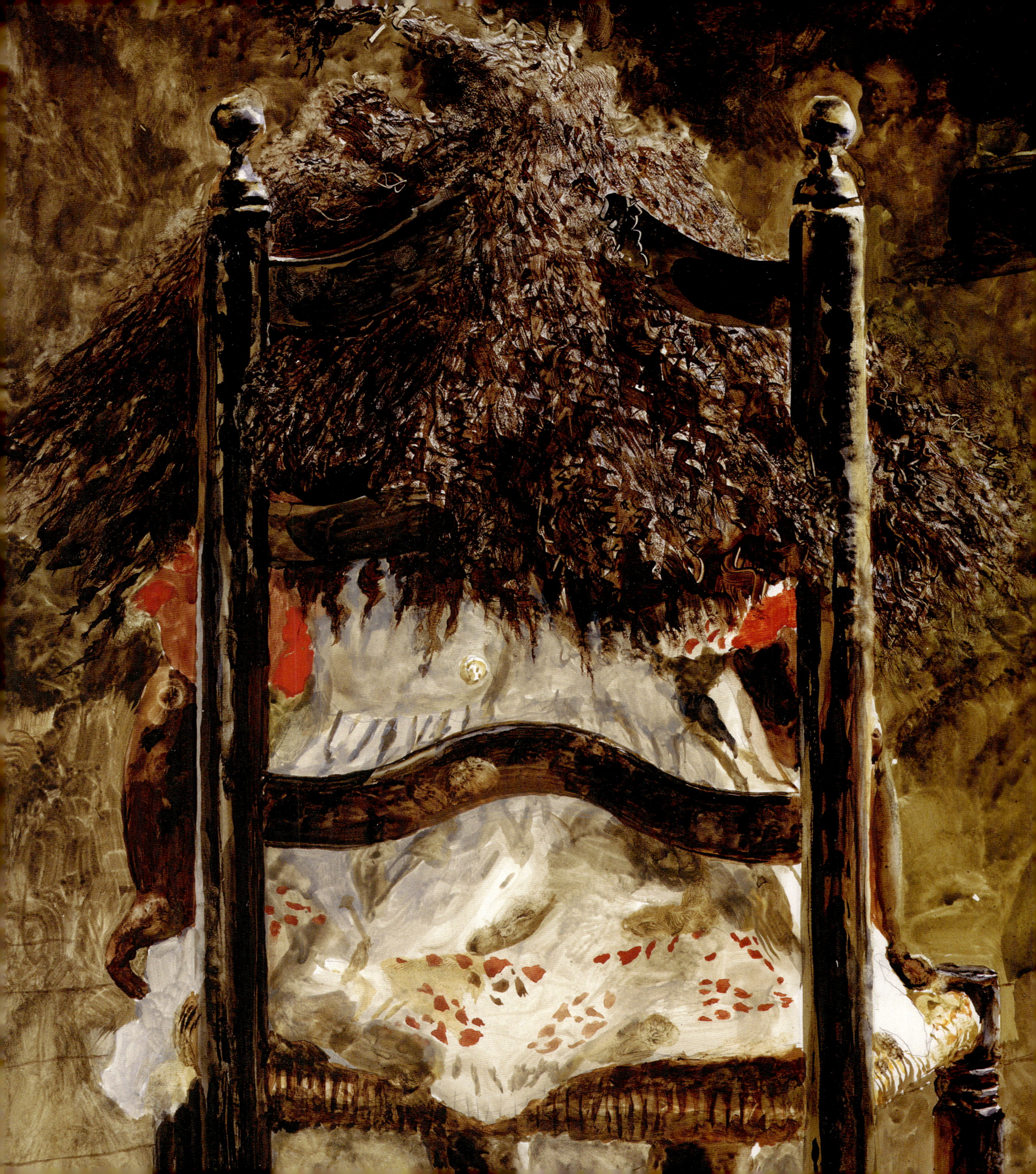

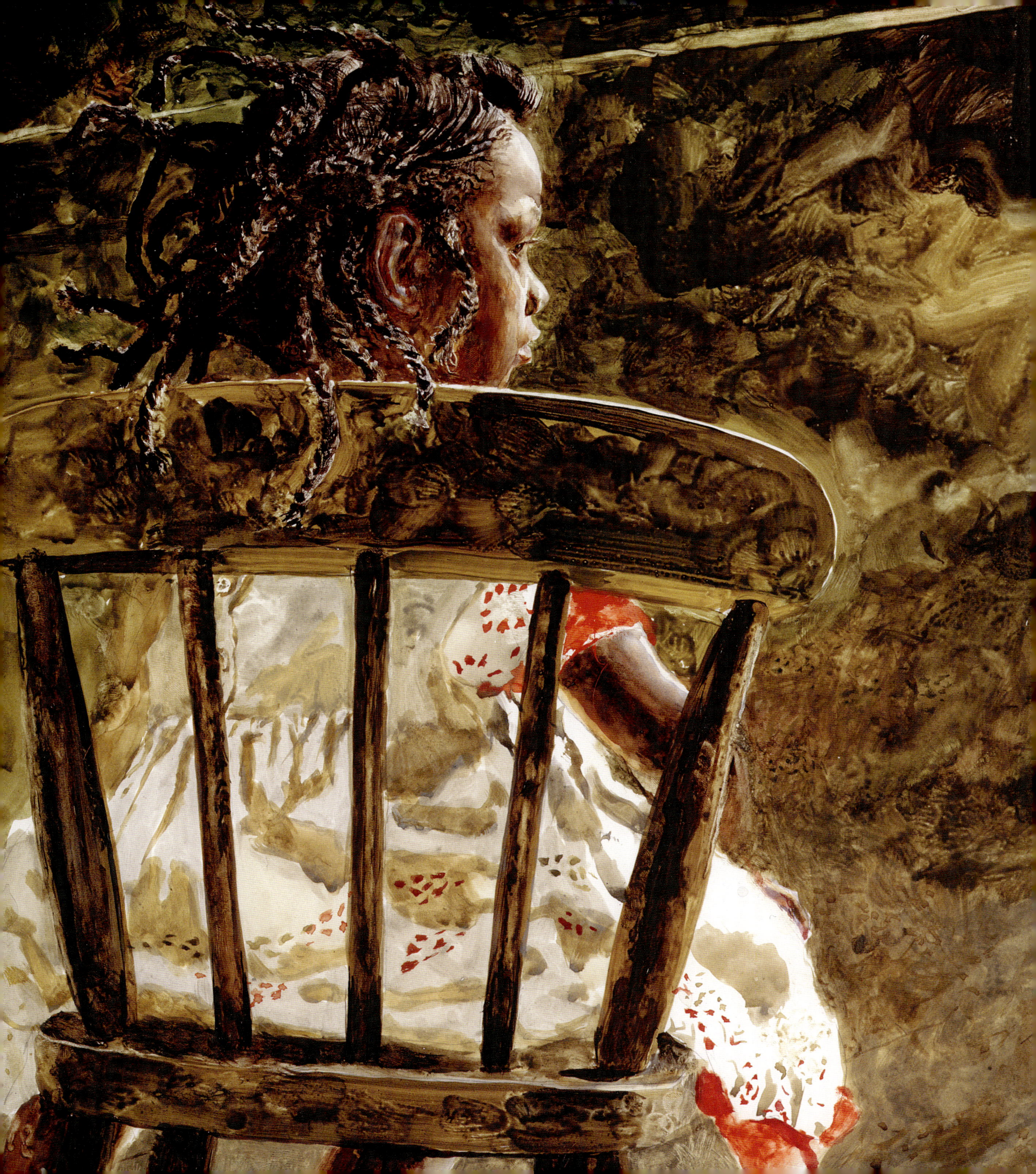

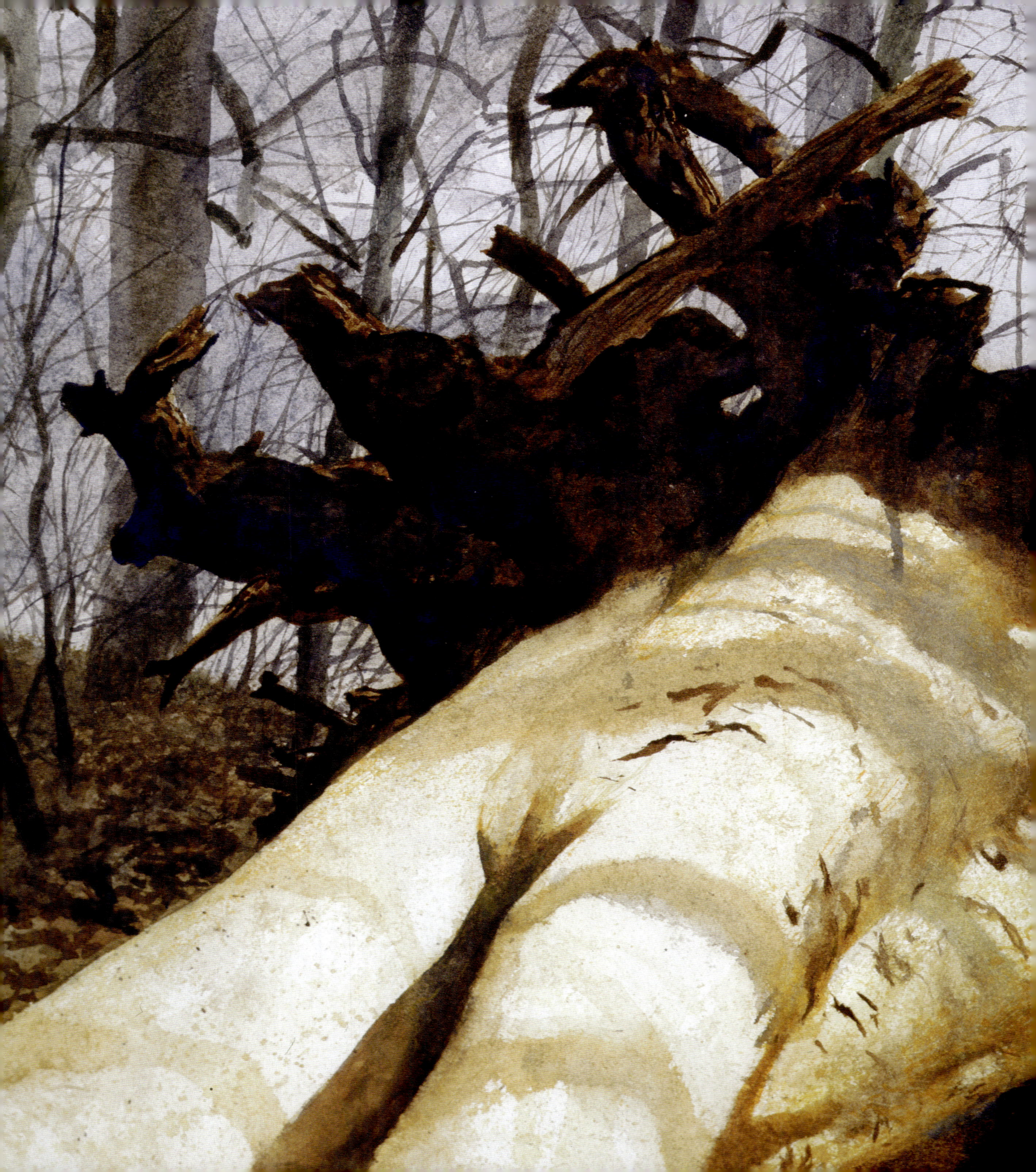

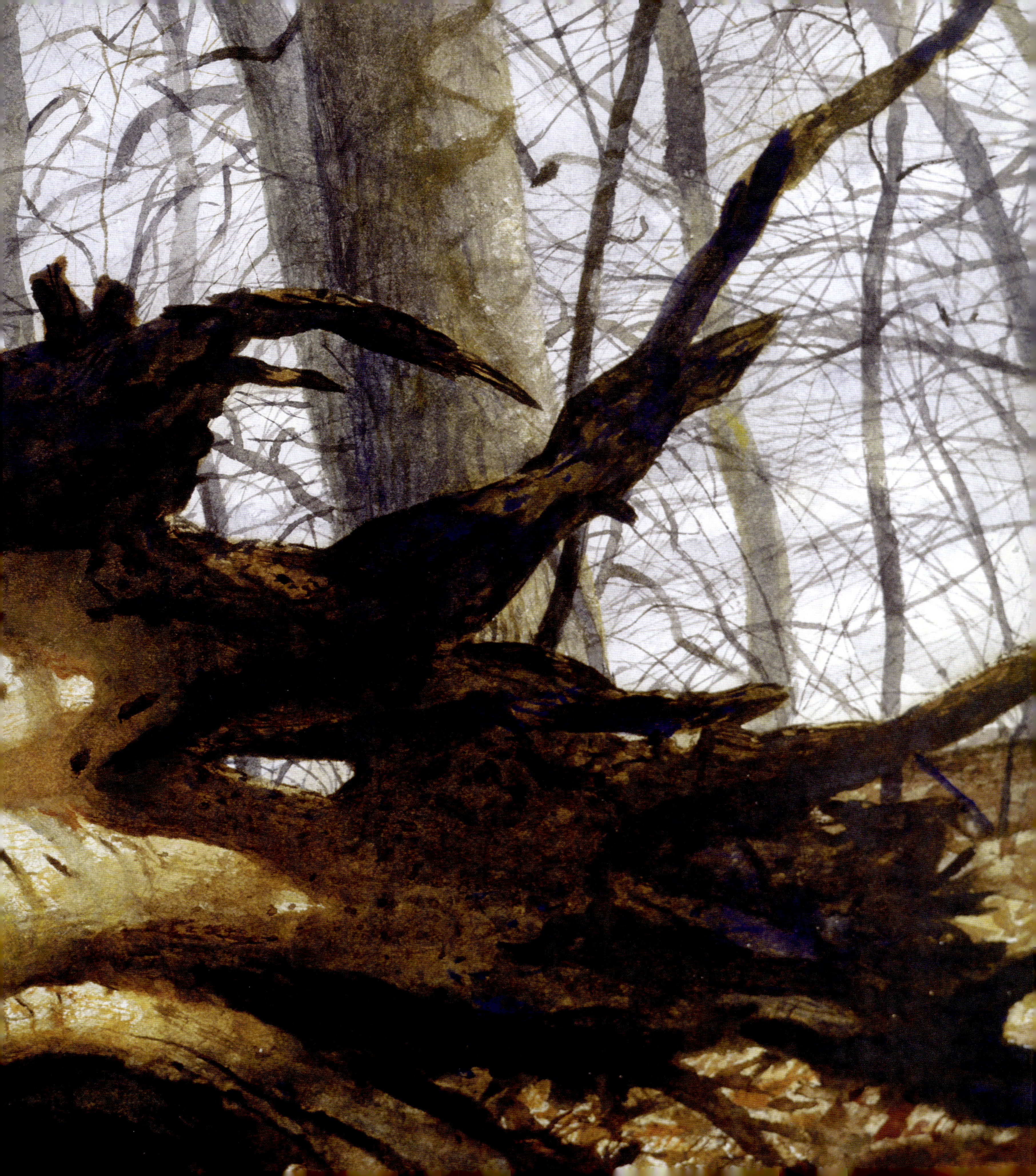

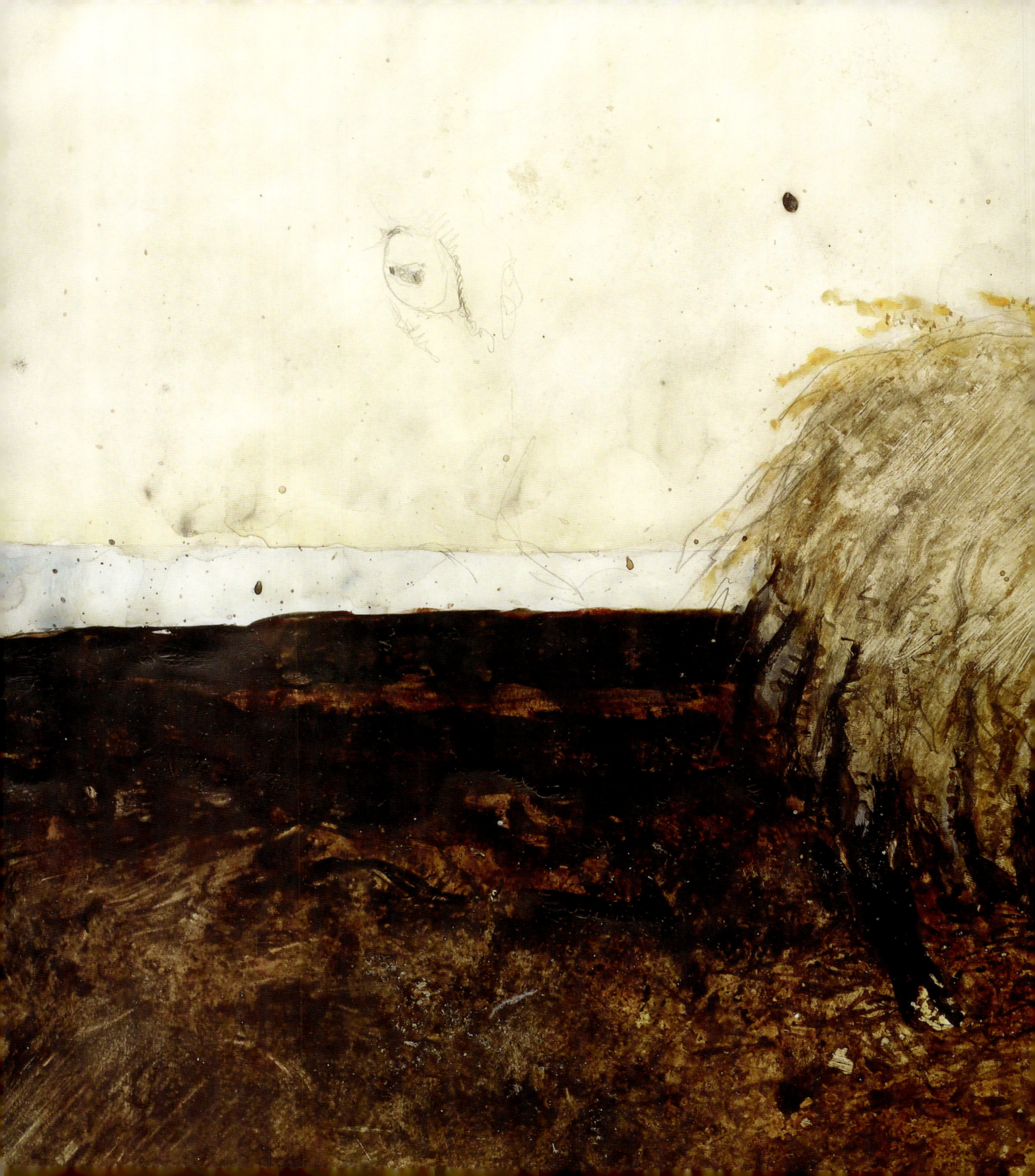

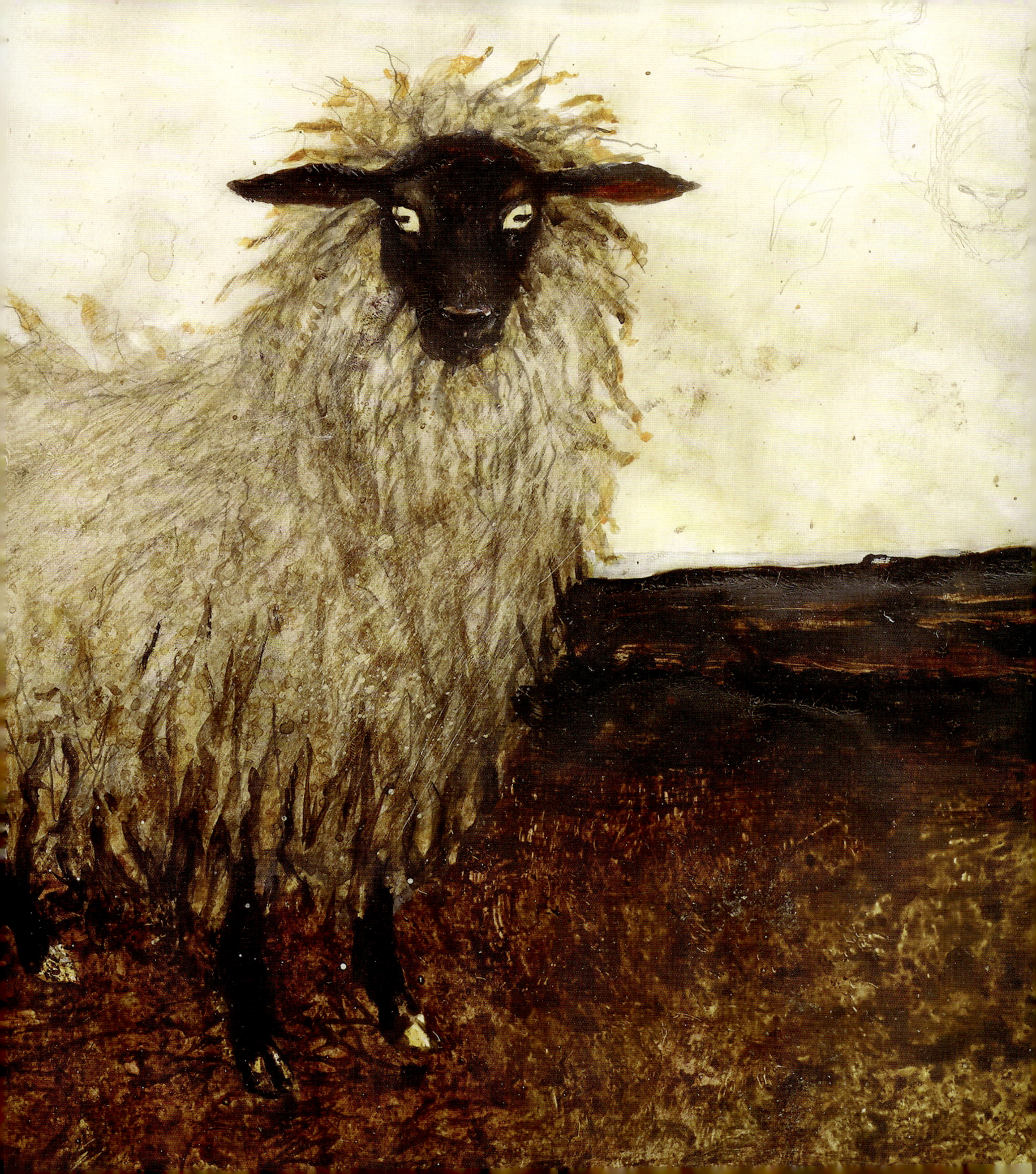

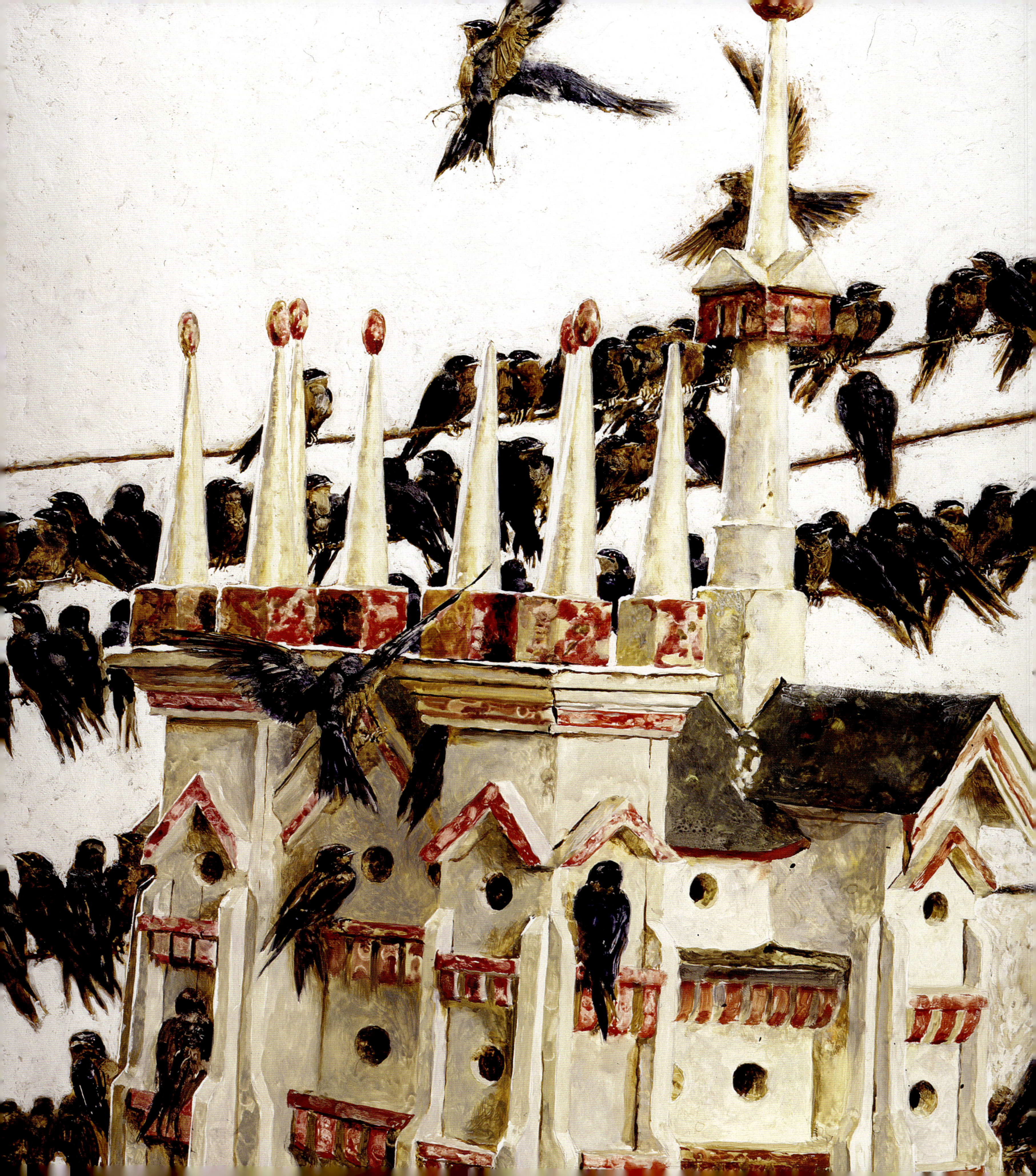

CHECKLIST OF THE EXHIBITION

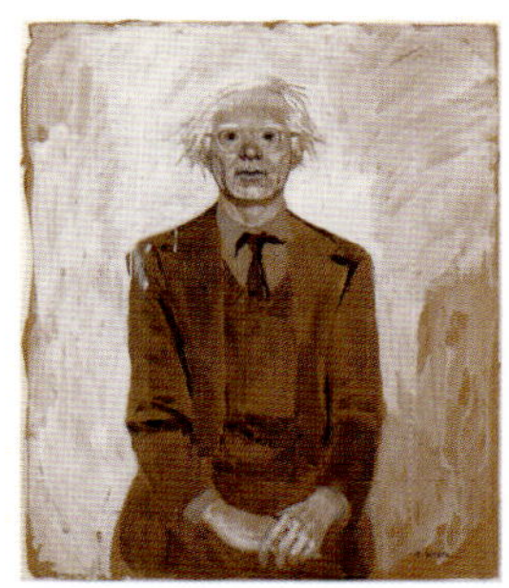

Andy Warhol on White (Andy Warhol Study), 1976
Watercolor on cardboard
40 × 38 in.
Farnsworth Art Museum, Rockland, Maine
Bequest of Betsy J. Wyeth, 2021

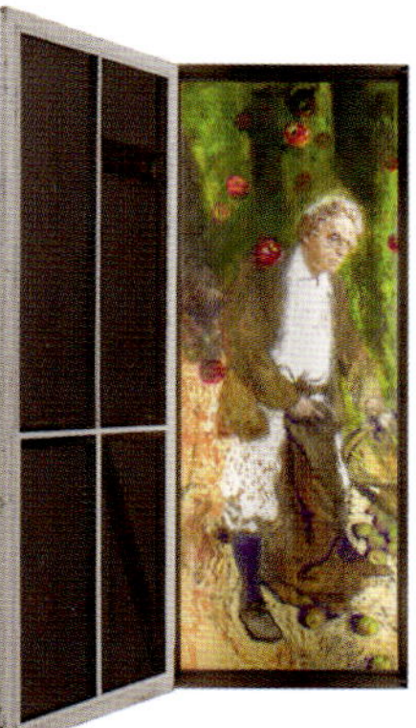

Apples: Fifth in the Screen Door Sequence, 2021
Assemblage
91½ × 36 × 11 in.
The Phyllis and Jamie Wyeth Collection

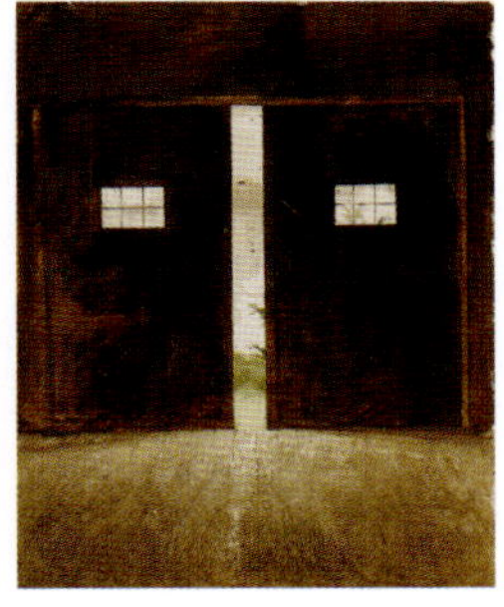

Barn Door, Broad Cove Farmhay, ca. 1965
Watercolor on paper
19⅜ × 15¾ in.
The Phyllis and Jamie Wyeth Collection

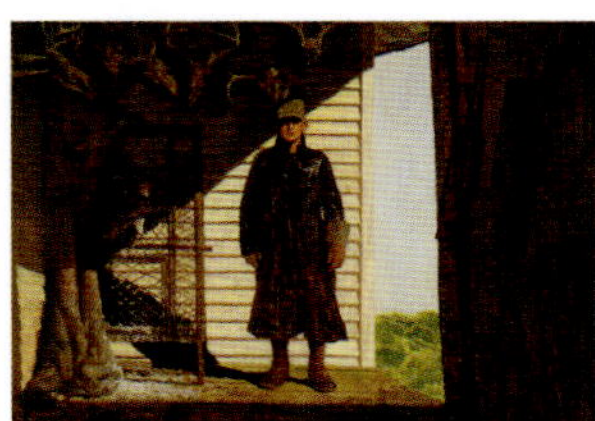

Bean Boots, 1985
Oil on panel
37 × 50 in.
Farnsworth Art Museum, Rockland, Maine
Gift of the Cawley Family, 2001.29.1

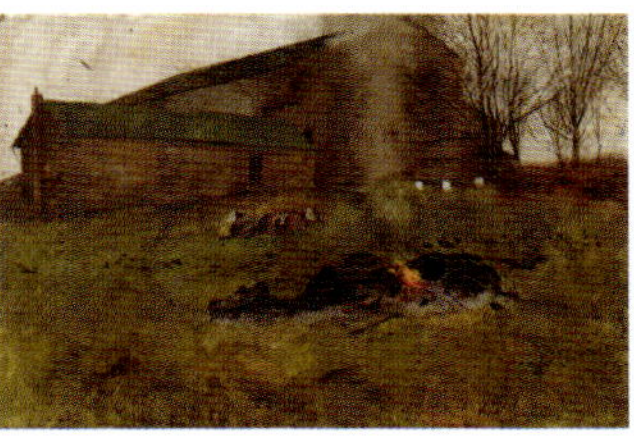

Below the Barn, 1965
Watercolor on paper
18⅞ × 27⅞ in.
Frye Art Museum
Museum purchase, 1982.006

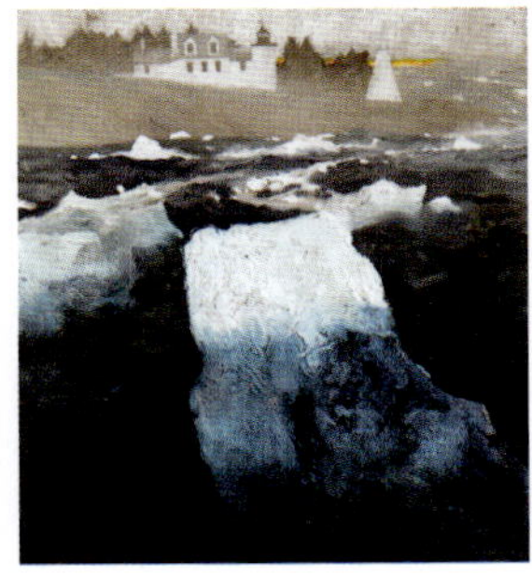

Berg, 2011
Watercolor, gesso, and enamel on joined rag boards
40¼ × 36 in.
Private collection

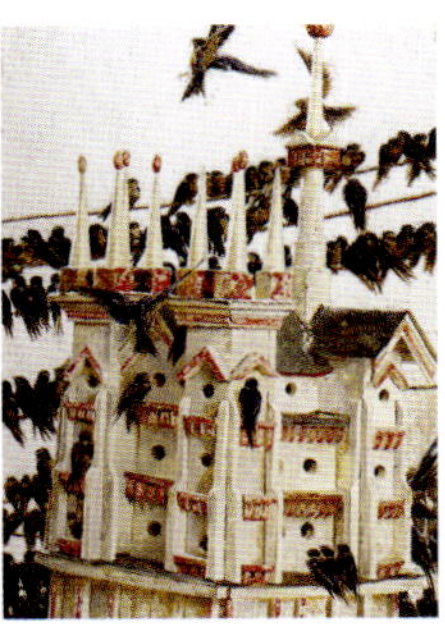

Birds' House, 1989
Watercolor and varnish on white Strathmore paper
30¼ × 21½ in.
Private collection

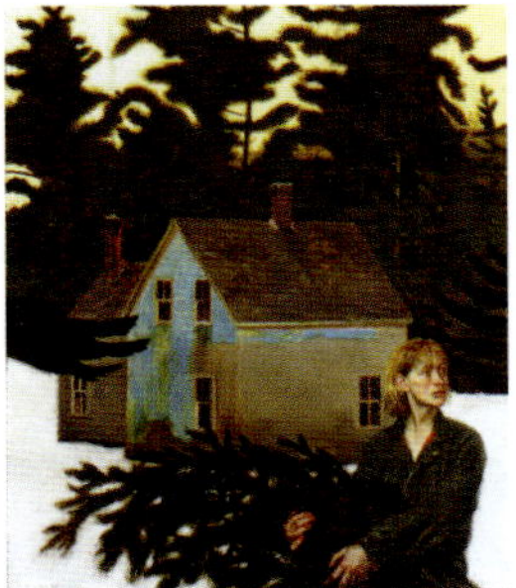

Black Spruce, 1994
Oil on panel
36 × 30 in.
Collection of the Kemper Museum of Contemporary Art, Kansas City, Missouri
Bebe and Crosby Kemper Collection,
Gift of the William T. Kemper Charitable Trust,
UMB Bank, n.a., Trustee, 2002.3

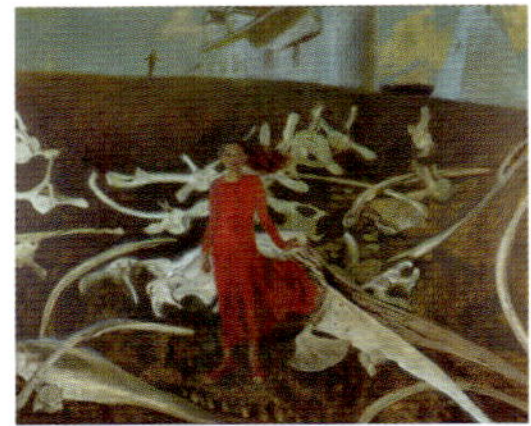

The Bones of a Whale, 2006
Oil on canvas
60⅛ × 72⅛ in.
Collection of the Kemper Museum of Contemporary Art, Kansas City, Missouri
Bebe and Crosby Kemper Collection,
Gift of the Enid and Crosby Kemper Foundation,
2006.19

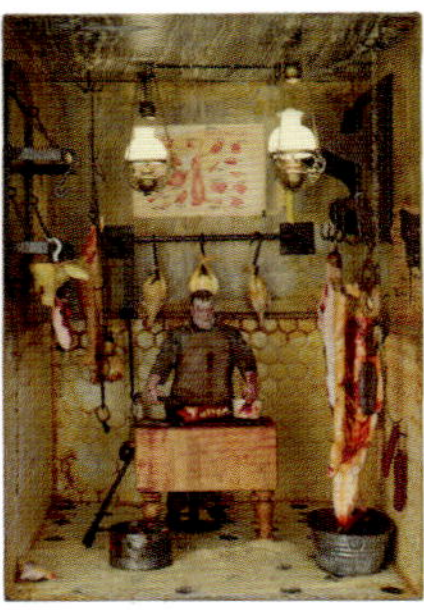

Butcher Shop, 2015
Tableau
25 × 18⅛ × 19½ in.
The Phyllis and Jamie Wyeth Collection

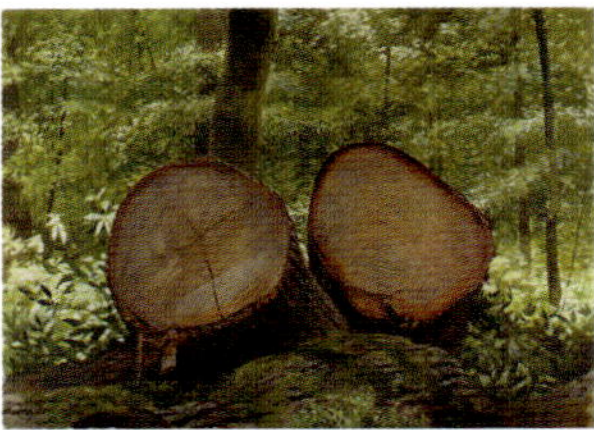

Butts, 1973
Watercolor on paper
21½ × 29⁹⁄₁₆ in.
Saint Louis Art Museum
Bequest of Edith J. and C. C. Johnson Spink

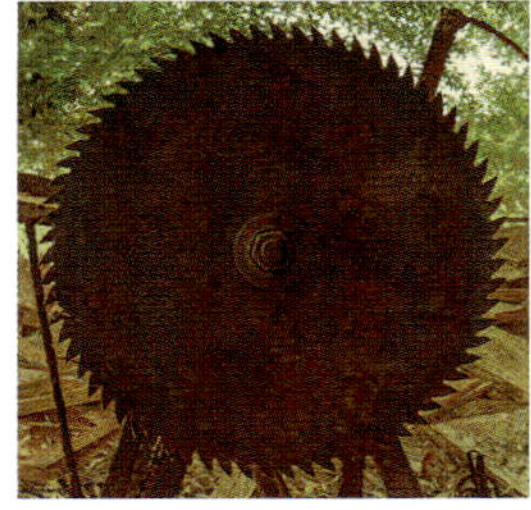

Buzz Saw, 1969
Oil on canvas
30 × 30 in.
Collection of Sherry Delk Kerstetter

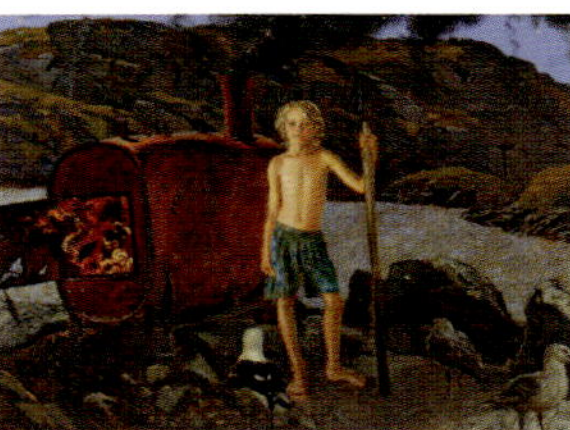

Cat Bates of Monhegan, 1995
Oil on panel
36 × 48 in.
Frye Art Museum
Museum purchase, 1996.002

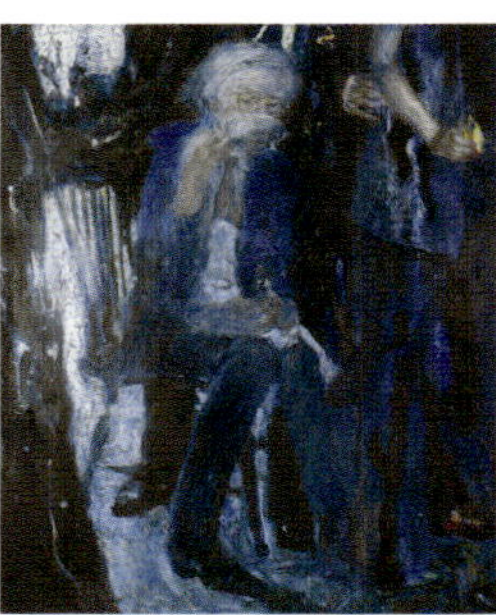

Consommé, 2013
Enamel, gesso, gouache, and watercolor on archival cardboard
47¼ × 39¼ in.
Greenville County Museum of Art, Greenville, South Carolina
Purchase with funds through the 2017 Art for Greenville campaign and the 32nd Antiques, Fine Art and Design Weekend, presented by United Community Bank

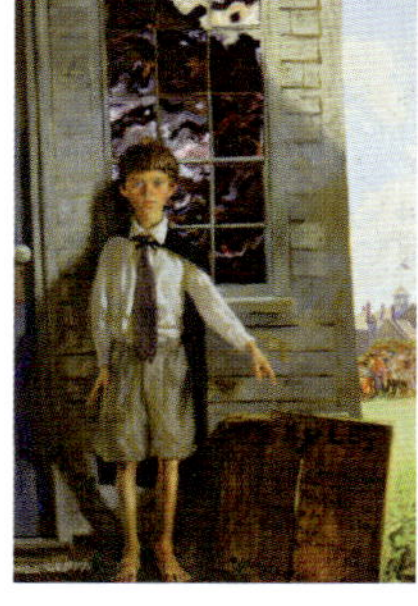

Dead Cat Museum, Monhegan Island, 1999
Oil on canvas
60 × 40 in.
Private collection

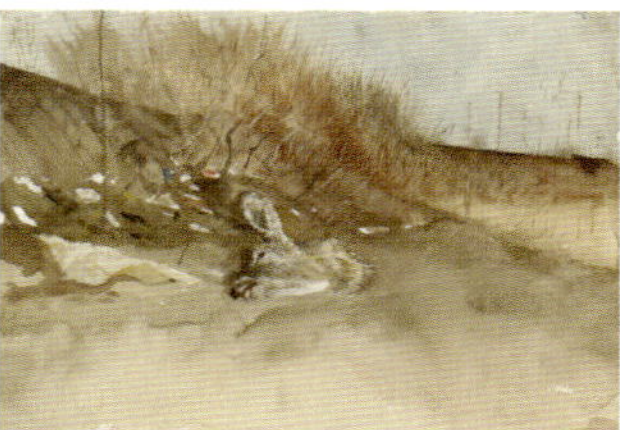

Deer Head I, ca. 1965
Watercolor on paper
14 × 20 in.
The Phyllis and Jamie Wyeth Collection

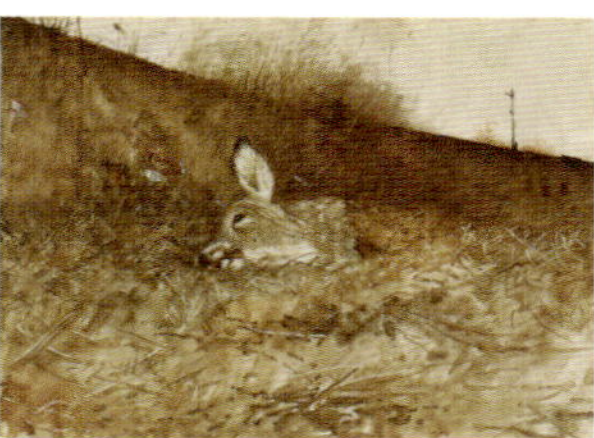

Deer Head II, ca. 1965
Watercolor on paper
11 × 15 in.
The Phyllis and Jamie Wyeth Collection

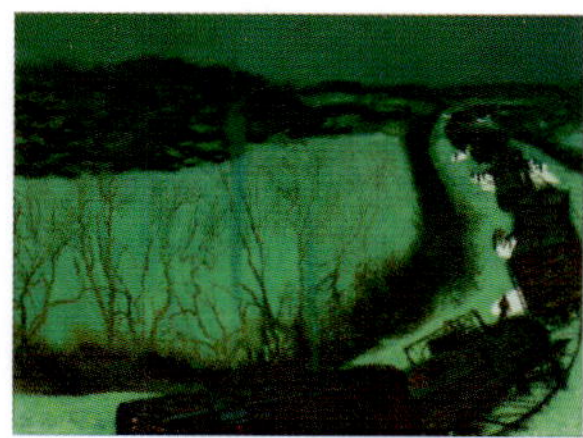

The du Ponts of Delaware Study, 2010
Oil on canvas
26 × 34 in.
The Phyllis and Jamie Wyeth Collection

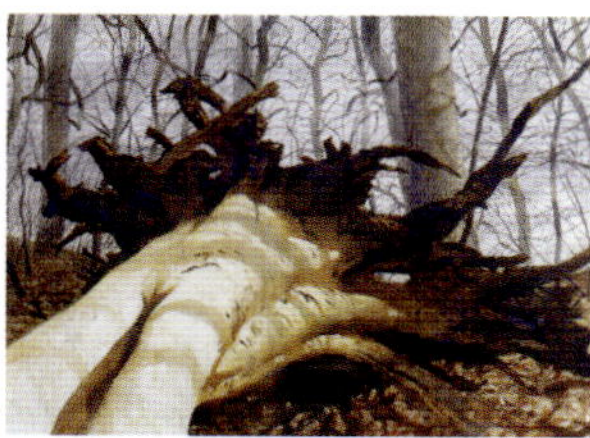

Fallen, 1975
Watercolor on paper
21 × 30 in.
Private collection

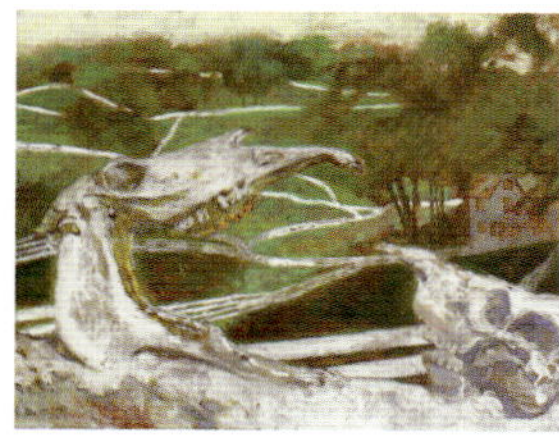

Farm Talk, 2016
Oil and gesso on panel
27 × 34 in.
Greenville County Museum of Art, Greenville, South Carolina
Purchase with funds through the 2020 Art for Greenville campaign and the 36th Antiques, Fine Art and Design Weekend, presented by United Community Bank Foundation

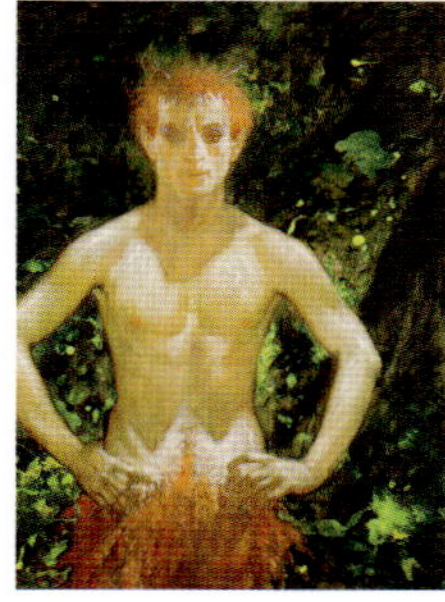

The Faune, 1977/2002
Oil on canvas
36 × 26 in.
Brandywine Museum of Art
Purchase made possible by the Robert J. Kleberg, Jr. and Helen C. Kleberg Foundation; the Roemer Foundation; the Margaret Dorrance Strawbridge Foundation of PA I, Inc.; and an anonymous donor, 2006

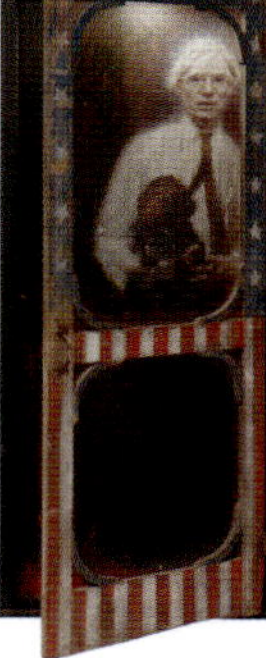

First in the Screen Door Sequence, 2015
Oil on canvas on honeycomb aluminum support with American folk art "found object" constructed of wood, metal screen, and hardware
82 × 33½ × 3⅞ in.
Brandywine Museum of Art
Gift of George A. Weymouth, 2016

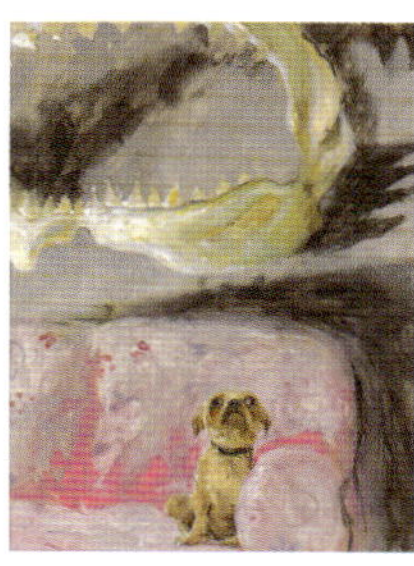

Great White Shark, 2011
Charcoal, oil, and watercolor on toned paper board
24 × 18 in.
Private collection

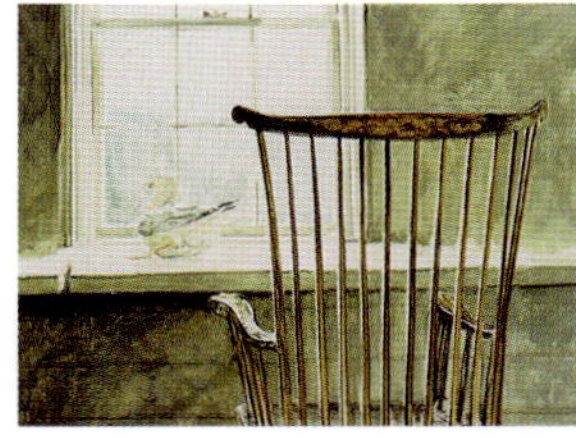

Gull and Windsor, 1993
Combined mediums on paper
19¾ × 25½ in.
Collection of Lindsay and Candice Hooper

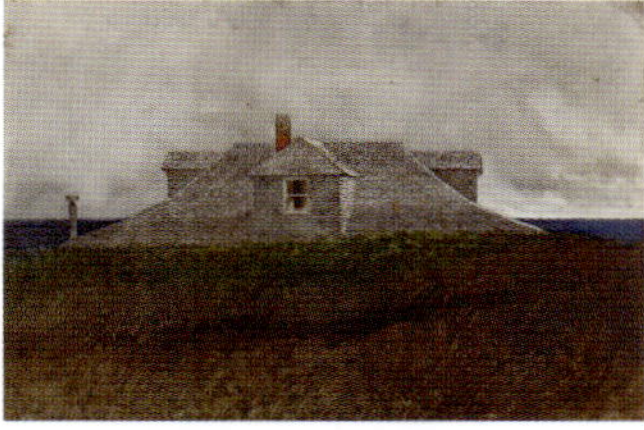

Hekking House, 1968
Watercolor on paper
18⅜ × 27⅜ in.
Brandywine Museum of Art
Gift of Mr. and Mrs. Andrew Wyeth, 1985

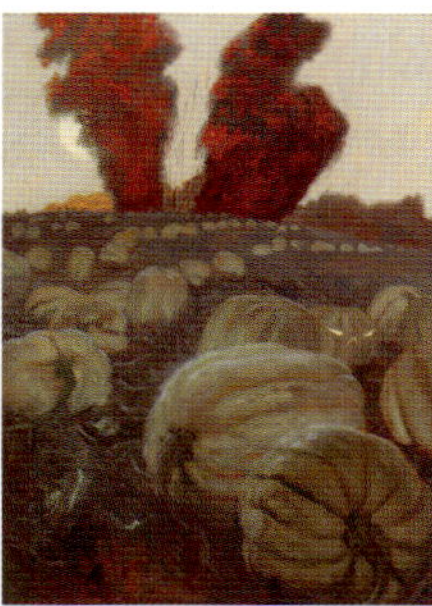

Hill Girt Farm, 2000
Oil on canvas
36 × 26⅛ in.
Brandywine Museum of Art
Museum Volunteers' Purchase Fund, 2000

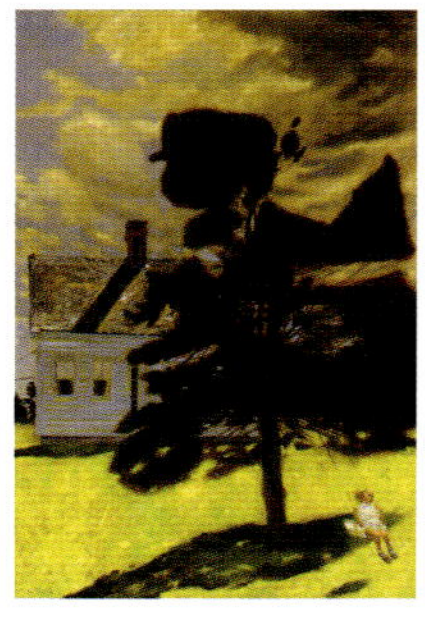

Julia on the Swing, 1999
Oil on canvas
60 × 40 in.
Private collection

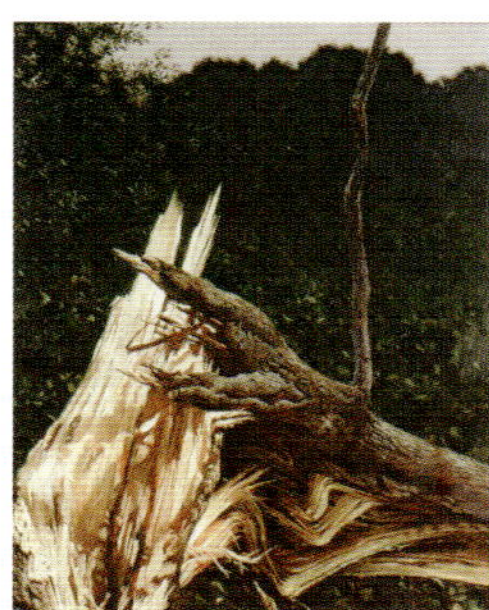

Lightning Struck, 1975
Oil on canvas
38¼ × 30¼ in.
Collection of Sherry Delk Kerstetter

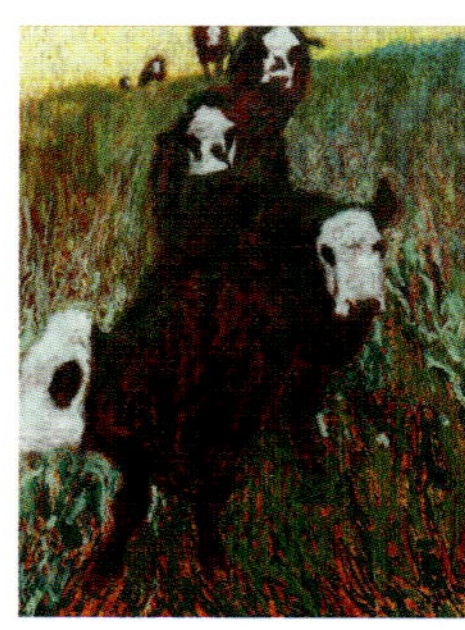

A Midsummer Night's Dusk, 2022
Oil, enamel, and acrylic on Claybord panel
39 × 29 in.
The Phyllis and Jamie Wyeth Collection

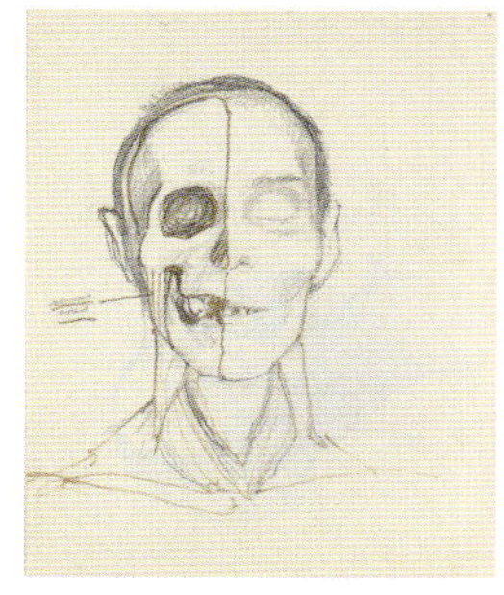

Morgue Sketchbook, 1965–66
Graphite on paper
14 × 11 in.
Brandywine Museum of Art
Gift of Robert J. Demarest, 2015

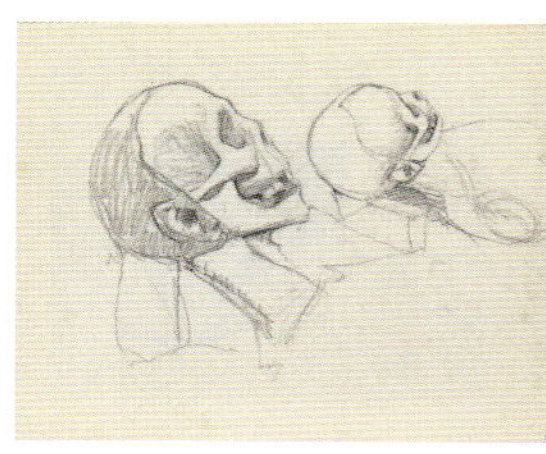

Morgue Sketchbook, 1965–66
Graphite on paper
11 × 14 in.
Brandywine Museum of Art
Gift of Robert J. Demarest, 2015

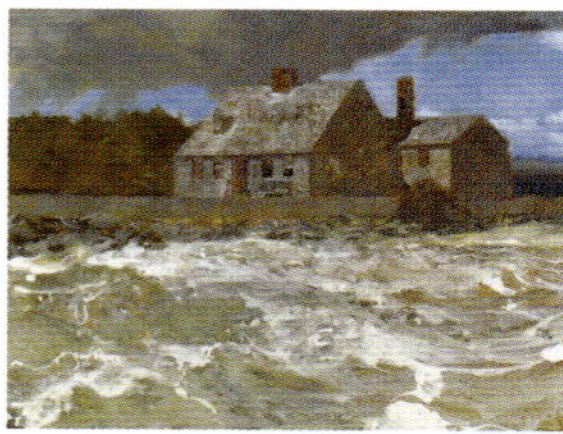

My Mother and the Squall, 2016
Acrylic, gesso, oil, and watercolor on panel
31 × 41½ in.
Private collection

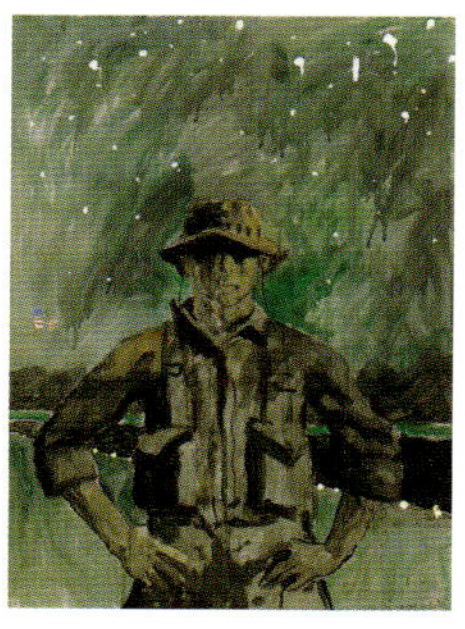

Night Vision Study II, 2002
Oil on canvas
39⅝ × 29¼ in.
The Phyllis and Jamie Wyeth Collection

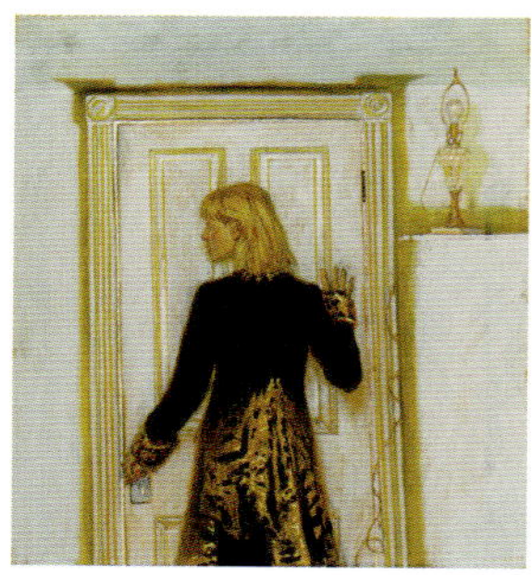

Other Voices, Study #1, 1995
Charcoal and gouache on cardboard
39¼ × 36 in.
The Phyllis and Jamie Wyeth Collection

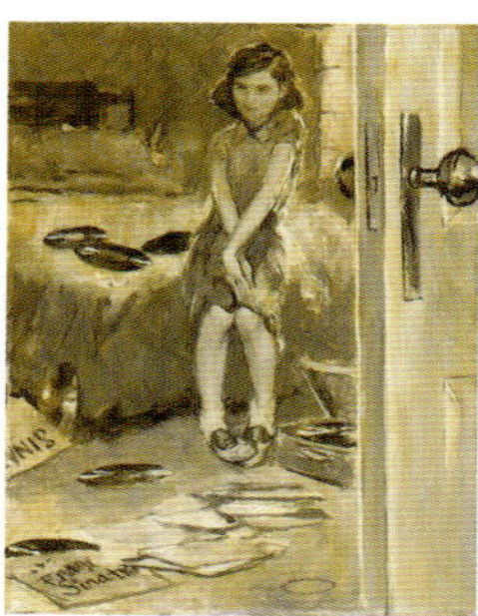

Patricia Kennedy Listening to Sinatra Records, 2013
Acrylic and gesso on canvas
14 × 11 in.
The Phyllis and Jamie Wyeth Collection

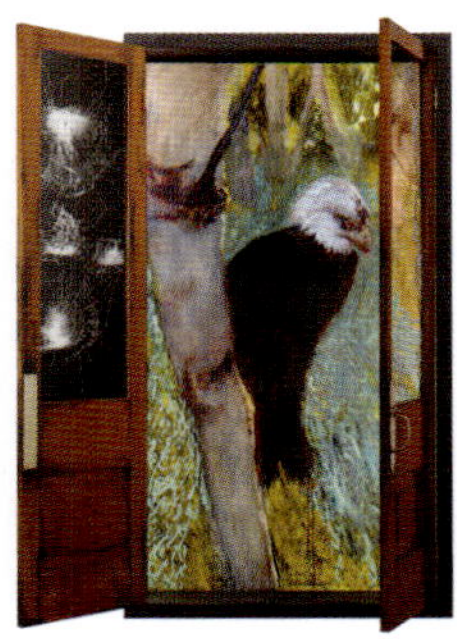

Poison: Seventh in the Screen Door Sequence, 2022
Assemblage
76¼ × 42 × 10½ in.
The Phyllis and Jamie Wyeth Collection

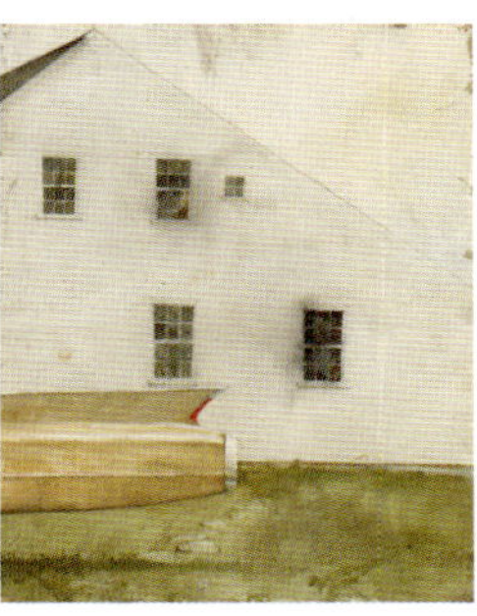

Pom Pom's Cadillac, Broad Cove Farm, ca. 1965
Watercolor on paper
24¾ × 19 in.
The Phyllis and Jamie Wyeth Collection

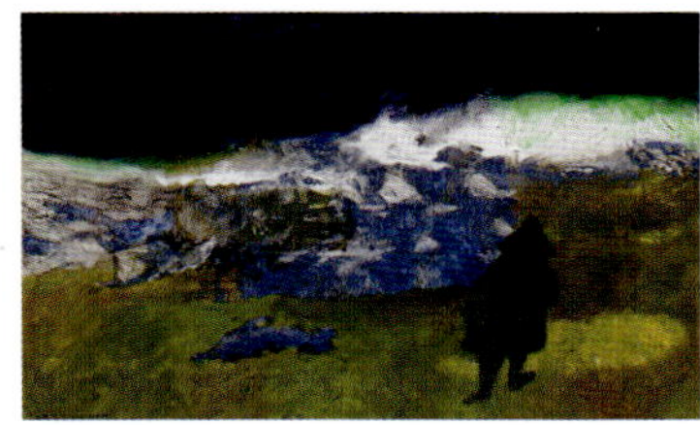

Portrait of a Moon Curser, Fifteenth in a Suite of Untoward Occurrences on Monhegan Island, 2020
Acrylic, gesso, and oil on canvas
25½ × 35½ in.
The Phyllis and Jamie Wyeth Collection

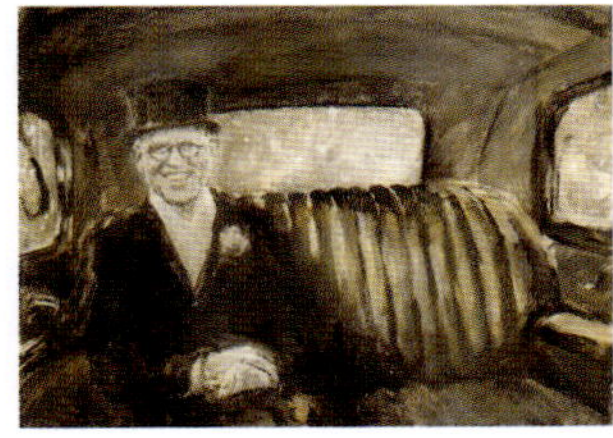

Portrait of Joseph P. Kennedy, 2013
Acrylic and gesso on canvas
12 × 16 in.
The Phyllis and Jamie Wyeth Collection

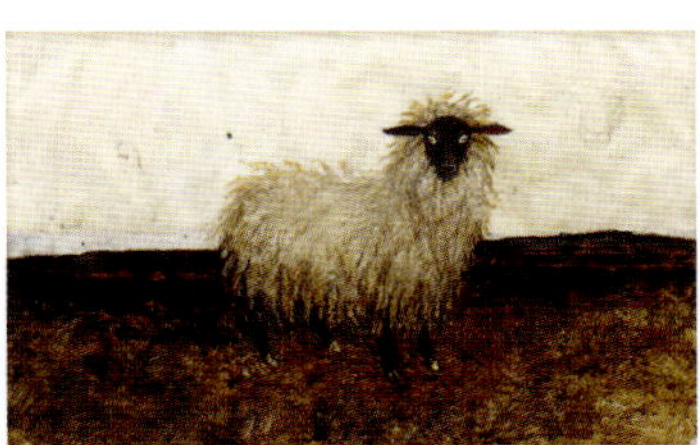

Portrait of Lady, Study #1, 1968
Watercolor on paper
14 × 22 in.
Private collection

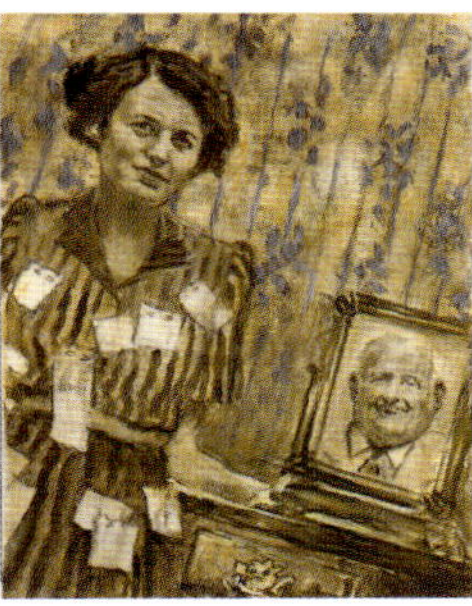

Portrait of Rose Kennedy with Her Father's Photograph, 2013
Acrylic and gesso on canvas
14 × 11 in.
The Phyllis and Jamie Wyeth Collection

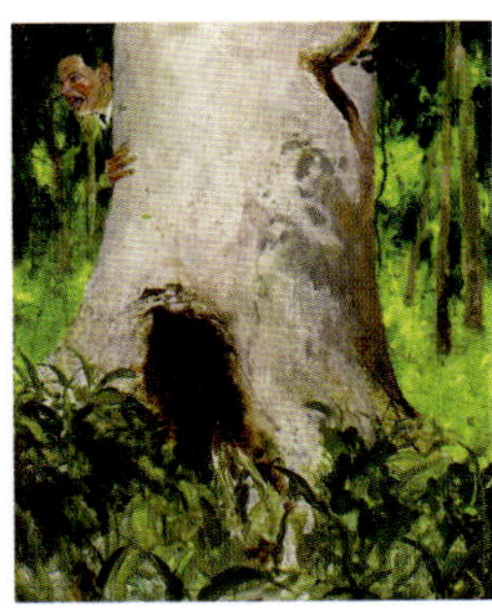

Ramps, 2013
Enamel, gesso, and watercolor on Strathmore paper
36 × 29½ in.
The Phyllis and Jamie Wyeth Collection

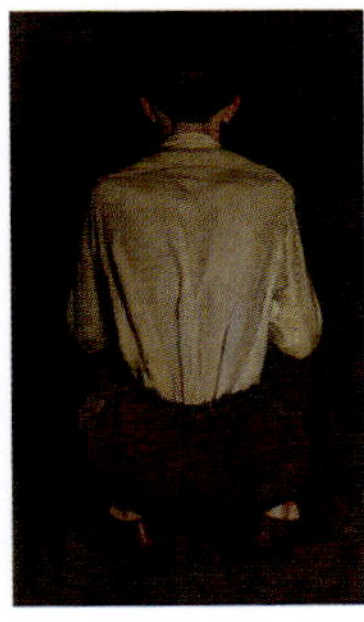

Record Player, 1964
Oil on canvas
47 × 28 in.
Collection of Lisa and David Spartin

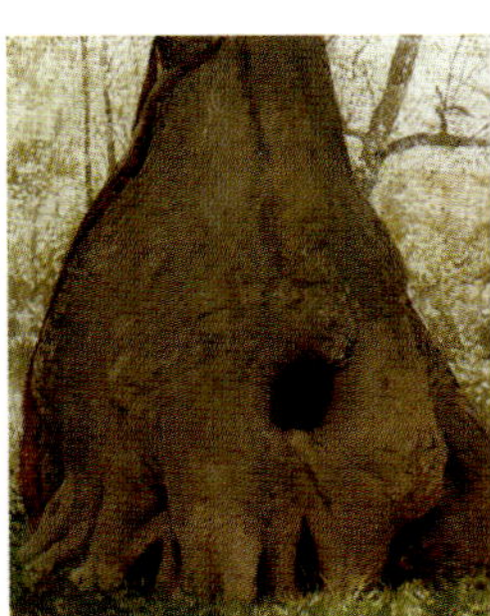

River Trunk, 1968
Watercolor on paper
24½ × 19½ in.
The Phyllis and Jamie Wyeth Collection

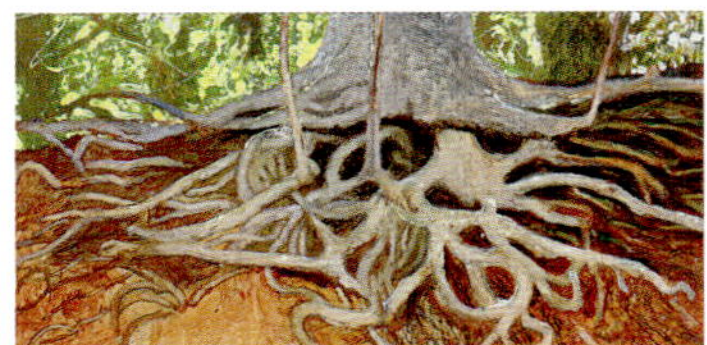

Roots, Revisited, 2019
Acrylic, oil, and enamel on panel
48 × 96 in.
The Phyllis and Jamie Wyeth Collection

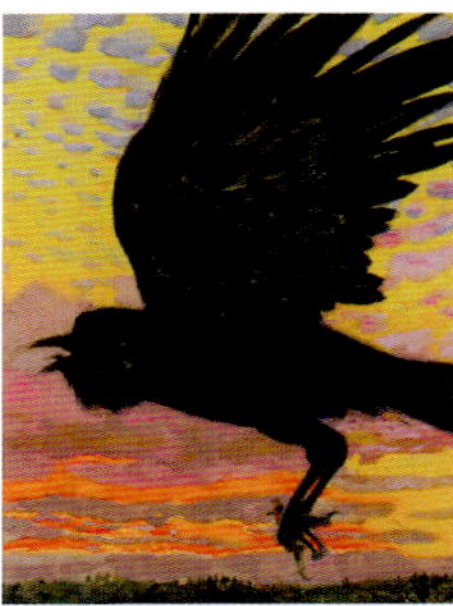

Rudolf Hess and the Raven, 1997
Combined mediums on wove board
24 × 18 in.
Collection of Jim and Jocelyn Stewart

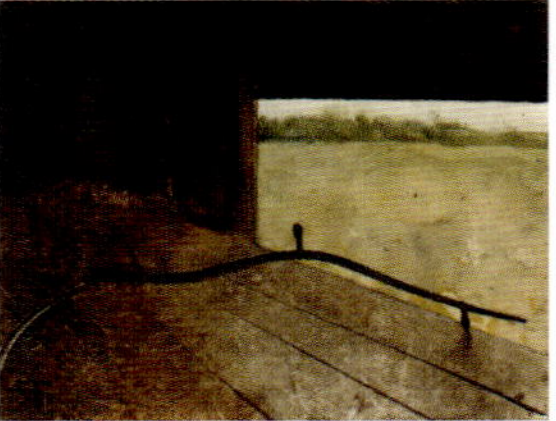

The Scythe, 1966
Watercolor on paper
18 × 24 in.
Hunter Museum of American Art, Chattanooga, Tenessee
Gift of the Benwood Foundation, 1975.2

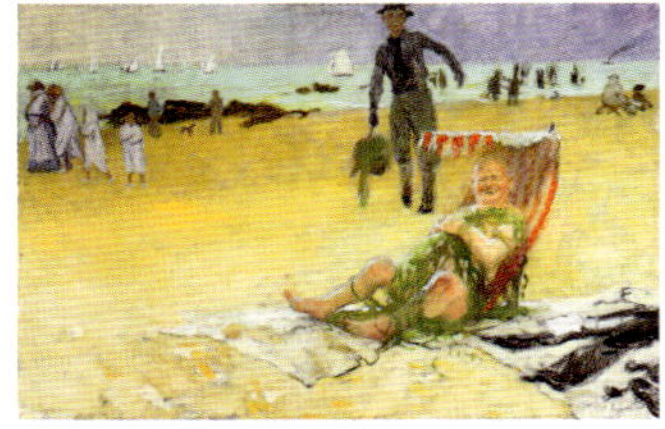

The Seaweed and Honey Fitz, 2014
Oil on canvas
19½ × 29½ in.
The Phyllis and Jamie Wyeth Collection

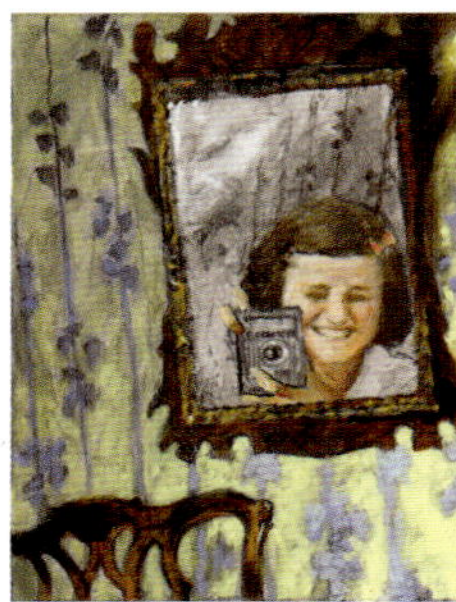

Self-Portrait of Jean Kennedy, 2013
Acrylic and gesso on canvas
16 × 12 in.
The Phyllis and Jamie Wyeth Collection

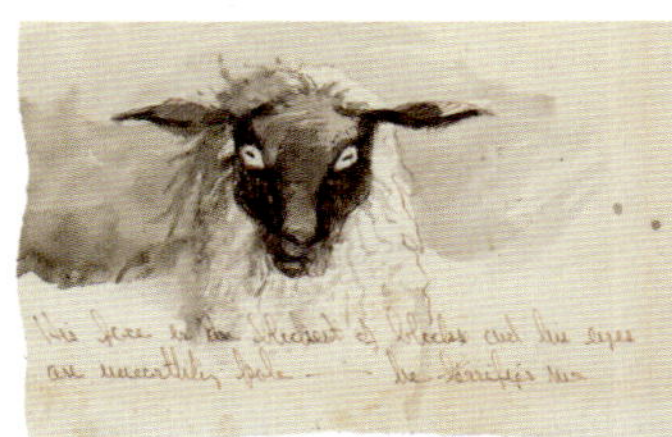

Sheep Drawing with Letter, 1968
Watercolor on paper
6¼ × 9½ in.
The Phyllis and Jamie Wyeth Collection

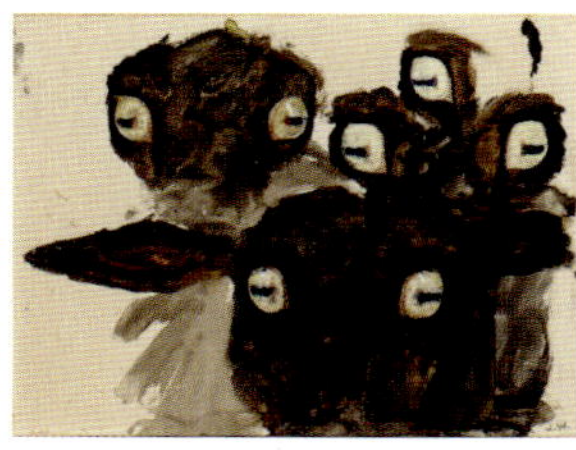

Sheep Eyes, 1968
Watercolor on paper
9 × 12 in.
The Phyllis and Jamie Wyeth Collection

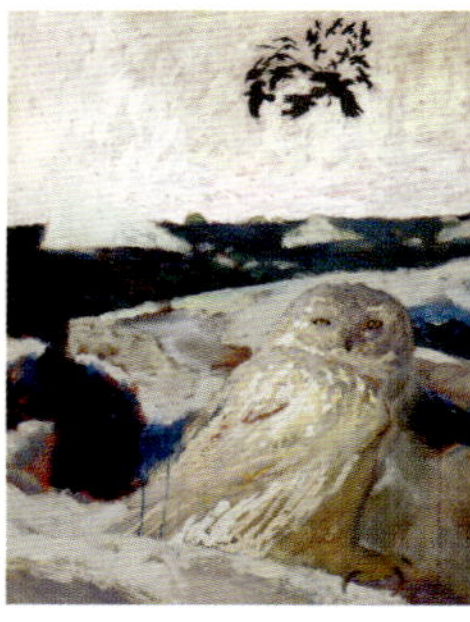

Snow Owl, Fourteenth in a Suite of Untoward Occurrences on Monhegan Island, 2020
Acrylic, oil, and watercolor on canvas
46 × 36 in.
The Phyllis and Jamie Wyeth Collection

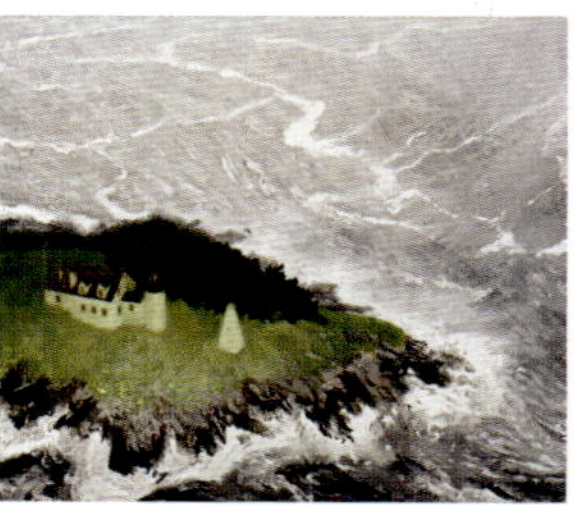

Spindrift, 2010
Oil on canvas
40 × 46 in.
The Phyllis and Jamie Wyeth Collection

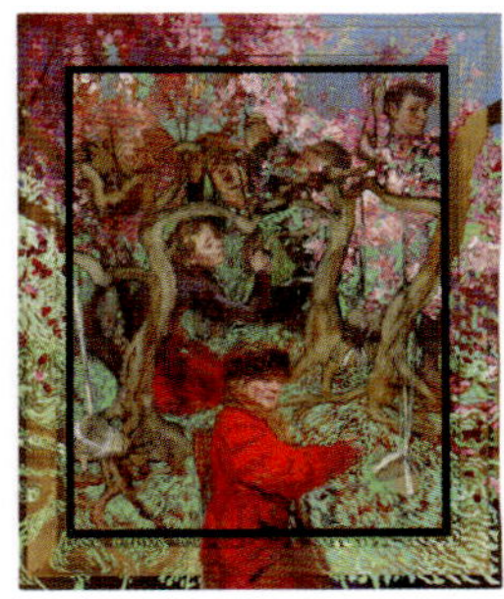

Spring, the Hanging of the Tree Rocks, 2017
Acrylic and oil on wood panel
46 × 36 in.
The Phyllis and Jamie Wyeth Collection

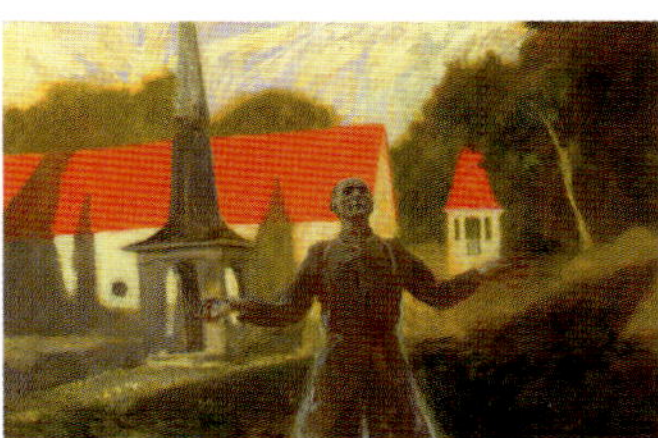

The Steeple Salesman, 2012
Oil on board
23¼ × 35½ in.
Greenville County Museum of Art, Greenville, South Carolina
Purchase with funds through the 2017 Art for Greenville campaign and the 32nd Antiques, Fine Art and Design Weekend, presented by United Community Bank

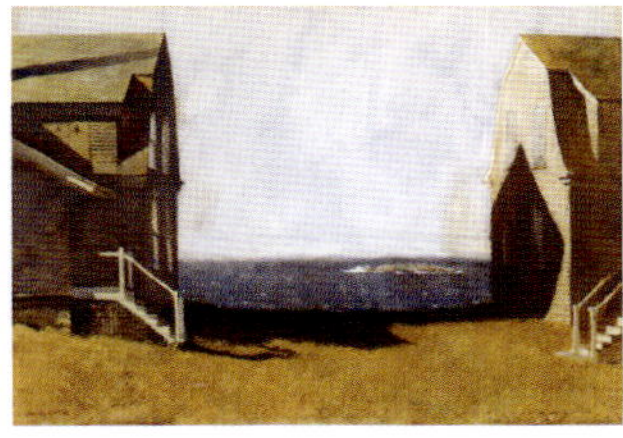

Summer House, Winter House, 1975
Watercolor on paper
21¾ × 30 in.
Farnsworth Art Museum, Rockland, Maine
Gift of MBNA America, 2003.3.8

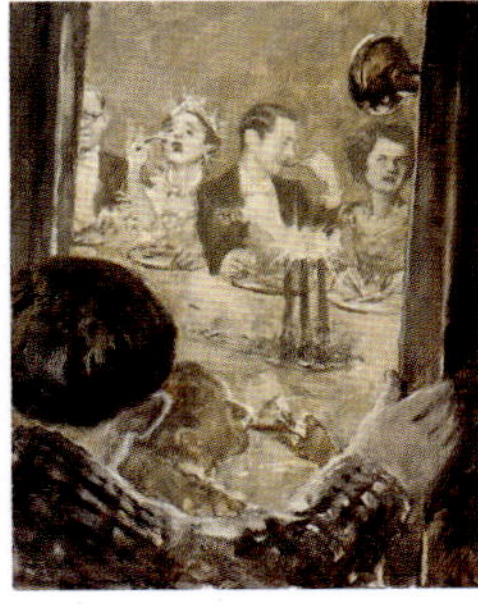

Teddy Kennedy Observing the King and Queen of England, 2013
Acrylic and gesso on canvas
16 × 12 in.
The Phyllis and Jamie Wyeth Collection

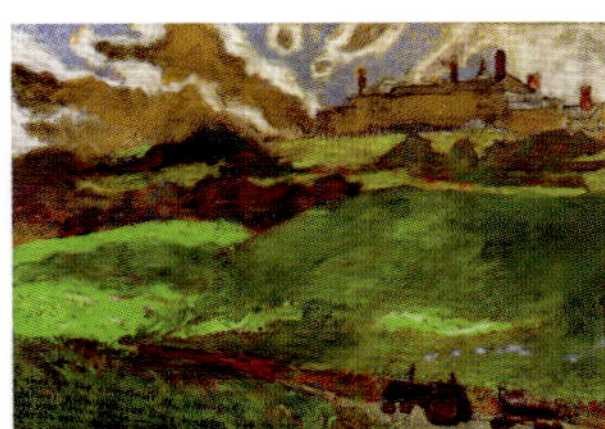

Through the Cornfields of Granogue, 2022
Acrylic and oil on canvas
25½ × 35½ in.
The Phyllis and Jamie Wyeth Collection

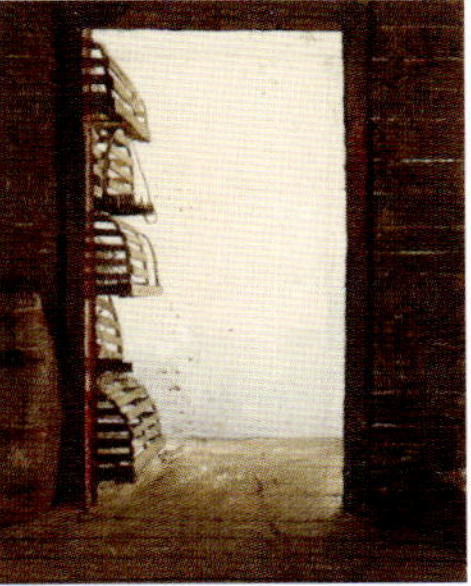

Traps, ca. 1965
Watercolor on paper
18½ × 24 in.
The Phyllis and Jamie Wyeth Collection

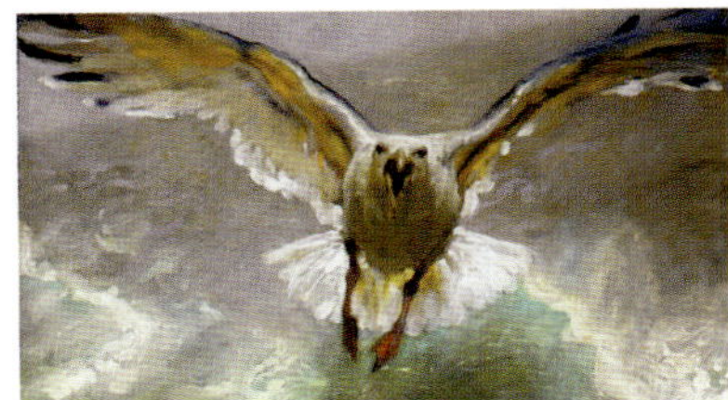

Wake, 2008
Gesso and oil on canvas
36 × 48 in.
The Phyllis and Jamie Wyeth Collection

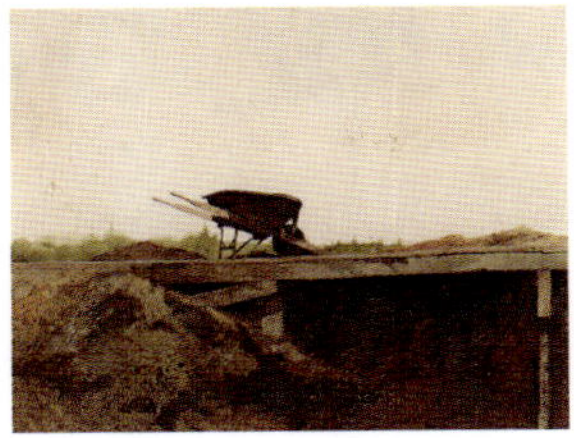

Wheelbarrow, 1963
Watercolor on paper
18⅝ × 23⅞ in.
Frye Art Museum
Museum purchase, 1985.006

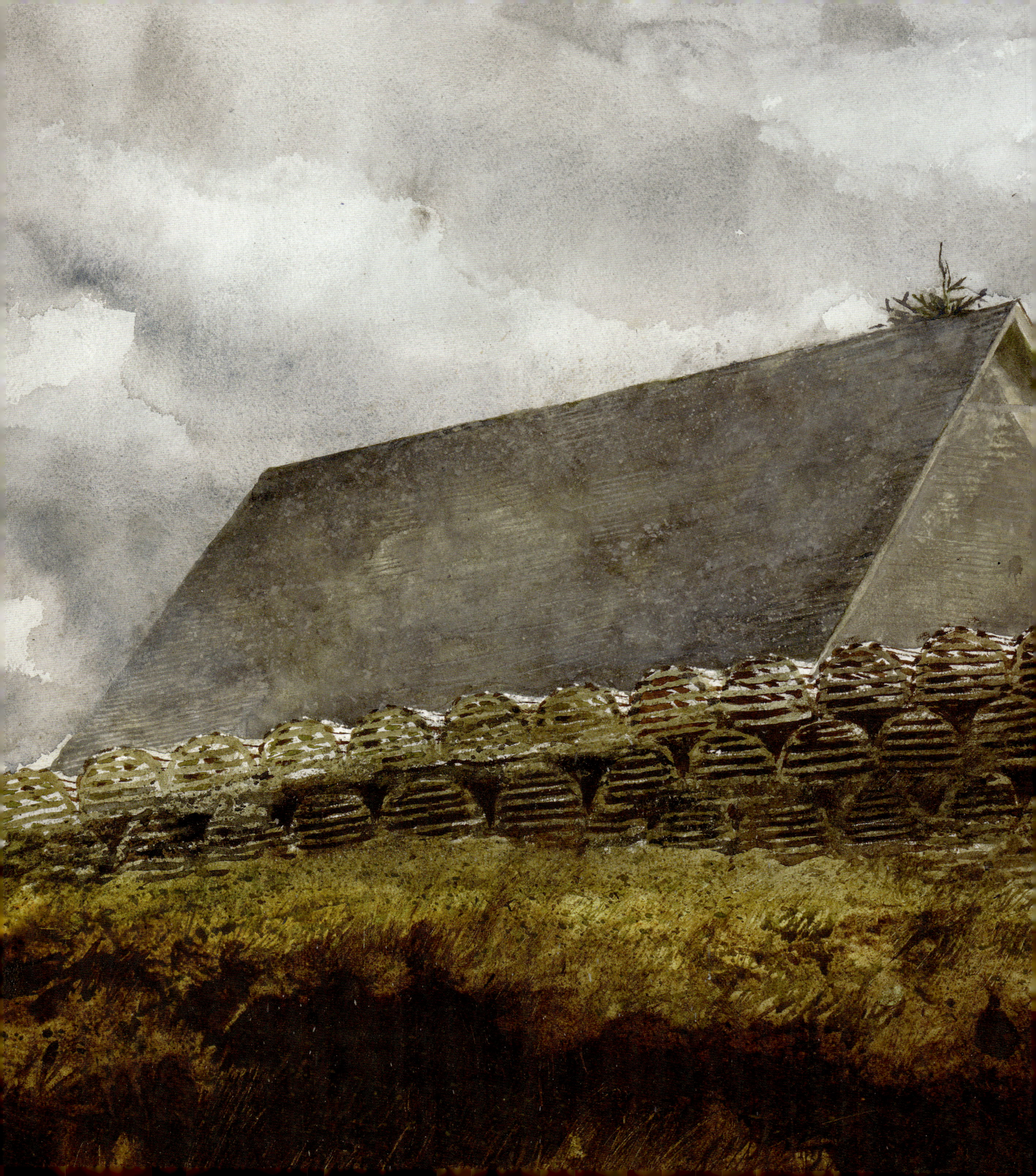

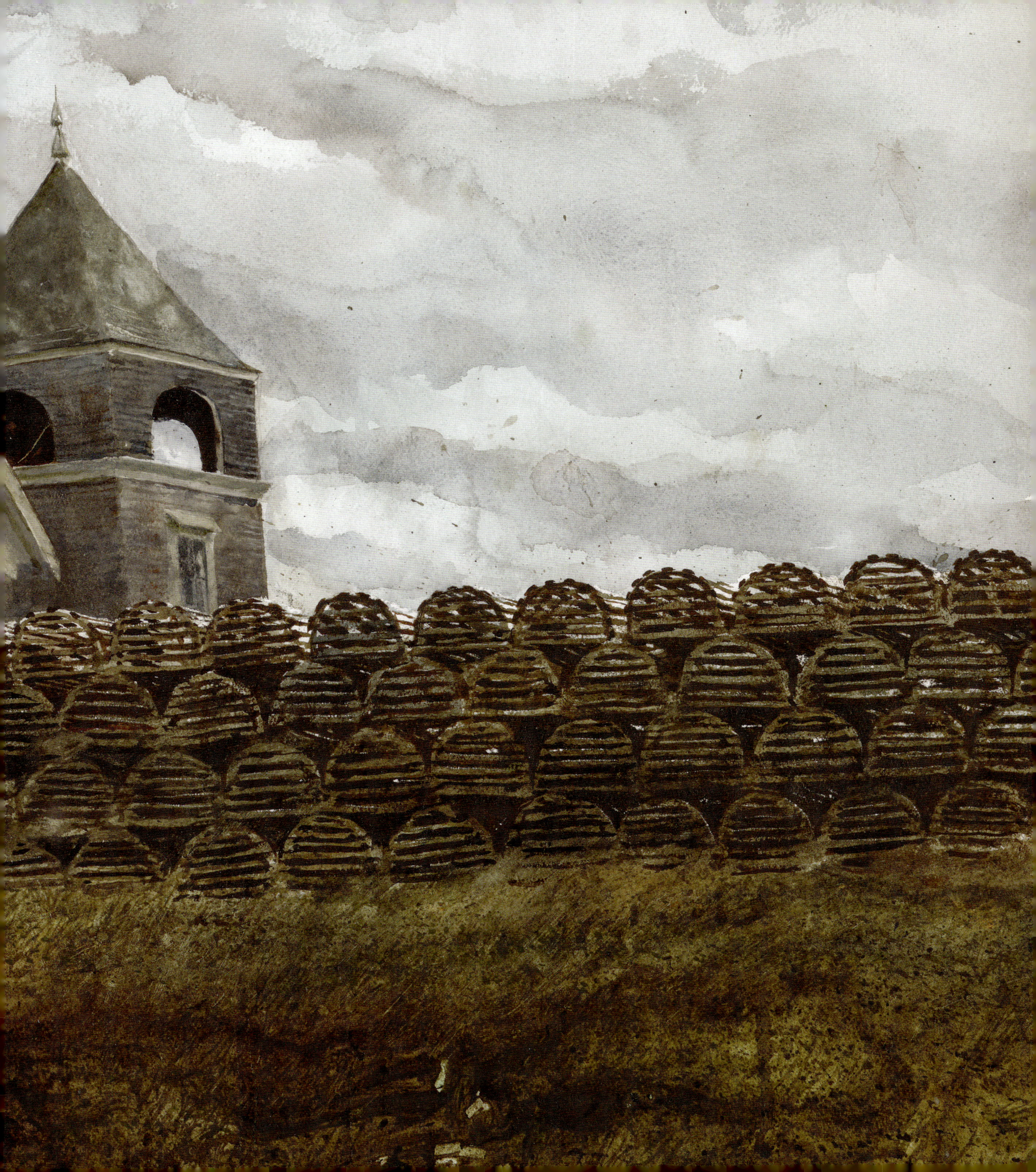

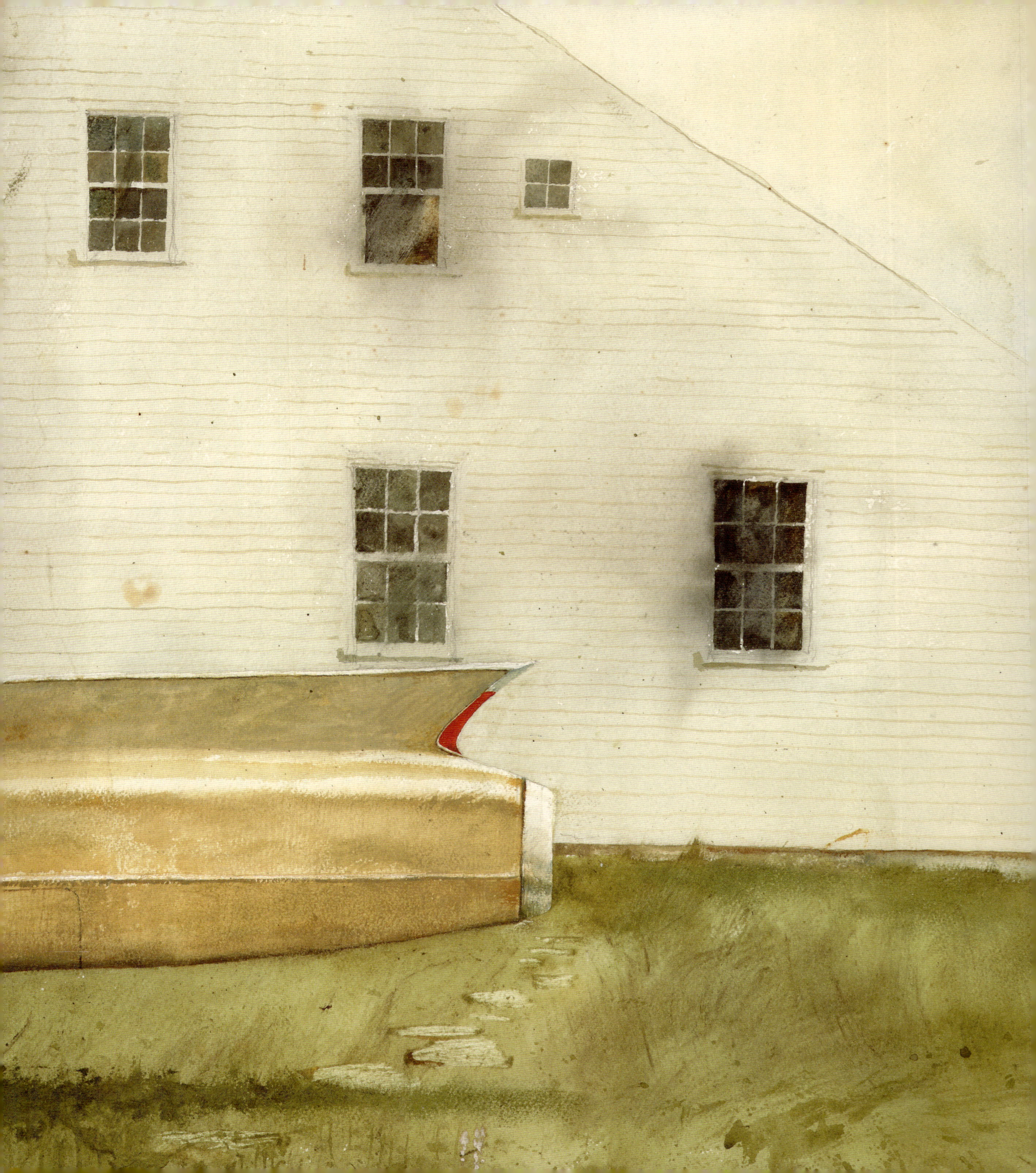

CONTRIBUTORS

Described as "a composer of profound sensibility," Scottish-American **Jennifer Margaret Barker** has received performances of her compositions on five continents. Her compositions have been performed by major orchestras and chamber and choral ensembles in the United States and at festivals in Brazil, Scotland, and Malta, among others, by an extensive list of international artists. She was the recipient of the 2022 Miriam Gideon Prize from the International Alliance for Women in Music; was the winner of the the 2022 New Ariel Piano Composition Competition; and received the 2021 Masters Fellowship Award from the Delaware Division of the Arts and awards from The American Prize in 2019 and 2020. Dr. Barker is Professor of Composition/Theory at the University of Delaware. In 2022, she received the University of Delaware College of Arts and Sciences Outstanding Scholarship Award.

A specialist in American art, **Amanda C. Burdan** is Senior Curator at the Brandywine Museum of Art, caring for both the collection of American art and the Museum's historic properties, including the N.C. Wyeth House and Studio, the Andrew Wyeth Studio, and the Kuerner Farm. She has worked on a number of exhibitions about the work of Jamie Wyeth, including a collaboration with the Farnsworth Art Museum, *Jamie Wyeth, Rockwell Kent and Monhegan,* in 2012–13, and another with the Museum of Fine Arts, Boston, on their Jamie Wyeth retrospective in 2014–15; and on a re-creation of his 1965 studio within the Andrew Wyeth Studio in 2023. At Brandywine she curates a rotating exhibition of Wyeth's work in a dedicated gallery alongside the works of his grandfather N.C. Wyeth.

Rena Butler hails from Chicago. She began her studies at The Chicago Academy for the Arts, studied both overseas at Taipei National University of the Arts in Taiwan and at the State University of New York, Purchase Conservatory of Dance. She has danced with many prestigious companies and has choreographed work for Hubbard Street Dance Chicago, BalletX in Philadelphia, Jacob's Pillow, and the Juilliard School. She served on the Consortium for Chicago Dancemakers Forum, was on the annual panel for Black Girls Dance in Chicago, and co-created and directed DanceLab—a free, choreographic course for Chicago teens, empowering participants of varying socioeconomic backgrounds and identities to find commonality in creation. In 2022, she choreographed the San Francisco Opera's production of *Orpheus and Eurydice*, and in 2023, she premiered her first work for The National Ballet of Canada.

Michael Kiley is a sound designer, composer, performer, and educator working in dance, theater, and public installation. His original works range from immersive vocal works to geo-locational soundwalks and community outreach collaborations, all centered in the investigation of the healing and transformative nature of sound and voice. He is a four-time nominee and two-time recipient of the Barrymore Award for Excellence in Theatre, and his work has been called "essential sound design" by the *Huffington Post*, and "dramatic and beguiling" by *The New York Times*. Kiley's collaborations include theatrical work with a number of Philadelphia-area cultural institutions. He is currently working on a book exploring the development of his own voice practice, which he calls Personal Resonance. He also records albums under the moniker The Mural and The Mint.

John Rusk is an Assistant Director and Producer of over fifty feature films and television shows. These include *Dead Poets Society*, *Avalon*, *A League of Their Own*, *Fearless*, *The Pelican Brief*, *Outbreak*, *Twelve Monkeys*, *The Sixth Sense*, *Unbreakable*, *Doubt*, and *Split.* Most recently, Rusk worked on *Hustle*, *Stranger Things*, and the upcoming *Dangerous Waters.* Rusk has collaborated with numerous Oscar-nominated directors, including three films with Peter Weir, three with Alan J. Pakula, and twelve with M. Night Shyamalan. Other prominent directors with whom he has worked include Barry Levinson, Wolfgang Petersen, Jonathan Demme, Terry Gilliam, John Patrick Shanley, Mark Rydell, and John Schlesinger. Rusk is a graduate of the University of Delaware and the DGA-Producer Assistant Director Training Program.

IMAGE CREDITS

Front cover, 2, 4–9, 13, 28, 34, 40, 69, 70, 71, 84–89, 92, 106, 115, 117, 122–26, 127, 129, 143, 144, 147, 164, 171, 174–75, 176–77, 180: Courtesy of the artist; pp. 10, 20–21, 103, 108–113, 120, 133, 134, 137, 138, 141, 142, 149, 153, 156, 157, 161–63, 169, 190, Back cover: Photos: Alan Lavallee; pp. 15, 16: Photos: Cig Harvey; pp. 22–23, 98, 102, 107, 150: Photos: Jamie Stukenberg Photography, Rockford, IL; pp. 24, 46, 91, 96, 105, 119, 121, 130, 140, 145, 158, 159, 165, 173: Photos: Peter Philbin, Brilliant Studio; p. 27 (top left): bpk Bildagentur; Hamburger Kunsthalle. Photo: Andres Kilger, Art Resource, NY; pp. 27 (bottom left), 35 (right): Archivio GBB / Alamy Stock Photo; p. 27 (right): © 2024 Andrew Wyeth/Artists Rights Society (ARS); p. 31 (left): The Art Institute of Chicago / Art Resource, NY; p. 31 (right): Allstar Picture Library Limited / Alamy Stock Photo; p. 33: Reproduced with permission of the Charles E. Burchfield Foundation; p. 35 (right): © Edward Hopper / ARS, NY. Digital Image © The Museum of Modern Art/Licensed by SCALA / Art Resource, NY; p. 37: Courtesy of David Campany; p. 39 (left): bpk Bildagentur, Nationalgalerie, Staatliche Museen, Berlin, Germany. Photo: Andres Kilger, Art Resource, NY; p. 39 (right): Gerry Bishop / Alamy Stock Photo; pp. 41, 74, 76: Photos: Edward C. Robison III; pp. 51 (right), 97, 135: Photos: Steve Morrison; p. 52: Courtesy of The Alan Mason Chesney Medical Archives of The Johns Hopkins Medical Institutions; p. 53 (left): Courtesy of frameset.app; p. 53 (right): Courtesy of betafilm.ai; p. 54: Courtesy of Michael Kiley. Photo: Byron Karabatsos; pp. 56, 62 (right): Photo 12 / Alamy Stock Photo; p. 59 (left): Courtesy of John Rusk; p. 59 (right): ScreenProd / Photononstop / Alamy Stock Photo; p. 61: Cinematic Collection / Alamy Stock Photo; p. 62 (left): AJ Pics / Alamy Stock Photo; pp. 64, 67, 93, 101: Photos: Rick Echelmeyer; pp. 68, 72: Courtesy of Rena Butler; p. 78: © George Crumb, 1973, by C. F. Peters Corporation, New York. Permission by C. F. Peters Corporation. All rights reserved; p. 95: Photo: Spike Mafford; p. 99: Photo: David Clough Photography; p. 116: Photo: Dan Wayne; pp. 139, 178–79: Photos: Tony Prikryl; p. 151: Photo: James Allison Photography; pp. 155, 168: Photos: Jueqian Fang; p. 170: Photo: Chris Oughtred, North Light Imaging

Detail captions
Front cover: *Julia on the Swing*, 1999. Detail
Back cover: *Pom Pom's Cadillac, Broad Cove Farm*, ca. 1965. Detail
p. 2: *Record Player*, 1964. Detail
pp. 4–5: *Squirrel Island*, 1986. Detail
pp. 6–7: *If Once You Slept on an Island*, 1996. Detail
pp. 8–9: *Roots, Revisited*, 2019. Detail
p. 10: *Berg*, 2011. Detail
p. 13: *Saltwater Ice*, 1997. Detail
pp. 20–21: *Deer Head II*, ca. 1965. Detail
pp. 22–23: *Farm Talk*, 2016. Detail
p. 24: *Buzz Saw*, 1969. Detail
p. 64: *Catching Snowflakes*, 2004. Detail
p. 74: *Carney Gull #3*, 2009. Detail
pp. 84–85: *Where W. Rat Lives*, 1978. Detail
pp. 174–75: *Channel 12*, 1992. Detail
pp. 176–77: *Fallen*, 1975. Detail
pp. 178–79: *Portrait of Lady, Study #1*, 1968. Detail
p. 180: *Birds' House*, 1989. Detail
pp. 188–89: *Island Church*, 1968. Detail
p. 190: *Pom Pom's Cadillac, Broad Cove Farm*, ca. 1965. Detail

The following works appear in the plate section but were not included in the exhibition:

PLATE 3
Channel 12, 1992
Combined mediums and Day-Glo enamel on Strathmore paper
22½ × 28½ in.
Private collection

PLATE 6
Light Station, 1992
Enamel and oil on panel
36 × 30 in.
Private collection

PLATE 14
Dormer: Third in the Screen Door Sequence, 2017
Oil on canvas and wood
50¼ × 39½ in.
Greenville County Museum of Art, Greenville, South Carolina. Purchase with funds donated by 2020 Visionaries and Friends of Jamie

PLATE 17
If Once You Slept on an Island, 1996
Oil on panel
30 × 36 in.
Private collection

PLATE 31
Roots, 1971
Watercolor on paper
21 × 30 in.
Private collection

PLATE 33
Where W. Rat Lives, 1978
Watercolor on paper
37 × 25½ in.
Private collection

PLATE 48
Saltwater Ice, 1997
Oil on gessoed panel
36 × 30 in.
Collection of F. E. Keeler III

PLATE 63
Squirrel Island, 1986
Watercolor on paper
21½ × 29¾ in.
Private collection

PLATE 65
Island Church, 1968
Watercolor on paper
19½ × 24½ in.
Private collection

PLATE 70
The Axe, 1964
Oil on gessoed panel
16 × 12 in.
Private collection